MUSIC IN THE
NINETEENTH CENTURY

Western Music in Context: A Norton History

Walter Frisch SERIES EDITOR

Music in the Medieval West, by Margot Fassler

Music in the Renaissance, by Richard Freedman

Music in the Baroque, by Wendy Heller

Music in the Eighteenth Century, by John Rice

Music in the Nineteenth Century, by Walter Frisch

Music in the Twentieth and Twenty-First Centuries, by Joseph Auner

MUSIC IN THE NINETEENTH CENTURY

Walter Frisch

Columbia University

W. W. NORTON AND COMPANY

NEW YORK • LONDON

W. W. Norton & Company has been independent since its founding in 1923, when William Warder Norton and Mary D. Herter Norton first published lectures delivered at the People's Institute, the adult education division of New York City's Cooper Union. The firm soon expanded its program beyond the Institute, publishing books by celebrated academics from America and abroad. By midcentury, the two major pillars of Norton's publishing program—trade books and college texts—were firmly established. In the 1950s, the Norton family transferred control of the company to its employees, and today—with a staff of four hundred and a comparable number of trade, college, and professional titles published each year—W. W. Norton & Company stands as the largest and oldest publishing house owned wholly by its employees.

Editor: Maribeth Payne
Associate Editor: Justin Hoffman
Assistant Editor: Ariella Foss
Developmental Editor: Harry Haskell
Manuscript Editor: Jodi Beder
Project Editor: Jack Borrebach
Electronic Media Editor: Steve Hoge
Marketing Manager, Music: Amy Parkin
Production Manager: Ashley Horna
Photo Editor: Stephanie Romeo
Permissions Manager: Megan Jackson
Text Design: Jillian Burr
Composition: CMPreparé
Manufacturing: Quad/Graphics—Fairfield, PA

Library of Congress Cataloging-in-Publication Data

Frisch, Walter, 1951-
    Music in the nineteenth century / Walter Frisch.—1st ed.
        p.cm. — (Western music in context: a Norton history)
    Includes bibliographical references and index.
    ISBN 978-0-393-92919-5 (pbk.)
    1. Music—19th century—History and criticism. I. Title.
    ML196.F75 2013
    780.9'034—dc23

                                                                    2012028569

W. W. Norton & Company, Inc., 500 Fifth Avenue, New York, NY 10110-0017
www.wwnorton.com

W. W. Norton & Company, Ltd., Castle House, 75/76 Wells Street, London W1T3QT

1 2 3 4 5 6 7 8 9 0

For Marilyn, Devin, Nick, and Simon
loving and supportive quartet

CONTENTS IN BRIEF

CONTENTS

ANTHOLOGY REPERTOIRE

SERIES EDITOR'S PREFACE

Western Music in Context: A Norton History starts from the premise that music consists of far more than the notes on a page or the sound heard on a recording. Music is a product of its time and place, of the people and institutions that bring it into being.

Many music history texts focus on musical style and on individual composers. These approaches have been a valuable part of writing about music since the beginnings of modern scholarship in the later nineteenth century. But in the past few decades, scholars have widened their scope in imaginative and illuminating ways to explore the cultural, social, intellectual, and historical contexts for music. This new perspective is reflected in the volumes of Western Music in Context. Among the themes treated across the series are:

- The ways in which music has been commissioned, created, and consumed in public and private spheres
- The role of technology in the creation and transmission of music, from the advent of notation to the digital age
- The role of women as composers, performers, and patrons
- The relationships between music and national or ethnic identity
- The training and education of musicians in both private and institutional settings

All of these topics—and more—animate the pages of Western Music in Context. Written in an engaging style by recognized experts, the series paints vivid pictures of moments, activities, locales, works, and individuals:

- A fourth-century eyewitness report on musical practices in the Holy Land, from a European nun on a pilgrimage
- A lavish wedding at the court of Savoy in the mid-fifteenth century, with music by Guillaume DuFay

- Broadside ballads sung on the streets of London or pasted onto walls, and enjoyed by people from all levels of society
- A choral Magnificat performed at a church in colonial Brazil in the 1770s, accompanied by an organ sent by ship and mule from Portugal
- The barely literate impresario Domenico Barbaia making a tidy fortune at Italian opera houses by simultaneously managing gambling tables and promoting Gioachino Rossini
- A "radio teaching piece" from 1930 by Kurt Weill celebrating the transatlantic flight of Charles Lindbergh

Each volume of Western Music in Context is accompanied by a concise anthology of carefully chosen works. The anthologies offer representative examples of a wide variety of musical genres, styles, and national traditions. Included are excerpts from well-known works like Aaron Copland's *Billy the Kid*, as well as lesser-known gems like Ignacio de Jerusalem's *Matins for the Virgin of Guadalupe*. Commentaries within the anthologies not only provide concise analyses of every work from both formal and stylistic points of view, but also address issues of sources and performance practice.

StudySpace, Norton's online resource for students, features links to recordings of anthology selections that can be streamed from the Naxos Music Library (individual or institutional subscription required), as well as the option to purchase and download recordings from Amazon and iTunes. In addition, students can purchase access to, and instructors can request a free DVD of, the Norton Opera Sampler, which features over two hours of video excerpts from fourteen Metropolitan Opera productions. Finally, for readers wanting to do further research or find more specialized books, articles, or web-based resources, StudySpace offers lists of further readings that supplement those at the end of each chapter in the texts.

Because the books of the Western Music in Context series are relatively compact and reasonably priced, instructors and students might use one or more volumes in a single semester, or several across an academic year. Instructors have the flexibility to supplement the books and the accompanying anthologies with other resources, including Norton Critical Scores and *Strunk's Source Readings in Music History*, as well as other readings, illustrations, scores, films, and recordings.

The contextual approach to music history offers limitless possibilities: an instructor, student, or general reader can extend the context as widely as he or she wishes. Well before the advent of the World Wide Web, the renowned anthropologist Clifford Geertz likened culture to a spider's web of interconnected meanings that humans have spun. Music has been a vital part of such webs throughout the history of the West. Western Music in Context has as its goal to highlight such connections and to invite the instructors and students to continue that exploration on their own.

Walter Frisch
Columbia University

AUTHOR'S PREFACE

Most of the Western classical compositions that form the core of today's repertory come from the nineteenth century: the symphonies of Beethoven and Brahms; the songs of Schubert and Schumann; the nocturnes of Chopin and etudes of Liszt; the operas of Rossini, Verdi, Bizet, and Wagner; the early works of Debussy and Mahler. These works are ever-present around the world in concert halls, opera houses, sound recordings, and on radio and high-definition video broadcasts.

An appreciation of this rich legacy requires more than frequent exposure. It demands an exploration of the historical, social, and cultural contexts in which the music was created and heard. Many music histories, written primarily as a narrative of great composers and works, fail to achieve this goal. What is left out, or pushed to sidebars, are the broader currents that affect musical life, as well as the people and institutions that animate it—performers, audiences, patrons, impresarios, critics, educators, and publishers. *Music in the Nineteenth Century*, in keeping with the goal of the Western Music in Context series, seeks to recover these and other contextual dimensions of nineteenth-century music and to fully integrate them into a discussion of the music and the composers, in a style that is accessible for undergraduate and graduate students, as well as for general readers.

Like other volumes in the series, *Music in the Nineteenth Century* is relatively concise. It provides a selective overview of the period in thirteen chapters. Chapters 1 to 12 are broadly chronological. After a general introduction to the century and the contextual approach in Chapter 1, Chapter 2 investigates Romanticism, a far-reaching set of principles that dominates the first half of the century. Chapters 3 to 6 explore music and musical life between about 1815 and 1850, from the later Beethoven through the generation that included Berlioz, Chopin, Robert and Clara Wieck Schumann, Felix Mendelssohn and Fanny Mendelssohn Hensel, Meyerbeer, and Liszt. Chapter 7 shows that in the latter part of the nineteenth century

Romanticism becomes tempered by other cultural values and practices, including realism, nationalism, and historicism. How these are manifested in opera, operetta, and symphony is the subject of Chapters 8 to 10, with a focus on composers that include Verdi, Bizet, Wagner, Brahms, and Tchaikovsky. In Chapter 11, we look at the interaction between home-grown and imported traditions in the United States, which in the nineteenth century burgeoned in population, landmass, and cultural diversity. Chapter 12 examines the rise of Modernism in composers coming to maturity in the 1890s, including Puccini, Strauss, Mahler, and Debussy. An important aspect of nineteenth-century music rarely treated in textbooks occupies the final chapter: the music's sound or physical presence, as revealed in contemporary documents and in the earliest recordings.

Music in the Nineteenth Century takes account of the most recent scholarly research and perspectives; to assure readability, endnotes and references are kept to a minimum. A short list of further readings at the end of each chapter points the student to some of this more specialized literature; an expanded bibliography is available on StudySpace, Norton's online resource for students. Frequent quotations from primary sources, many drawn from *Strunk's Source Readings in Music History*, keep the narrative lively. For readers who wish to explore these sources in more detail, page references for both the single-volume and seven-volume editions of *Strunk* appear in parentheses after quotations drawn from this text. Bibliographic information for other source readings appears in endnotes.

The text is also sparing in its use of musical examples and analytical remarks. For those who want to delve deeper into individual works, twenty-three full musical scores, each with detailed commentary, are included in the in the accompanying *Anthology for Music in the Nineteenth Century*. Links to recordings of anthology repertoire are available on StudySpace.

ACKNOWLEDGMENTS

Many colleagues have been generous with their time and expertise as this volume was in preparation. Helen M. Greenwald, Stephen Huebner, and Susan Youens provided thorough preliminary reviews for W. W. Norton. Matthew Gelbart, Karen Henson, Marilyn McCoy, and Larry Stempel read later drafts of many chapters and offered valuable suggestions. Kristy Riggs checked the copyedited manuscript and had excellent ideas for final revisions. Others who read individual chapters, shared materials, or provided prompt answers to queries include John Deathridge, Mark Everist, Denise Gallo, Giuseppe Gerbino, Christopher Gibbs, Dana Gooley, Philip Gossett, Thomas Grey, Hans-Joachim Hinrichsen, D. Kern Holoman, Steven Huebner, Benjamin Korstvedt, Hugh Macdonald, Peter Manuel, Rena Mueller, Jann Pasler, Christopher Peacocke, John Roberts, and Robin Wallace.

Students in my undergraduate music history survey at Columbia in spring 2009 read an earlier draft of the book in a classroom "test drive," and their reactions and comments were extremely helpful. My fellow authors in the series, Joseph Auner, Margot Fassler, Richard Freedman, Wendy Heller, and John Rice, have been supportive in countless ways—reading drafts of my chapters, class-testing some of them, and readily sharing ideas that improved not only my book, but the series as a whole. Wendy Heller suggested the image for the book's cover during an inspired moment as we toured the nineteenth-century galleries at the Metropolitan Museum of Art.

I am supremely grateful to the team at Norton (past and present), especially Maribeth Payne, a friend and colleague of long standing and the foresightful music editor with whom I began planning Western Music in Context just over a decade ago; and Jack Borrebach, Ariella Foss, Harry Haskell, Courtney Hirschey, Justin Hoffman, Steve Hoge, Imogen Howes, Graham Norwood, and Stephanie Romeo. All have been professional, proactive, patient, and at every step fully dedicated to bringing this volume and the series as a whole to completion.

Walter Frisch

CHAPTER ONE

Nineteenth-Century Music and Its Contexts

The nineteenth century began with Beethoven's colossal, complex Third (*Eroica*) Symphony in imperial Vienna, and with the simple elegance of choral hymns by William Billings in the newly formed United States. It ended with the adventurous orchestral soundscapes of Claude Debussy in Paris, and with the catchy syncopations of the *Maple Leaf Rag* for piano, written by Scott Joplin in Sedalia, Missouri. The diversity of such composers and works, and the fact that they span what are often called classical and popular styles, present a formidable challenge for anyone seeking to construct a coherent narrative of nineteenth-century music.

Even the chronological boundaries of such a narrative are difficult to pin down. As John Rice chronicles in his volume in this series, *Music in the Eighteenth Century*, the musical path that would lead toward the *Eroica* began back in the 1780s and 1790s in the works of Mozart and Haydn. And as Joseph Auner shows in *Music in the Twentieth and Twenty-first Centuries*, the compositional principles of Debussy and Mahler continued to have resonance well beyond 1900.

No history of nineteenth-century music can do justice to its subject while remaining strictly within the bounds of the years 1800 and 1900. Historians have long felt a need to release the nineteenth century from those arbitrary calendrical moorings. Some have posited a "long" nineteenth century in western Europe, bounded by two seminal events, the French Revolution in 1789 and the outbreak of World War I in 1914, and punctuated near the middle by the wave of democratic revolutions that broke out in 1848. Other historians have suggested that the nineteenth century really begins in 1814–15 with the Congress of Vienna, which brought an end to the Napoleonic Wars, redrew the map of Europe, and ushered in a period of relative political stability.

Broadly speaking, historians can adopt two different approaches to a period. A diachronic approach emphasizes the succession of events in a chronological continuity; a synchronic one stresses context by examining things that happened concurrently. A history of nineteenth-century music, like other kinds of history, should resist the exclusive use of either approach. Music of the nineteenth century cannot be tidily organized by date or by subject; it is a dense web of composers, performers, publishers, promoters, notated scores, oral traditions, audiences, institutions, cities, and nations. The present volume acknowledges this complexity by weaving these varied topics into a narrative that is both chronological and contextual, diachronic and synchronic. Moving forward in time across the nineteenth century, it seeks to place the music in a broader cultural, historical, social, and intellectual setting. For reasons that will become clear in this introductory chapter, we will adopt the years around 1815 and the decade of the 1890s as the chronological beginning and ending points of our survey.

AROUND 1815

In the aftermath of the Congress of Vienna, Europe consisted of several large kingdoms and empires, including those of England, France, Spain, Austria, Prussia, and Russia, as well as smaller states, duchies, or principalities, especially in Italian and German areas (see Fig. 1.1). The German regions were linked together in a large but relatively loose German Confederation. Exhausted by decades of revolution and war, Europeans took refuge in a political climate that was conservative and even reactionary. Paradoxically, the same regimes that tended to suppress political dissent also managed to stimulate artistic expression.

In musical terms, the year 1815 coincides with the emergence of new genres and styles, and with sociocultural developments relevant to musical life. It is around this time that Franz Schubert and Gioachino Rossini arrive on the musical scene, breathing new life into the German lied (art song) and Italian opera, respectively. This younger generation, born in the last decade of the eighteenth century, begins to eclipse Beethoven, then in his mid-forties. Though still esteemed by many as the greatest living composer, Beethoven retreats from the

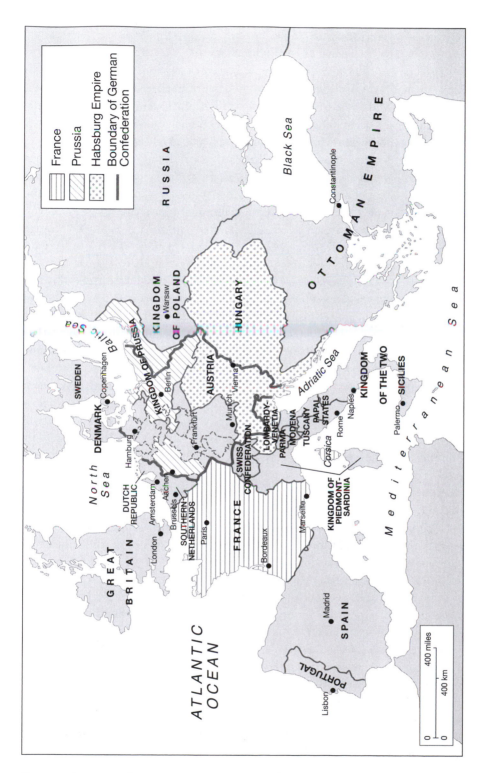

Figure 1.1: *Europe after the Congress of Vienna, 1815*

public eye around 1815 and cultivates a more hermetic style that, with a few exceptions, is not aimed at a broad audience.

The years around 1815 also witness a great expansion of music-making in both amateur and professional spheres. The former includes private homes, where music could be heard in parlors or salons; the latter includes larger public concert halls and opera houses. These developments were largely fueled by a growing middle class that was passionate about music and had resources to spend on it. In music histories, the first quarter of the nineteenth century has sometimes been called "the age of Beethoven" or "the age of Rossini," because those figures are seen as most representative. It could with equal justification be called "the age of Diabelli," after the most prominent music publisher; "the age of Paganini," after its greatest virtuoso; or, as we will see in Chapter 3, "the age of Metternich," after its most powerful statesman.

Between 1818 and his retirement in 1851, the music publishing house of Anton Diabelli (1781–1858) issued almost 10,000 works aimed at middle-class consumers. These included dances and marches for piano, arrangements for guitar and voice of the most popular arias of the day, and lieder. To look through the catalogues of Diabelli's publications is to see a side of nineteenth-century musical life very different from that encompassed by the more rarified piano sonatas or string quartets of Beethoven. Diabelli's is music on the ground and in the marketplace.

Diabelli is responsible for one of the cleverest musical marketing ideas of the period. In 1819 he sent a simple waltz theme of his own creation to many composers, inviting each to write a variation upon it, all of which he would then publish together. Eventually, 52 composers participated (including Franz Schubert and the young Franz Liszt). Beethoven took the assignment so seriously that he chose to write his own independent set of 33 variations on the theme. His *Diabelli* Variations, Op. 120, issued by the publisher in 1823 as Part 1 of the project, is one of the most monumental piano works in the history of music. With his approach, Beethoven effectively removed his own work from the popular marketplace inhabited by the other composers, most of whom wrote mere melodic decorations upon Diabelli's theme.

These responses point up a striking divide in the musical world of the early nineteenth century. Beethoven was writing for only the most accomplished professional pianist, and also for performers and listeners of generations to come; he hoped to enhance his reputation as a "great" composer. The other contributors were writing for the middle-class consumer who would buy the music, enjoy it in the parlor, then move on to other pieces. "Greatness" was probably not an overriding concern for Hieronymus Payer, Wenzel Plachy, and Michael Umlauf, to mention just three composers whose variations were included in Diabelli's collective set. And that is perhaps why their names do not feature in music histories, which tend to focus on composers like Beethoven, for whom greatness and reputation become strong motivating values.

The nineteenth-century parlor, which sought out music that was pleasing and playable, was also a gendered space. Amateur music-making was strongly associated with well-bred middle-class women, who were expected to learn to play the piano and to sing. They constituted much of the market for the piano music published by Diabelli and others, which often appeared with inscriptions like "to the ladies." Around 1840, Beethoven's pupil and prominent Viennese teacher Carl Czerny wrote that piano playing is "one of the most charming and honorable accomplishments for young ladies." The novels of Jane Austen are filled with scenes in which young English women like Elizabeth Bennet (*Pride and Prejudice*) or Emma Woodhouse (*Emma*) play for family or assembled guests in a drawing room.

At the opposite extreme of amateurs playing Diabelli's publications in parlors were the virtuosos beginning to dominate the concert stage. The Italian violinist Nicolò Paganini used his dazzling technique and enormous personal charisma to captivate—and even terrify—audiences during thousands of concerts across Europe and the United States between 1810 and 1835. His repertory consisted largely of showpieces he had written or arranged. Paganini's playing seemed so superhuman that some people believed he was assisted by the devil. He earned hefty sums for his concerts and helped create a culture of virtuosity and showmanship that was perpetuated by the pianist Franz Liszt and continues with superstars like the late rock guitarist Jimi Hendrix and the late singer-dancer-songwriter Michael Jackson.

Virtuosity also dominated the opera stage in the early part of the nineteenth century, which was the era of the *prima donna* (literally, "first lady") and of the impresarios who hired them. Sopranos like Giuditta Pasta, renowned for the naturalness of her acting and singing, commanded enormous fees and had a devoted following. More than just an interpreter, Pasta actually influenced the styles of the greatest composers of Italian opera, including Rossini, Vincenzo Bellini, and Gaetano Donizetti, all of whom created roles for her. As important as prima donnas like Pasta were the impresarios or producers like Domenico Barbaia in Italy and Louis Véron in France, who literally ran the show—selecting the composers, librettists, designers, and singers. Female amateurs, impresarios, virtuosos, and publishers all deserve a place in any history that seeks to provide a context for the music of Beethoven, Schubert, and Rossini.

THE FINAL DECADE OF THE CENTURY

A logical ending point for this book is marked by developments in the 1890s that are often linked under the term *Modernism*. Modernism is not a single phenomenon, but a range of attitudes and techniques shared by creative artists working in the decades around 1900. Out of the many important Modernist composers, we will focus on a cluster born around 1860, including Debussy, Gustav Mahler, Richard Strauss, and Giacomo Puccini. Each has strong ties to the past but also moves away from nineteenth-century traditions, with a greater emphasis on color, sonority, dissonance, and often a more naturalistic depiction of speech and dramatic action. After the turn of the century, and especially after the outbreak of World War I in 1914, Modernism departs still more radically from the past, in ways that Joseph Auner treats more fully in the next volume in this series.

Puccini's most beloved opera, La bohème (Bohemian Life), which had its premiere in 1896, might not be a work we immediately associate with Modernism. La bohème depicts the joys and heartbreaks of young lovers in Paris; it is full of soaring melodies that show the legacy of Rossini and Giuseppe Verdi. But in aiming for a newer kind of dramatic realism, Puccini and his librettists are characteristic early Modernists. Much of the opera consists of dialogue delivered musically in a manner that comes close to everyday speech. Shorter lyrical passages or exchanges between characters often take the place of traditional larger arias or duets. The most aria-like number in La bohème, Musetta's Waltz in Act 2, is part of a complicated, extended ensemble that eventually involves everyone on stage—a large cross-section of the Parisian population—in a kind of collage of different musical elements.

Collage-like treatment is also a characteristic of Mahler, an early Modernist composer very different from Puccini in outlook and style. At the very opening of his First Symphony, completed in 1888, Mahler juxtaposes diverse sound elements—fanfares, birdcalls, hunting horn melodies, a sinuous chromatic theme in the cellos, and the interval of a descending fourth—all within an orchestral frame created by the note A sounding in the strings across seven octaves. No composer before Mahler had created a musical tableau like this. But as with Puccini, the gestures take place within a recognizable nineteenth-century tradition, here one of symphonic composition that includes Beethoven and Hector Berlioz.

In La bohème Puccini captures an urban sound world; in the First Symphony, Mahler evokes a natural one. Like other early Modernists, neither composer is aiming for conventional beauty. Instead, their collage techniques convey something of the sense of fragmentation and alienation that was pervasive in the last part of the nineteenth century. The world had been expanded by advances in commerce, science, and technology. Railways and new means of telecommunication could connect people across vast distances. But this kind of progress and the increasing urbanization that accompanied it led to a widespread feeling of depersonalization.

Modernist alienation is also evident in the changing relationship of the artist to his or her audience. On the face of it, by the final decade of the nineteenth century concert and opera life was thriving in ways unimaginable in 1815. Established opera companies and symphony orchestras played subscription seasons in specially built large houses or halls. Solo instrumental and song recitals and chamber music abounded. Mahler and Strauss pursued successful careers as conductors or music directors of major opera companies and orchestras.

But as time passed, the generally harmonious relationship between artist and audience began to shift to a more adversarial one. Late-nineteenth-century audiences and repertories tended to be conservative; concert halls and opera houses became acoustic museums dominated by works of the past. Even though Mahler was widely admired as a conductor of the standard repertory, his First Symphony was met with puzzlement and even hostility (including hissing) by many in the audience and with disapproval from the critical establishment. A discouraged Mahler put the work aside for three years before revising it. *La bohème* was also received coolly by many, including one critic whose comments seem especially ironic in light of the opera's subsequent status as one of the most popular in the entire repertory: "*La bohème*, just as it left no impression on the minds of its listeners, will not leave much of a mark on the history of our lyric theatre."

By the first decades of the twentieth century, audiences and critics were increasingly, and even aggressively, intolerant. Some new works, like Arnold Schoenberg's First Chamber Symphony of 1906 and Igor Stravinsky's *Le sacre du printemps* (Rite of Spring) of 1913, were greeted with catcalls, whistling, and fistfights among the audience, and scathing reviews in the press—only to be accepted as masterpieces within a generation.

FROM 1815 TO THE 1890s

Taking 1815 and the 1890s as our temporal or diachronic frame, we will look at musical repertories, institutions, and personalities within a wide range of historical and cultural contexts. Chapter 2 investigates Romanticism as a key element in the creative imagination of artists in the first half of the century. Like Modernism, Romanticism was no monolithic phenomenon, but a range of beliefs and practices expressed in the writings of such figures as Friedrich Schlegel and E.T.A. Hoffmann in Germany, François-René de Chateaubriand in France, and Giuseppe Mazzini in Italy.

Chapter 3 considers Beethoven's late style, Schubert's new lyrical voice, and the rising cult of virtuosity, all in the context of a more stable but repressive political climate after 1815—largely the creation of Prince Klemens Wenzel von Metternich—in which a burgeoning middle class was encouraged to stay out of public affairs and focus on domestic and artistic pursuits. In Chapter 4 we look at the fusion of music and commercial interests in the big, international business of opera. Major composers of early Romantic opera included Rossini and Bellini in Italy, Giacomo Meyerbeer in France, Carl Maria von Weber in Germany, and Mikhail Glinka in Russia. We also look at the importance in the opera industry of star singers like Pasta.

The next chapters consider the careers of a new generation of musicians that comes to maturity in the 1830s and actively engages the public through musical criticism and performance, as well as composition. Chapter 5 examines writings by Berlioz, Robert Schumann, and Liszt; the conducting career of Felix Mendelssohn; musical salons led by Fanny Mendelssohn Hensel; and the piano recitals of Clara Wieck Schumann. In Chapter 6 we discuss the musical works of some of these same figures (plus Frédéric Chopin) in the context of heated debates about musical expression and program or illustrative music.

As Chapter 7 shows, the midpoint of the nineteenth century marks a significant dividing point in musical culture. In the aftermath of the mostly unsuccessful revolutions of 1848 and in light of new developments in science and technology, the Romantic worldview yields to attitudes exemplified by nationalism, historicism, materialism, and realism. The only "ism" of the period attached to a composer, Wagnerism, is treated in Chapter 8, which examines the dramatic theories, works, and influence of Richard Wagner. His mature operas from the decades after 1850, including *Tristan und Isolde* and the four-opera cycle *Der Ring des Nibelungen* (The Ring of the Nibelung), resonate in European culture far beyond his native Germany.

Chapter 9 looks at other composers for the musical stage in the later nineteenth century, who sought a broad audience while still maintaining high artistic standards. In Italy, Verdi dominated all rivals with his musically rich and dramatically powerful operas. In France, Georges Bizet's Spanish-inflected *Carmen* created a unique blend of exoticism and realism. And in France, England, and Austria, respectively, the immensely popular operettas of Jacques Offenbach, W. S. Gilbert and Arthur Sullivan, and Johann Strauss, Jr., turned a comic mirror on contemporary society.

Chapter 10 examines the development of a concert culture in Europe in the decades after 1850, which saw the growth of permanent orchestras, halls to house them, and works written to be played by them. We will discuss the most prestigious genre of instrumental music, the "great" or large-scale symphony, as exemplified in works by Johannes Brahms, Anton Bruckner, César Franck, Camille Saint-Saëns, and Pyotr Il'yich Tchaikovsky.

Chapter 11 moves across the Atlantic to the United States in the nineteenth century. In American musical culture, homegrown and popular elements blend (and sometimes clash) in distinctive ways with imported and more rarified ones. We will examine figures as geographically and musically diverse as the Spanish priest and choir director Narciso Durán in California, the songwriter Stephen Foster in Pennsylvania, and two pianist-composers, Louis Moreau Gottschalk in New Orleans and Amy Beach in New England. Chapter 12 treats early Modernism in the 1890s in ways outlined in the above discussion of Puccini and Mahler. The final chapter of the book, Chapter 13, steps outside the narrative chronology to consider the sound world of nineteenth-century music as captured through contemporary witnesses and early recordings. We focus on the rapidly evolving technology of the piano and of orchestral instruments, and on the human voice, especially the development of the tenor across the century.

THE "TRISTAN" CHORD

When we establish contexts for works, the impetus is naturally to radiate outward from the music. In keeping with that goal, this book, like the others in the series, avoids detailed analysis of music, which is to be found in the commentary in the accompanying score anthologies. But musical style—how the notes sound and how they are shaped into larger forms—is always an essential element of the music's context: a work exists as part of a sonorous universe that includes pieces by other composers, and in other genres.

To conclude this chapter, and by way of introduction to the technical aspects of nineteenth-century music, let us work outward from a single harmonic sonority, perhaps the most famous one of the era. The "Tristan" chord, as it is often called, appears at the beginning of the Prelude to Wagner's opera *Tristan und Isolde* (1859) and then is heard countless times throughout the opera as a symbol of the unfulfilled longing of the two lovers (Ex. 1.1). The "Tristan" chord is all about context: its meaning depends on how it is resolved harmonically. Wagner's chord is intentionally ambiguous, its tonal implications undefined. It is a dissonant chord that is not prepared, that is, not approached from a consonance. Nor does it move toward a consonance; it resolves to another dissonance, a dominant seventh, which in turn is left unresolved. Also distinctive about the "Tristan" chord—indeed part of its identity—is the scoring. Above the last note of the initial melodic fragment from the cellos, the chord is played by a closely spaced array of woodwinds, including oboes, clarinets, bassoons, and the English horn, whose, plaintive, melancholy tone color suffuses Wagner's opera.

Example 1.1: *Wagner,* Tristan und Isolde, *Prelude, mm. 1–3*

The opening sonorities of Wagner's *Tristan* are unique and unforgettable. Yet they did not emerge from a vacuum. Wagner did not invent the "Tristan" chord. In a different voicing or spacing—and in a different context—its notes form a half-diminished seventh chord, which is most commonly encountered in the minor mode as a ii⁷ harmony that leads to the dominant (V). Beethoven uses the chord this way in his Piano Sonata in E♭ Major, Op. 31, No. 3, written in 1802, many decades before Wagner's *Tristan* Prelude. Where Wagner more or less drops the chord upon us, Beethoven prepares it carefully. Unlike in *Tristan*, the tonal context of Beethoven's sonata is clear: the first cadence of the movement (shown in Ex. 1.2a) leaves no doubt that we are in the key of E♭. Beethoven begins with a ii ⁶₅ chord in its normal form for E♭ major, with a C♮. A bit later in the exposition, the opening chord appears in its half-diminished form, with a C♭, instead of C♮ (Ex. 1.2b), and this opens the way to the "Tristan" chord, which appears at the exact same pitches, and with something of the same intense longing, that it will have in Wagner (shown with an x). No more than Wagner did Beethoven invent this harmony, but its striking appearance in the E♭-Major Sonata marks a moment near the start of the nineteenth century when a single harmonic gesture could take on a unique character.

Example 1.2: *Beethoven, Piano Sonata in E♭ Major, Op. 31, No. 3, movement 1*

(a) mm. 1–8

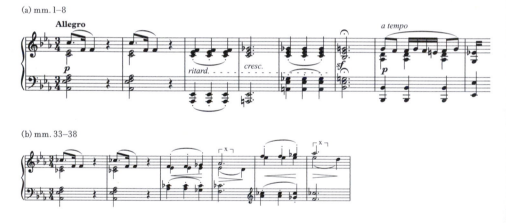

(b) mm. 33–38

At the other end of the century, during the decade of early Modernism, and in still another context, the "Tristan" chord serves as the first sonority of *En sourdine* (Muted), a *mélodie* or song composed by Claude Debussy in 1891 to a text by the Symbolist poet Paul Verlaine (Ex. 1.3). The chord appears in exactly the same spacing and at the same pitches as in Wagner. But how utterly different the effect is! The title *En sourdine* says it all: the harmony is understated, discreet. It is allusive, not declarative. Unlike Beethoven, Debussy does not appear to derive the chord from its origins as a ii⁷ harmony; at the close of the nineteenth century composers often sought to avoid such a logical process. Nor does Debussy invest the chord with the enormous tension it has in Wagner. In *En sourdine*, the "Tristan" chord sits languidly underneath an oscillating melodic figure in the

Example 1.3: *Debussy,* En sourdine, *mm. 1–5*

Calm in the twilight

right hand and a repeated low D♯ in the voice. The bass note, E♯, moves up by half step to F♯, then sinks back down. The gesture is all about stasis, not forward motion. Debussy is clearly interested in the "Tristan" harmony for its coloristic or Impressionistic qualities.

These three examples reveal a change in the harmonic language whose nodal points have been plausibly identified with Classicism (Beethoven), Romanticism (Wagner), and Modernism (Debussy) in music. We see a shift from a harmonic language that is "functional," able to be explained and rationalized within a tonality, to one that has an ambiguous identity and can move to different key areas, to one which is almost wholly nonfunctional and static.

Beethoven's style did not inevitably "lead to" Wagner, nor Wagner's to Debussy. Rather, all three composers are part of the larger historical context for the kind of chromatic language exemplified by the "Tristan" chord. That context includes not only other works by these composers—Beethoven's piano sonatas, Wagner's operas, Debussy's songs—but also the cultural universe into which these pieces were born. This complex, untidy world of performers, critics, publishers, institutions, and creative artists working in other media will be explored in the chapters that follow as we attempt to build a contextual account of music in the nineteenth century.

FOR FURTHER READING

The Cambridge History of Nineteenth-Century Music, ed. Jim Samson (Cambridge and New York: Cambridge University Press, 2002)

Dahlhaus, Carl, *Nineteenth-Century Music*, trans. J. Bradford Robinson (Berkeley and Los Angeles: University of California Press, 1989)

Gildea, Robert, *Barricades and Borders: Europe 1800–1914*, 3rd ed. (Oxford and New York: Oxford University Press, 2003)

Plantinga, Leon, *Romantic Music: A History of Musical Style in Nineteenth-Century Europe* (New York: W. W. Norton & Company, 1985)

Taruskin, Richard, *Music in the Nineteenth Century* (Oxford and New York: Oxford University Press, 2009)

ⓢ Additional resources available at wwnorton.com/studyspace

CHAPTER TWO

The Romantic Imagination

We can sympathize with the French writer F. R. de Toreinx, who in his History of Romanticism of 1829 became exasperated when trying to clarify the term under discussion. "Do you know it? Do I? Has anyone ever known it? Has it ever been defined concisely and exactly?" he asked. "No!" he responded. "Romanticism is just that which cannot be defined!" Almost a hundred years later, in 1924, the intellectual historian Arthur Lovejoy could still write, "The word 'romantic' has come to mean so many things that, by itself, it means nothing." Romanticism remains a slippery concept, even though it was arguably the most pervasive phenomenon in the culture—and the music—of Western Europe in the first half of the nineteenth century.

Not until about 1850 were Classicism and Romanticism seen as comprising distinct historical periods or definable artistic styles. Before that, they were understood as referring to attitudes and practices that had appeared at various epochs of Western culture, even at the same time. Broadly speaking, Romanticism from the 1790s through the first few decades of the nineteenth century represented a reaction against Enlightenment values of rationality and universality. It celebrated subjectivity, spontaneity, and the power of emotions. In Romantic music, more open-ended structures and sonorities tended to replace or inflect the forms and standard harmonic patterns of the later eighteenth century, which, as John Rice has shown in the previous volume in this series, were not perceived as "Classical," but rather as moving on a spectrum between "galant" and "learned" styles.

Aspects of Romanticism had been prefigured well before 1800. Although he never used the term Romanticism, the great philosopher and writer Jean-Jacques Rousseau (1712–1778) articulated the individualism that would lie at the heart of the movement. Rousseau began his autobiographical *Confessions* of 1769 by writing: "Myself alone. I feel my heart and I know men. I am not made like any that I have seen; I venture to believe that I was not made like any that exist. If I am not more deserving, at least I am different." In his novels and philosophical tracts, Rousseau celebrated the worth of individuals as opposed to larger political and social structures. He valued man in his "state of nature," in his original, unfettered being. Rousseau's ideas became influential during the French Revolution (1789–99) and for many generations thereafter.

A beautiful description of the new directions that would be associated with Romanticism came from the English poet William Wordsworth (1770–1850) in the Preface to his *Lyrical Ballads* (1800):

> Poetry is the spontaneous overflow of powerful feelings: it takes its origin from emotion recollected in tranquillity: the emotion is contemplated till by a species of reaction the tranquillity gradually disappears, and an emotion, kindred to that which was before the subject of contemplation, is gradually produced, and does itself actually exist in the mind.

Wordsworth—who also did not use the term Romanticism—emphasizes the role of feeling and of the lack of restraint, but also stresses that a poem (or by extension any work of creative art) is based not upon the direct experience of an emotion, but upon the reflection that comes afterward. In true art, feelings are always mediated by contemplation and craft.

These passages from Rousseau and Wordsworth capture many of the qualities of artworks created in the first half of the nineteenth century and identified at the time, or later, as Romantic. As we will see in Chapter 7, the term is less well suited to the latter part of the century. In what follows we will survey more general aspects of Romantic thought and art, then turn to music, which played an especially large role in the Romantic imagination. A short chapter cannot provide a comprehensive account of the different regions where Romanticism appeared. We will focus primarily on the German-speaking world, in part because it was there that Romanticism was originally defined and self-consciously practiced, and secondarily on France and Italy.

THE REACTION AGAINST CLASSICISM

The values and artistic practices of the ancient Greeks were much praised and emulated in the later eighteenth century. In 1755 Johann Joachim Winckelmann

(1717–1768) extolled Greek art for its "noble simplicity" and "tranquil grandeur." Winckelmann saw in Greek sculpture and painting the pinnacle of artistic beauty, especially for the perfection of the forms, the contours, the positions of the bodies, and the representation of clothing. He urged contemporary artists to model their works on the Greeks, just as Raphael and Michelangelo had done in the Renaissance.

Winckelmann's influence on thinkers and artists helped to usher in a Neoclassical phase in late-eighteenth-century art. The French painter Jacques-Louis David (1748–1825), who worked in Rome for five years, created large canvases on classical subjects, such as *Oath of the Horatii* (1784), renowned for its sharply outlined human figures posed with a frozen, sculptural quality (see Fig. 2.1). In the 1780s, after an extended trip to Italy, the writer Johann Wolfgang von Goethe (1749–1832) experienced a conversion to the ideals of Classical art. Living in the town of Weimar in Germany, Goethe, together with his friend Friedrich Schiller (1759–1805), shaped what came to be known as Weimar Classicism, manifest especially in their dramatic works. In Hamburg and Berlin, Gotthold Lessing (1729–1781) achieved something similar with his plays based on Aristotelian principles of dramatic unity.

Figure 2.1: *Jacques-Louis David,* Oath of the Horatii, *1784*

The self-conscious inventors of Romanticism were a group of like-minded young thinkers gathered in the German city of Jena in the 1790s. They were part of a newer generation, most born in the early 1770s, who found the ideals of Greek art more limiting than inspiring. They included the brothers August Wilhelm and Friedrich Schlegel (1767–1845 and 1772–1829), Ludwig Tieck (1773–1853), Friedrich Schleiermacher (1768–1834), and Friedrich Schelling (1775–1854). The Jena group gave a name—*Romantik* in German—to an art that they believed to be more open-ended, more spiritually vibrant than Classical art. This "Romantic" art could be found in many places and eras: Gothic cathedrals, and the early Renaissance drawings of Albrecht Dürer, and the plays of Shakespeare were all considered Romantic. Figure 2.2 shows a painting from 1815 in which the artist Karl Friedrich Schinkel sets a Gothic church on a rock by the sea at sunset. The subject is medieval, but the treatment is fully Romantic in spirit: the church, placed on a dramatic outcropping, is backlit by a sun setting under scattered clouds that reflect its light.

The most influential early formulation of a specifically Romantic worldview came in 1797 from Friedrich Schlegel in the journal *Athenäum*, which he founded with his brother August Wilhelm. *Athenäum* was distinctive for publishing "fragments" or short paragraphs instead of full-fledged essays. (The fragment

Figure 2.2: *Karl Friedrich Schinkel,* Gothic Church on a Rock by the Sea, *1815*

became one of the most innovative literary forms of Romanticism.) In one, Schlegel defines "Romantic poetry" as "progressive" and "all-embracing." By "poetry" he really means the original Greek sense of *poesis*, or making. Schlegel writes: "Other kinds of poetry are complete and can now be fully and critically analysed. The Romantic kind of poetry is constantly developing. That in fact is its true nature: it can forever only *become*, it can never achieve definitive form. . . . It alone is infinite. It alone is free." Schlegel sees the Romantic outlook as expanding rather than excluding or superseding the Classical one. (The title of the journal *Athenäum* is itself a classical reference to a cultural institution in ancient Rome named after the goddess Athena.)

Friedrich Schlegel's ideas, virtually the credo of Romantic art, were taken up at greater length by August Wilhelm Schlegel, who in his "Lectures on Dramatic Art and Literature" of 1808 noted that the term Romantic had been coined to differentiate the new and unique spirit of modern art from that of ancient or Classical art. As Schlegel observed, the term derived from "romance," the name applied to the vernacular languages that had developed from Latin and Germanic tongues of the later Middle Ages.

Acknowledging Winckelmann, Schlegel observes that the ancient Greeks cultivated an art of "refined and ennobled sensuality." But, he says, they were too much confined to the present, and not enough concerned with the infinite. For Schlegel, it took the spread of Christianity to regenerate "the decayed and exhausted world of Classical antiquity." The Christian attitude, with its emphasis on eternity, helped foster a more Romantic perspective. The ancient Greeks held human nature to be self-sufficient. The Christian outlook is opposed to this: "Everything finite and mortal is lost in contemplation of the eternal; life has become shadow and darkness." In a beautifully expressed contrast between the Classical and Romantic outlooks, Schlegel says: "The poetry of the ancients was the poetry of possession, while ours is the poetry of longing. The former is firmly rooted in the present, while the latter hovers between remembrance and anticipation." These statements—however misguided they might be about the true nature of Classical Greek art—capture the essence of Romanticism.

The first generation of French Romantics echoed many of these sentiments. François-René de Chateaubriand (1768–1848) shared the German Romantics' love of the medieval, the Gothic, and the Christian, as well as their mistrust of Enlightenment rationality and secularism. His book *Génie du christianisme* (Genius of Christianity, 1802) sees Christianity as a higher, more spiritual— hence more Romantic—culture than that of ancient Greece and Rome.

The fullest expression of these trends in French Romanticism comes with Victor Hugo (1802–1885; Fig. 2.3), whose best-known works were the novels *Les misérables* (The Wretched) and *Notre-Dame de Paris* (The Hunchback of Notre Dame). Hugo's preface to the play *Cromwell* (1827) became a key manifesto of Romanticism. In it, Hugo, like Chateaubriand and the Schlegels, argued that

Figure 2.3: *Victor Hugo, Romantic French author, after a photograph by Nadar*

Christianity had ushered in a new era for the arts and intellectual life, whose worldview was very different from that of antiquity. Romantic art, going forward from Christian spiritualism and melancholy, would embrace many different styles and moods, including the sublime and the grotesque. As for Friedrich Schlegel, "poetry," in the following excerpt from Hugo's preface, really means all artistic expression:

> Christianity leads poetry to the truth. . . . Everything in creation is not humanly *beautiful* . . . the ugly exists beside the beautiful, the unshapely beside the graceful, the grotesque on the reverse of the sublime, evil with good, darkness with light. . . .
>
> Then it is that, with its eyes fixed upon events that are both laughable and redoubtable, and under the influence of that spirit of Christian melancholy and philosophical criticism . . . poetry will take a great step, a decisive step, a step which, like the upheaval of an earthquake, will change the whole face of the intellectual world. It will set about doing as nature does, mingling in its creations—but without confounding them—darkness and light, the grotesque and the sublime; in other words, the body and the soul, the beast and the intellect; for the starting-point of religion is always the starting-point of poetry. All things are connected.

Hugo's comments reflect or anticipate many characteristics of Romantic music, which is often deliberately hard to listen to and breaks traditional rules to portray extreme emotional contrasts. Many of Beethoven's later compositions from the 1820s—including the C♯-Minor Quartet, Op. 131, which we will examine in the next chapter—manifest a sharp juxtaposition of the heavenly and the down-to-earth, the sublime and the comical, the lyrical and the gruff. Berlioz's *Symphonie fantastique* (Fantastic Symphony) of 1830 conspicuously mixes the sublime, the humorous, the religious, and the grotesque. The *March to the Scaffold* (the fourth movement) and the *Witches' Sabbath* (the fifth) are perfect musical embodiments of the grotesque in music.

The first movement of the symphony reflects a series of strongly contrasting emotional states like those Hugo describes: the movement depicts, according to Berlioz's program, "the passage from this state of melancholy reverie, interrupted by a few fits of groundless joy, to one of frenzied passion, with its movements of fury, of jealousy, its return of tenderness, its tears, its religious consolations." Even the main theme of Berlioz's symphony, the recurring *idée fixe* (fixed idea, or obsession) that represents the beloved, captures within itself the wide range of feelings or moods characteristic of Romantic art. At 40 measures (the beginning is shown in Ex. 2.1), this is likely the longest, most complex theme that had been written in European art music. With its irregular phrases, its long notes frequently tied over the barline, and its sharp, oddly placed accents, the *idée fixe* is by turns impulsive, reflective, hesitant, insistent, and yielding.

Example 2.1: *Berlioz, Symphonie fantastique, movement 1, mm. 72–79, idée fixe (beginning)*

ROMANTIC LONGING

Berlioz's theme is also the perfect embodiment of another Romantic preoccupation, that of longing or unfulfilled desire. In Chateaubriand's semi-autobiographical novel *René* (1802), the young hero suffers from world-weariness and aimless longing, which the author describes with the term *vague des passions*, the emptiness or void of passions, a phrase picked up directly in the *Symphonie fantastique*, whose hero is described by Berlioz as being afflicted by it. In such a state, one's passions can fixate on an object of desire, as do those of Berlioz's hero on the beloved, whom he represents in the *idée fixe*. The theme contains chains of long appoggiaturas that delay melodic resolution, and the tonic C major is nowhere stated clearly until the very last cadence. These are the musical techniques of longing—or, to return to the terms of the Schlegel brothers, of becoming rather than being.

In German poetry, fiction, and music of the early nineteenth century, we encounter frequent references to *Sehnen, Sehnsucht,* or *Verlangen,* the terms for longing or desire. A characteristic example is the brief two-stanza lyric from

1823 by Heinrich Heine (1797–1856), whose poems were set to music by Robert Schumann in the magnificent song cycle *Dichterliebe* (Poet's Love, 1840):

Im wunderschönen Monat Mai,	*In the wonderful month of May,*
Als alle Knospen sprangen,	*When all the buds come out,*
Da ist in meinem Herzen	*Then in my heart*
Die Liebe aufgegangen.	*Love burst forth.*
Im wunderschönen Monat Mai,	*In the wonderful month of May,*
Als alle Vögel sangen,	*When all the birds were singing,*
Da hab' ich ihr gestanden	*Then I confessed to her*
Mein Sehnen und Verlangen.	*My yearning and longing.*

All the images of the poem—buds bursting, love springing, birds singing—prepare for the final words, "Sehnen und Verlangen," so characteristic of Romanticism. In the Schlegels' terms, Schumann's music captures striving rather than being, desire rather than possession (Ex. 2.2). He sets the final words to a melodic line that climbs upward but droops at the end, never reaching its goal, the tonic or home key of F♯ minor. The last word is accompanied by a dissonance, here a dominant seventh chord, which remains unresolved and unfulfilled; it literally, to recall A. W. Schlegel, hovers between remembrance and anticipation. (The next song in *Dichterliebe* begins in A major, thus providing a surprise resolution for the dissonant chord.)

Example 2.2: *Schumann, Dichterliebe, No. 1, Im wunderschönen Monat Mai, mm. 22–26*

mm. 22-23, 26

My yearning and longing.

After Berlioz and Schumann, it was Richard Wagner who would create the most powerful musical language of Romantic longing, especially in his opera *Tristan und Isolde.* Completed in 1859, almost twenty years after *Dichterliebe,* *Tristan* depicts a searing passion that goes well beyond the more innocent love pangs represented by Berlioz, Heine, and Schumann. The love between Tristan and Isolde is at once all-powerful and ill fated; it is literally "consuming" in that it can be fulfilled only in death.

Wagner captures the lovers' situation with intensely chromatic music in which the individual lines move by half-step motion and rarely settle into stable consonant chords. The result is constant musical flux or yearning. The most famous musical emblem of this phenomenon is the "Tristan" chord, which is heard at the opening of the Prelude (see Ex. 1.1 in Chapter 1) and then recurs frequently throughout the opera. Just as the passion between Wagner's lovers is more intense than that suggested by Heine and Schumann, so too the "Tristan" chord, a half-diminished seventh chord in an unusual inversion, is more dissonant than Schumann's dominant seventh.

The longing depicted in Wagner's *Tristan* is far removed from that described by the Schlegels or Chateaubriand. It is modeled on the ideas of another important early Romantic, the philosopher Arthur Schopenhauer (1788–1860). Schopenhauer's major work, *Die Welt als Wille und Vorstellung* (The World as Will and Representation), was written and published before 1819, but its impact was delayed until the second half of the century. Wagner discovered the work in 1854, wrote extensively about it and its influence upon him, and finally created in *Tristan und Isolde* the musical and dramatic embodiment of Schopenhauer's philosophy.

For Schopenhauer, who is fundamentally pessimistic, longing is an inevitable state of permanent suffering in life. He posited a basic force or principle he called the Will, a blind, fundamental drive that longs for satisfaction but never reaches it. All Will is founded in need, he wrote, and thus in suffering. Only in death is the suffering completely alleviated—as happens in Wagner's opera. And yet, according to Schopenhauer, there are other means at least to quiet or calm the Will. One of these is music, which, as we shall now see, played a large role in Romantic thought.

MUSIC IN THE ROMANTIC IMAGINATION

The years around 1800 can be seen as a period of liberation for instrumental music, thus marking a key development in Romanticism. Until then, among most aestheticians and philosophers, instrumental music had second-class status, below the prestigious forms of opera and vocal music. Its origin was understood to lie in dance and in more popular genres, like serenades or the opera overture, which were dismissed by some philosophers or aestheticians as displaying empty sensuousness. Instrumental music was deemed to be incapable of independent expression; it could only represent specific, predefined emotional states (as in the eighteenth-century theory of "affects") or imitate external phenomena (birds, storms). These views began to change in the last decades of the eighteenth century. In 1785, the French musician and writer Michel-Paul Guy de Chabanon argued in favor of nonrepresentational instrumental music that could speak directly to the emotions and to the sensory pleasure of the ear.

In the ensuing decades instrumental music was increasingly valued, and deemed Romantic, because of the same abstract qualities that had been seen as its limitations—its ineffability and apparent indistinctness. In what came to be a renowned essay on Beethoven's instrumental music, E.T.A. Hoffmann in 1813 expressed this view clearly: "When we speak of music as an independent art, should we not always restrict our meaning to instrumental music, which, scorning every aid, every admixture of another art (the art of poetry), gives pure expression to music's specific nature, recognizable in this form alone? It is the most romantic of all the arts—one might almost say, the only genuinely romantic one—for its sole subject is the infinite" (SR 160:1193; 6/13:151). Here Hoffmann picks up and applies to music the rhetoric of the Schlegels, especially the celebration and exploration of the infinite in Romantic art.

Schopenhauer further developed early Romantic ideas about the special qualities of music. He worked more specifically than the Schlegels or Hoffmann in the framework developed by the philosopher Immanuel Kant (1724–1804). Kant had not held music in high esteem; indeed, he condemned it as a mere play of sensations, of little cultural value. But Kant also noted music's potential to communicate normally inexpressible thoughts. Developing this idea, Schopenhauer understood music as the most immediate expression of the Will, which as we saw above was his term for the essence of all things, and which Kant had called the *Ding an Sich* (thing-in-itself). All life was a manifestation or representation (*Vorstellung*) of the Will, which like Kant's thing-in-itself can be experienced directly only under certain circumstances. Music is the one art that can achieve an unmediated expression of the Will. The other arts objectify the Will only indirectly, by means of ideas, says Schopenhauer. But music,

> since it passes over the Ideas, is also quite independent of the phenomenal world, positively ignores it. . . . Thus music is as *immediate* an objectification and copy of the whole *will* as the world itself is. . . . Music is by no means like the other arts, namely a copy of the Ideas, but a *copy of the will itself*. . . . For this reason the effect of music is so very much more powerful and penetrating than is that of the other arts, for these others speak only of the shadow, but music of the essence.

This problem of how to understand the relationship of music to the world—whether the more metaphysical world beyond our perception or the more materialistic bourgeois, everyday world—is a central issue of Romantic thought. So is the idea that music, especially autonomous instrumental music, has a special connection or a direct pathway to the "essence" of things.

THE RELIGION OF ART

In the early nineteenth century, the idea of art as something that transcends the real world also enabled it to become a substitute for religious worship. We have already seen how in early Romantic aesthetics art was associated specifically with a Christian viewpoint, and with the contemplation of the infinite. It is only a small step from that attitude to having an artistic experience stand in for a religious one, in what came to be called art-religion, or *Kunstreligion*.

Nowhere is the association between religious fervor and artistic experience expressed more effectively than in the novella by Wilhelm Wackenroder (1773–1798), *Das merkwürdige musikalische Leben des Tonkünstlers Joseph Berglinger* (The Remarkable Musical Life of the Musician Joseph Berglinger; 1797). Joseph grows up in a family headed by a conscientious and hard-working doctor who has no diversions. His five sisters are described as "pitiable" and "lonely." Joseph feels out of place in this family, because his "whole life was a beautiful fantasy and a heavenly dream." He is drawn to music, studies piano, and attends many musical events in churches and concert halls. Here he has profound experiences that lift him out of the everyday world. The sound of music in church makes him feel

> as though his soul had all at once unfurled great wings . . . he soared up into the radiant sky. . . . The present sank away before him; his being was cleansed of all the pettiness of this world—veritable dust on the soul's luster; the music set his nerves tingling with a gentle thrill, calling up changing images before him. (SR 149:1063; 6/2:21)

Joseph's reaction is similar at concerts, where "he seated himself in a corner, without so much as glancing at the brilliant assembly of listeners, and listened with precisely the same reverence as if he had been in a church—just as still and motionless, his eyes cast down to the floor in the same way" (SR 149:1064; 6/2:22). Here is the perfect expression of art-religion—the contemplation of the musical work is done in spiritual isolation, away from the real world. Such beliefs would strongly influence a new code of audience etiquette that grew up in the decades after 1815 and culminated in a behaviorally circumscribed "concert culture" to be discussed in Chapter 10. Socializing, eating, or coming and going during musical performances were no longer acceptable, as they had been in earlier eras. Music was meant to be listened to with full concentration or devotion.

Joseph goes on to become a professional musician, a kapellmeister (music director) for the bishop, and he lives in considerable splendor. Yet he becomes increasingly unhappy, feeling an irreconcilable conflict between his inner musical world and the outer world. "How far more ideally I lived in those days when I merely enjoyed art, in youthful innocence and peaceful solitude, than I do now that I practice it, in the dazzling glare of the world, surrounded only by silk, stars and crosses of honor, and people of culture and taste!" (SR 149:1069; 6/2:27).

Art in the Romantic view is thus almost too pure, too perfect to be sullied by contact with the real world. This is the paradox of the Romantic worldview. Its interiority—what Schumann called *Innigkeit*, a designation he often put at the beginning of pieces of his music—is in many ways incompatible with the inherent exteriority of musical performance, or of a musical profession. Joseph Berglinger falls ill and dies, we are told, "in the bloom of his years": "Alas, his lofty fantasy was what destroyed him" (SR 149:1071; 6/2:29).

FANTASY VERSUS REALITY

One of the images to emerge from Wackenroder's tale of Joseph Berglinger is a gap between the world of the artist-creator and the "real" world. The artist feels underappreciated, or at least not adequately understood, by the more materialistic world of commerce. This kind of split did not exist before about 1800, when the patronage system prevailed. Most artists were servants of nobility and produced their art on demand. Joseph Haydn spent most of his career in service to the aristocratic Esterházy family. Wolfgang Mozart was also supported by patrons, although less consistently. Later in life, both composers began to work on a more freelance basis. Joseph Berglinger's career is on the cusp of these kinds of changes. He is a kapellmeister in service to a bishop, but he also feels himself an artist, one who should be above all worldly things.

After 1800, many artists and thinkers found it increasingly hard to reconcile the bourgeois, capitalist world with the realm of art. Looked at from a more metaphysical or philosophical point of view, the relationship between the artist and society may be said to have embodied the split posited by Kant between the phenomenal world (the world of appearances) and the noumenal world (the world we cannot see). Artists began to view the phenomenal world with scorn; they longed for the noumenal world, the world of artistic fantasy.

The theme of the artist in isolation from, and often in conflict with, the real world, is common in Romanticism. We see it with particular force in the stories of E.T.A. Hoffmann, where the sensitive protagonist is often trapped or torn between the everyday bourgeois world and a supernatural realm to which only he has access. In *The Mines of Falun*, Elis Fröbom is enticed by magnificent lodes deep inside a mine—lodes that no one else can see—and eschews the surface world of love, marriage, and family. Like so many Hoffmann characters, Elis feels "split in half." In *The Golden Pot*, one of Hoffmann's greatest tales, Anselmus is a poor, beleaguered student who rejects the real world into which he fits awkwardly (he rips his coat on a nail, loses his hat while bowing, breaks things easily, and so on) and flees

Figure 2.4: *E.T.A. Hoffmann, drawing of*
The Kapellmeister Kreisler Going Mad,
1822

to a fantasy world of green-gold snakes, bronze-gold palm trees, and tropical birds who make music when they fly.

Hoffmann's greatest fictional creation is the kapellmeister Johannes Kreisler, who appears in numerous works of fiction and whom Hoffmann also captured in a whimsical drawing (Fig. 2.4). Like Berglinger, Kreisler is an eccentric conductor and composer who is utterly devoted to his art but is awkward and ill suited for the real bourgeois world of which he is a part. He even views himself as partly mad, signing his letters "Johannes Kreisler, Kapellmeister and Crazy Musician par excellence." In one of Hoffmann's major works of fiction, *Lebens-Ansichten des Katers Murr* (The Life and Opinions of Tomcat Murr), the biography of Kreisler is interwoven with the memoirs of the cat, who is writing them on the reverse sides of paper he has recovered from the trash on which the memoirs of Kreisler are contained.

Hoffmann's stories had wide appeal throughout the nineteenth century. The French composer Jacques Offenbach (whom we discuss in Chapter 9) used five of them as the basis for his best-known opera, *Les contes d'Hoffmann* (The Tales of Hoffmann, 1880). Robert Schumann steeped himself in Hoffmann's writings. He entitled one of his major piano cycles *Kreisleriana* (1838). And on three occasions he used the term *Fantasiestücke* (Fantasy Pieces) for a set of short pieces, a likely reference to Hoffmann's collection of writings *Fantasiestücke in Callots Manier* (Fantasy Pieces in the Style of Callot [a French artist]). Above all, Schumann, like Hoffmann, saw a conflict between the real and imaginary worlds. In his own music criticism and in the titles of some of his piano pieces, Schumann (drawing on a biblical rivalry) pitted the "Philistines," who were the general public and conservative musicians, against the "*Davidsbund*," the Band of David, who saw their goal to fight against the poor taste of the bourgeoisie (see Chapters 5 and 6). Schumann especially took issue with the prevailing enthusiasm for (as he saw it) salon-style and empty virtuoso piano music. He championed great composers of the remote and recent past like Bach, Handel, Mozart, Beethoven, and Schubert, and composers of his own time like Chopin and Liszt.

ROMANTIC IRONY

The problems of split identity in Hoffmann's tales and novels reveal an important dimension of early Romantic aesthetics: irony. Irony was an ancient rhetorical practice, that of saying or implying the opposite of what you really mean. In Romanticism, irony became more than just a strategy; it became a worldview. In part Romantic irony consisted in acknowledging, and even celebrating, the divide between the real and imaginary worlds. For Friedrich Schlegel, writers had a duty to employ irony as a way of acknowledging the contradictory, unresolvable qualities of the relationship between an individual and the world. This attitude accounts for the apparently bizarre practices of Romantic writers like Hoffmann, who often undercut any clear story line or single authorial stance by stepping outside the narrative, or, as in *Tomcat Murr*, by constantly shifting the point of view. In one play by Ludwig Tieck, the characters gang up at the end and murder the author. Schlegel described the key aspect of Romantic irony as the destruction of illusion.

Romantic irony figures heavily in the poetry of Heine and was captured musically in Schumann's *Dichterliebe*. The text of the song *Ich grolle nicht* claims that the poet never complains, even when his heart is broken, even when love is lost:

> Ich grolle nicht, und wenn das Herz auch bricht,
> Ewig verlor'nes Lieb! Ich grolle nicht.
>
> *I don't complain, even when my heart is breaking,*
> *Love forever lost! I don't complain.*

This is classic irony in the sense that the text is saying more or less the opposite of what is really meant: the poet *is* certainly complaining. Schumann captures this irony perfectly with his musical setting—an accompaniment of continually unresolved dissonance, with angrily throbbing chords in the right hand and powerful octaves in the left (see Ex. 2.3).

As the nineteenth century wore on, Romantic irony lost much of its sense of innocence. The philosopher Friedrich Hegel (1770–1831) had little use for Schlegel's variety of Romantic irony, which he dubbed "trifling with everything,"

Example 2.3: *Schumann,* Dichterliebe, *No. 7,* Ich grolle nicht, *mm. 1–8*

which "can transform all things into show," and in which "all noble or divine truth vanishes away or becomes mere triviality." Hegel believed in tragic irony, as understood by Socrates and practiced by the ancient Greek playwrights. Tragic irony presented individuals in the grip of forces largely beyond their control and awareness. Here was the foundation of what Hegel called the "universal irony of the world," or what Heine would label "world irony." Such irony was fundamental to the actual processes of history, in which the events characteristic of tragic drama are projected onto the world stage.

Wagner's mature operas, written between about 1850 and 1880, capture this later phase of irony. In Wagner's *Ring of the Nibelung*, the main characters Wotan, Siegfried, and Brünnhilde are caught up in events they often neither understand nor can control, but through which they come to accept their fate. Events or individual actions are directed ultimately toward the destruction of the gods, a cataclysm that occurs at the end of the final opera, *Götterdämmerung* (Twilight of the Gods). Wagner was following Schopenhauer's pessimism, which adds a darker, more personal twist to Hegel's world irony. Wagner's rich orchestra, with its succession of leitmotifs representing certain characters or ideas (to be discussed in Chapter 8), seems to offer an ironic commentary on the situations in which they find themselves.

ROMANTICISM AND NATIONALISM

It may seem from the foregoing that Romanticism was concerned mainly with an artist's self-expression, and that the relationship to the real world was usually one of separation and isolation. In fact, Romanticism also had a strongly political and social side, which sometimes complemented and sometimes contradicted the artists' individual beliefs. One of the precursors of Romanticism in Germany, Johann Gottfried Herder (1744–1803), argued that geographical, ethnic, and linguistic identity was essential in shaping the culture and art of a people. In a period where contemporaries like Winckelmann were extolling the virtues of Greek art, Herder praised the native traditions of Germany. His published collections of folk poetry would inspire generations of Romantic artists, including the Brothers Grimm, who in 1812 compiled a renowned collection of German fairy tales that would go through seven editions up to 1857.

The French Revolution also contributed to the rise of Romanticism. Writers, painters, thinkers, and musicians were inspired by the revolution to believe in the power of ideals and values, including artistic ones, to change the world. The first generation of Romantics in France grew up in the aftermath of the revolution. Many maintained its nobler ideals, but were appalled at some of its actual consequences. One of the most famous of all Romantic paintings, *Liberty Leading the People* (1830) by Eugène Delacroix, shows a woman waving the *tricolore* (three-color flag) of the French Revolution as she guides the people forward over the bodies of the fallen (see Fig. 2.5). The painting was inspired by the so-called July Revolution of 1830 that overthrew King Charles X. Victor Hugo resolutely opposed the restoration of the monarchy in France in 1814. In 1852, when Louis-Napoleon Bonaparte (nephew of Napoleon) declared himself emperor, an outraged Hugo went into self-imposed exile from France for almost twenty years.

In England, Wordsworth at first embraced the French Revolution and its goals. He wrote in his autobiographical poem *The Prelude*, "Bliss was it in that dawn to be alive / But to be young was very heaven!" Yet after witnessing the bloody aftermath of the revolution, Wordsworth became disillusioned. Later in *The Prelude* he wrote of the Reign of Terror:

Most melancholy at that time, O Friend!
Were my day-thoughts, my nights were miserable;

Figure 2.5: *Eugène Delacroix,* Liberty Leading the People, *1830*

Through months, through years, long after the last beat
Of those atrocities, the hour of sleep
To me came rarely charged with natural gifts,
Such ghastly Visions had I of despair,
And tyranny, and implements of death.

In a poem of 1809 Wordsworth described Napoleon as

. . . ruthless, undismayed;
And so hath gained at length a prosperous Height,
Round which the Elements of worldly might
Beneath his haughty feet, like clouds, are laid.

In Italy, Romanticism, politics, and music were directly connected in the figure of Giuseppe Mazzini (1805–1872), who was both a philosopher and a statesman. Mazzini would play a large role in the revolutions of 1848, and then in the 1850s and 1860s as a leader in the Risorgimento, the movement to create a unified Italy (discussed in Chapters 7 and 9). Earlier, in his *Philosophy of Music* of

1836, Mazzini urged his countrymen to transcend narrow nationalism in musical styles. He saw European music as divided into two strains, northern and southern, or primarily German and Italian. As much as he admired Beethoven, Rossini, and their successors, none was deemed adequate to fulfill the Romantic ideals of human expression and communication:

> Italian music lacks the sanctifying concept of all efforts: the moral thought that stimulates the forces of the mind, the blessing of a mission. German music lacks the energy to carry it out, the actual instrument of the conquest; it lacks, not the sentiment, but the concrete form of the mission. Italian music is rendered barren by materialism; German music is uselessly consumed in mysticism. (SR 152:1091–92; 6/5:49–50)

Mazzini called for music that represents a "European synthesis" of these strands, which he saw already present in the other arts. In a beautiful phrase, he describes music as "the algebra of the immanent soul of humanity," and demands that it not be left out of this synthesis of the arts. Mazzini goes on to say that "when the time is ripe," a musical genius will appear who will achieve that synthesis and rescue European music.

We have seen in this chapter that, despite the frustrations of Toreinx and others in trying to define it, Romanticism was a genuine phenomenon in the early nineteenth century. Romanticism comprised no single worldview, no specific set of artistic styles. It thrived as an array of attitudes and practices that strongly affected literature, philosophy, aesthetics, the arts, and politics. Romanticism reacted against the closed, finite nature of Classical structures and systems of thought. It explored the relationship between real and imagined worlds, and was strongly drawn to the latter, to the realm of fantasy. Romanticism also turned art into a kind of substitute religion.

Music played a central role in these developments. For many writers and thinkers, it came to the fore as the most Romantic of the arts, the one best equipped to communicate longing, to broach the infinite and the imaginary. In the chapters that follow we will examine how the ideals of Romanticism were adapted to the activities and the products of musical life in the first half of the nineteenth century.

FOR FURTHER READING

Abrams, M. H., *The Mirror and the Lamp: Romantic Theory and the Critical Tradition* (Oxford and New York: Oxford University Press, 1971)

Breckman, Warren, *European Romanticism: A Brief History with Documents* (New York: Bedford/St. Martin's, 2008)

Ferber, Michael, *Romanticism: A Very Short Introduction* (New York and Oxford: Oxford University Press, 2010)

Hoffmann, E.T.A., *Tales of E.T.A. Hoffmann*, ed. and trans. Leonard Kent and Elizabeth Knight (Chicago and London: University of Chicago Press, 1969)

Honour, Hugh, *Romanticism* (New York: Westview Press, 1979)

le Huray, Peter, and James Day, *Music and Aesthetics in the Eighteenth and Early-Nineteenth Centuries*, abridged ed. (Cambridge and New York: Cambridge University Press, 1988)

Ⓢ Additional resources available at wwnorton.com/studyspace

CHAPTER THREE

Music and the Age of Metternich

He was a powerful politician whose name has come to symbolize an entire era in Europe. As chancellor of Austria, Klemenz Wenzel von Metternich (1773–1859) became the chief architect and enforcer of European geopolitics in the period from 1815 up to the revolutions of 1848. In 1814–15 he hosted the Congress of Vienna, which would affect not only the power structure of the continent but also the culture of the arts and music.

Broadly speaking, two trends emerge in musical life during the Metternich era. One fostered private or semiprivate music-making; the other brought music into the larger public spheres of the concert hall and opera house. Although these two realms, private and public, would become associated with different genres of music, many composers and performers participated actively in both. In this chapter we will focus first on the Austro-German realm, specifically on Ludwig van Beethoven (1770–1827) and Franz Schubert (1797–1828), who negotiated the Metternich era in different ways and whose careers and works can be understood in relation to its cultural values. Then we will turn to the new phenomenon of virtuoso performers. Opera will be treated in Chapter 4.

THE CONGRESS OF VIENNA

"Comment ça marche?" (How is it going [literally, walking]?), the Prince de Ligne was supposedly asked in 1815 about the Congress of Vienna. "Le congrès ne marche pas; il danse" (It's not walking; it's dancing), came the response. Taken literally, the prince's comment would probably refer to the waltz, a dance in triple meter that became popular at the Congress as a high-class version of the earthy Austrian ländler. (It was also distinct from the earlier minuet, which was in triple meter as well.) The waltz would be cultivated by countless composers, from Schubert and Chopin, to Johann Strauss, Jr. (the "Waltz King"), to Verdi and Mahler. Figure 3.1 shows a ball given by Prince Metternich at the Congress of Vienna.

In politics as in music, the Congress of Vienna would cast a long shadow across the nineteenth century. However much they danced and caroused, the diplomats and heads of state who assembled in the capital city of the Austro-Hungarian Empire between September 1814 and June 1815 were occupied with serious business. Their main task was to reconstruct Europe after the disruptions and devastations of the Napoleonic Wars. Anxious to put an end to the turbulence dating back to the French Revolution, the participants in the Congress of Vienna restored strong monarchies in France, Spain, and the Netherlands, awarded parts of the Italian territories and Poland to other sovereignties, and reshaped the defunct Holy Roman Empire into a German Confederation dominated by Austria and Prussia. These decisions were to have important

Figure 3.1: *Ball given by Prince Metternich at the Congress of Vienna in 1815*

consequences in the coming decades, including revolutions that broke out across Europe in 1848 and the strong push for independent national status in Germany, Italy, and among peoples in Central and Eastern Europe.

The new rulers of Europe placed heavy restrictions on personal liberty and freedom of expression. Nowhere was this more apparent than in the German Confederation, which was supervised with an iron fist by Metternich. In the aftermath of the murder of a prominent diplomat by young liberals, he imposed the repressive Carlsbad Decrees of 1819 on private citizens and institutions, including universities and the press. The arts were also affected by the clampdown on politics and other public activities. Schubert's friend Eduard von Bauernfeld, writing in 1872, characterized life in Vienna in the 1820s in this way: "Today's youth cannot imagine the humiliating pressure on our creative spirits under which we, as young people—aspiring writers and artists—suffered. The police in general and censorship in particular weighed on us all like a monkey we could not get off our back." Schubert, although he kept a low profile, had his own brush with the law when he was arrested one evening in 1820 along with several members of his circle. The police report noted the aggressive behavior of the poet Johann Chrysostomus Senn and added that Schubert had "chimed in against the authorized official in the same tone, inveighing against him with insulting and opprobrious language." Schubert was released with a reprimand, but Senn, whose liberal views were well known to the authorities, was imprisoned for 14 months, then banished from Vienna.

BIEDERMEIER CULTURE

A natural reaction to the repressive atmosphere of the Metternich era was to turn away from the world of politics, inward to the home. Especially within Austro-German culture and society, the era ushered in by the Congress of Vienna and lasting until the revolutions of 1848 has been called the Biedermeier period, after the name of a fictitious schoolteacher featured in a series of humorous poems that appeared in a Munich periodical in the 1850s. Biedermeier has come to indicate a range of values associated with domesticity and the middle class, as manifested in styles of furniture, interior decoration, jewelry, clothing, painting, literature, and even music. The Biedermeier celebration of the cozy life is captured vividly in a memoir about the post-Congress decades by the German novelist Karl Gutzkow:

> What charm there is in the intimate sociability of a cultured home! . . .
> The orderliness and the solicitude spread everywhere a warmth and comfort that stir the soul as well as the senses. The women's little worktable by
> the window, the workbasket with its little spools of thread, its blue English needle-papers, its little lacquer stars for winding silk, the thimbles,

the scissors, and the pincushions on the little table, alongside the piano with its music, hyacinths in forcing-glasses on the windowsill, a bird in a pretty brass cage, a carpet that softens with every footstep, engravings on the walls, all merely transient necessities cleared away into distant rooms, the gatherings of the family all together in mutual reverence and contentment—no uproar, no running and dashing about.

One could scarcely assemble a list of more domesticated images. Significantly, along with birds, flowers, and pincushions, there is the piano and "its music." Just what might this music have been? Most likely a waltz, a song, or a duet to be played at one piano.

The first half of the nineteenth century saw an explosion of just such sheet music destined for middle-class homes. Stars in the publishing firmament, some still in business in the twenty-first century, were Chappell and Novello in London, Pleyel in Paris, Diabelli and Doblinger in Vienna, and Breitkopf & Härtel in Leipzig. To increase production and extend print runs of music, these publishers began to replace the older method of engraving, in which the notation was cut into a copper plate by a sharp tool, with the newer, more efficient method of lithography, invented in 1796, in which the surface remains smooth and the notation is drawn with an oil-based substance.

As we saw in Chapter 1, the house of Anton Diabelli made handsome profits by issuing thousands of works for domestic consumption, including lighter music for piano solo, for piano four-hands (that is, for two pianists at the same instrument), for guitar, and for voice. Diabelli also published weightier piano sonatas and string quartets by Beethoven. At this time, many members of the middle class had passable musical skills. Young women were trained on the piano, men often on string instruments. Many pieces published by Diabelli were arrangements of popular opera arias; others were dances like waltzes, ländler, écossaises (originally from Scotland), and deutsche (literally, German).

These works were enjoyed in settings like the one described by Gutzkow and also as depicted in the watercolor from 1821 reproduced as Figure 3.2. Here the Viennese artist Leopold Kupelwieser happened to include one prominent musician of the day—Franz Schubert, who is seated at the piano. Next to him is a dog, a perfect symbol of domesticity. Schubert's friends are engaged in an innocent and far-from-subversive pastime: a game of charades about Adam and Eve. This event most likely took place at a "Schubertiad," one of the frequent informal gatherings of the composer and his friends at which Schubert's music was performed. His initial reputation as a composer spread not through publications of his music or public concerts, but through events like these, much in the spirit of Biedermeier culture.

If these activities of Schubert and his circle represent one side of musical culture in the Metternich era—convivial domesticity—Beethoven represents

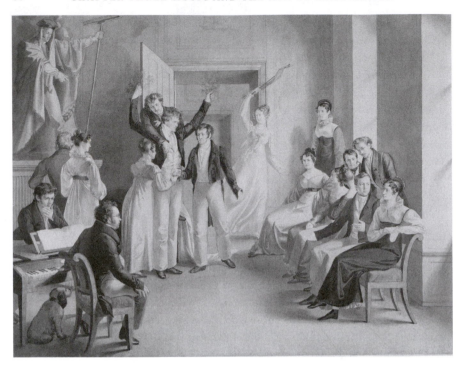

Figure 3.2: *Leopold Kupelwieser,* Charade among the Schubert Circle in Atzenbrugg: Expulsion from Paradise, *watercolor, 1821*

the other. In the years after the Congress of Vienna, Beethoven, deaf, eccentric, and misanthropic, largely withdrew from Viennese society. His later music, difficult both to play and to hear, and not intended primarily for the parlor, points up a divide between two "cultures" of music—roughly, the popular and the elite. Schubert was very comfortable in the former, Beethoven much less so. This split—which survives today in our distinction between "popular" and "classical" music—was articulated clearly by the critic Friedrich Rochlitz (1769–1842) in an 1828 review of a posthumous publication of some of Beethoven's last works:

> We must consider the public as belonging to two very different classes in regard to music, much as in regard to reading matter and many other things, according to sensibility and inclination. . . . The first only wants to amuse itself with music, whether hearing or practicing it—to create an agreeable pastime. The second wants, as regularly as possible, to excite, engage, reanimate, uplift, strengthen, and advance its whole inner person.

Rochlitz clearly places Beethoven's late works in the latter category, which "uplifts" rather than entertains.

Some middle-class people would have partaken of both cultures—playing ländler in their parlors one day and listening to Beethoven symphonies in the concert hall on another. But Rochlitz's comments show the beginnings of a fundamental divide between the arts as "entertainment" and as what the Germans would call *Bildung*, meaning education or intellectual formation, and whose sense is perfectly captured in Rochlitz's phrase "uplift, strengthen, advance its whole inner person." The gap between popular and classical music continued to grow during the nineteenth century, leaving behind the musical culture of the later eighteenth century, when a work like Mozart's opera *Die Zauberflöte* (The Magic Flute, 1791) could smoothly integrate both styles.

Rochlitz's comments about Beethoven appeared in a musical journal he had founded in 1798, the *Allgemeine musikalische Zeitung* (General Music Magazine). Published weekly without interruption until 1848 (and later revived), the *Zeitung* was a part of an important phenomenon of the early nineteenth century—the profusion of music journals in a whole range of European cities. Experts were eager to share their ideas with a growing musical public of both professionals and amateurs. They sought to improve musical *Bildung*, to "uplift and strengthen" musical life, and the public was eager to learn. Issued by Breitkopf & Härtel in Leipzig, the *Allgemeine musikalische Zeitung* was by no means a simple "house organ" used to promote the firm's own composers or interests. Under Rochlitz's leadership—he edited the journal until 1818 and continued to write for it well into the 1830s—it provided a model for music journalism that is still familiar to us today. Each issue included essays, biographical information, reviews of theoretical works and of music, descriptions of instruments, and news items from German, Austrian, Italian, French, Russian, and eventually American venues.

LUDWIG VAN BEETHOVEN

During the first decade of the nineteenth century, in what would later become known as his "middle" or "heroic" period, Beethoven established his reputation in the Austro-German sphere as a composer advancing in bold new directions. In works like the Third (*Eroica*) Symphony, Op. 55 (1803), and the three *Rasumovsky* String Quartets, Op. 59 (1806), traditional forms are expanded by a propulsive rhythmic and thematic language, and by broad harmonic designs. In their intensity these works clearly partake of the Romantic spirit outlined in Chapter 2. Indeed, one of the chief spokesmen of Romanticism, E.T.A. Hoffmann, claimed Beethoven's middle-period symphonic music as fully Romantic in that it touches on the "immeasurable" and awakens "endless longing" (SR 160:1194; 6/13:152). We recall that striving for the immeasurable or infinite, as well as a sense of longing, were essential components of the Romantic imagination. Also Romantic are Beethoven's view of art as a kind of sacred calling, like the art-religion discussed in Chapter 2, and his increasing claim to independence from societal norms.

At the beginning of the second decade of the nineteenth century, Beethoven was living in relative comfort and isolation on a generous annuity provided by a group of Viennese noblemen, in an arrangement probably unique in the history of musical patronage. According to this agreement, Beethoven did not have to compose or perform on demand; all he had to do was reside in Vienna or another city in the Austrian empire. But serious devaluation of the Austrian currency in 1811 meant that Beethoven could not rely on his annuity alone. He began to reach for popular acclaim and financial success in the concert hall, reemerging into the public eye with *Wellington's Victory*, Op. 91, composed early in 1813 to celebrate the defeat of the French army at the Battle of Vittoria. (Nine years earlier, Beethoven's disillusionment with Napoleon's autocratic tendencies had prompted him to revoke the dedication of his Third Symphony.) During the Congress of Vienna, Beethoven contributed the triumphal cantata *Der glorreiche Augenblick* (The Glorious Moment), Op. 136, set to a patriotic text by the poet Alois Weissenbach. Often dismissed today as anomalies of Beethoven's output, such works in fact reflect the strongly nationalistic dimension of political Romanticism outlined in the last chapter. Beethoven had come to oppose French domination and influence, and to advocate a stable monarchy as necessary for spiritual and social reform.

Although his nationalistic works were greeted enthusiastically by the Viennese public, this wave of popularity soon receded. Beethoven's late musical style began to emerge with the Piano Sonata in A Major, Op. 101 (1815), and by 1818 it was in full swing with three more piano sonatas (Opp. 109, 110, 111), and the beginnings of the Ninth Symphony, Op. 125, which would be completed in 1824 (see Fig. 3.3). In that year Beethoven also embarked on what were to

Figure 3.3: *Beethoven in 1824, at the time he completed his Ninth Symphony, by Johann Stefan Decker*

be his final works, a group of string quartets (Opp. 127, 130, 131, 132, and 135). The Ninth Symphony was in some ways a throwback to the heroic manner of Beethoven's middle-period works, a style associated with the *Eroica* Symphony. The Ninth has expansive dimensions, bold rhythmic energy, and a final movement with chorus and vocal soloists singing Friedrich Schiller's poem *Ode to Joy*, an Enlightenment-inspired hymn to universal brotherhood. Yet the strong contrasts in the symphony—a broad political-social message juxtaposed with moments of interiority and spirituality—also make it a characteristically Romantic work.

From 1812 on, not only was Beethoven understood by some as a Romantic, but he began himself to read widely in the contemporary literature of Romanticism. His reported comments and his later compositions suggest a growing belief in the roles of fantasy, transcendence, and the infinite. In the early 1820s Beethoven remarked that the genuine artist "sees unfortunately that art has no limits; he has a vague awareness of how far he is from reaching his goal; and while others may perhaps be admiring him, he laments the fact that he has not yet reached the point whither his better genius only lights the way for him like a distant sun."

Beethoven's later works often show an indifference to Biedermeier culture and values. We recall from Chapter 1 how he redefined Diabelli's collective variation project on his own terms, turning a kind of public Biedermeier party game into an occasion for his monumental set of 33 *Diabelli* Variations, Op. 120 (1819–23). Beethoven's late works also display experimentation—even downright quirkiness—not intended to appeal to a wider middle-class audience. Some have an unusual number of movements (as few as two, as many as seven). Childlike tunes alternate with jagged melodies, simple harmonies with harsh dissonances. In Beethoven's later works, expressive and structural contrast is the norm rather than the exception.

The C♯-Minor String Quartet, Op. 131, composed in 1825–26, shows clearly how Beethoven could explore the conventions and conflicts of his cultural milieu. String quartets became the most prestigious type of chamber music during the later eighteenth century, from Haydn and Mozart on. Audiences, critics, and amateur performers alike enjoyed the communal intimacy of the quartet, which was sometimes described as a dialogue or discussion. Composers appreciated the opportunity to write more complex and contrapuntal music in which (unlike in piano music) each part could be clearly heard. These ideals are confirmed by the music theorist Heinrich Koch, who observed in 1793 that in a quartet

> there are four main voices which alternately predominate and sometimes this one, sometimes that one forms the customary bass.

While one of these parts concerns itself with the delivery of the melody, the other two melodic voices must proceed in connected melodies which promote the expression without obscuring the main melody. From this it is evident that the quartet is one of the most difficult of all kinds of compositions, which only the composer completely trained and experienced through much practice may attempt. (SR 126:814; 5/5:80)

Beethoven's dominance in the genre of the string quartet was confirmed in 1808 by the composer and critic Johann Friedrich Reichardt (1752–1814), who reported on a performance in Vienna by a group led by the professional violinist Ignaz Schuppanzigh:

Three works were played, one by Haydn, then one by Mozart, and finally one by Beethoven; this last was particularly good. It was very interesting to me to observe in this succession how the three . . . each according to his individual nature, have further developed the genre. Haydn created it out of the pure, luminous fountain of his charming, original nature. . . . Mozart's more robust nature and richer imagination gained further ground, and expressed in many a piece the heights and depths of his inner being. . . . Beethoven built a bold and defiant tower on top of which no one could easily place anything more without breaking his neck. (SR 147:1036; 5/26:302)

We do not know which quartet of Beethoven was played on this occasion in 1808, but Reichardt's positive reception would not necessarily have been repeated two decades later for Beethoven's more idiosyncratic works in the genre. Here is how another critic, Ignaz Seyfried, writing in 1828, a year after Beethoven's death, reacted to the C♯-Minor Quartet: "The author was undoubtedly in a soul-sick frame of mind, at odds with himself, probably even visited by tormenting misanthropy, in order to have produced this night piece in Rembrandt's manner, brightened by so few points of light." Seyfried also pointed out how the unbroken continuity of movements in the quartet taxed the capabilities of both performers and listeners, and suggested a bit of trimming might be appropriate: "It was his [Beethoven's] will for all of the movements, big and little alike, to form an uninterrupted chain, which must manifestly exhaust the players as well as the audience through its length, and for this reason it would be advisable at least to make a few cuts at perfect cadences." Many critics of the 1820s and beyond saw the later Beethoven as no longer capable of writing coherent music; they were puzzled by the apparent lack of clear structure, the length of some movements, and the sustained level of dissonance.

Beethoven's Op. 131 is in many outward respects a traditional work. It has the skeleton of the four basic movement types—a sonata-form allegro; a slow movement; a scherzo; and a finale. But these are embedded in a sequence of seven numbered movements or sections, which follow each other without interruption and thus obscure the conventional structures discussed by Koch and Reichardt. The sonata-form allegro (2) is preceded by a slow fugue (1) more than twice its length and too massive to be considered a "slow introduction" in the eighteenth-century mold. A transitional passage (3) links the sonata-form movement (2) and subsequent slow movement (4), and another (6) links the scherzo (5) and finale (7). As with any Classical work, a principal key, here C♯ minor, serves as anchor:

(1) C♯ minor – (2) D major – (4) A major – (5) E major – (7) C♯ minor

But Beethoven's design is unusual in restricting the tonic to the outer movements—most works of the late eighteenth and early nineteenth centuries have an inner movement in the main key—and especially in placing the second movement in the remote key of the Neapolitan, or lowered second degree, D major.

In its sharp juxtaposition of styles, which as we saw in Chapter 2 was a characteristic of Romantic art, the C♯-Minor Quartet veers between the serious and the parodic. The opening fugue, with its ultra-serious counterpoint, evokes the "learned" style of the eighteenth century (Ex. 3.1; see Anthology 1). The fugue gives way to the second movement's swirling, somewhat frenzied dance in D major, a half step above the tonic of the work. We have the feeling of being tonally and emotionally several inches off the ground, as if Beethoven is poking fun at the world of light Biedermeier music.

Example 3.1: *Beethoven, String Quartet in C♯ Minor, Op. 131, movement 1, mm. 1–8*

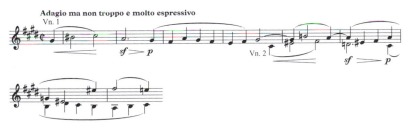

In the breathless scherzo Beethoven seems to be saying, "Here's how far I can push the form toward expressive mania." The last movement is built from themes that contrast sharply with one another. First comes a Hungarian dance, of the kind that became popular in Vienna in the first decades of the nineteenth century and was exploited by many composers for "local color." Beethoven's Hungarian dance has a stomping furor that tears off any Biedermeier veil (Ex. 3.2a). It gives way to a theme whose contour directly recalls the initial motive of the fugue of the first movement, both in its regular form and in inversion (see *x* in Ex. 3.2b). Beethoven thus seeks to round off his quartet by bringing things full circle.

Example 3.2: *Beethoven, String Quartet in C♯ Minor, Op. 131, movement 7*

(a) mm. 6–9

(b) mm. 21–24

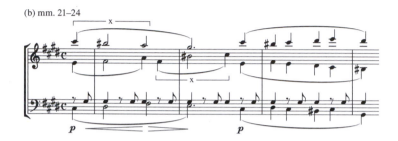

In its time the C♯-Minor Quartet was often greeted with incomprehension. Today we can recognize in it the summit of Beethoven's skills as an artist, especially his ability to bind together into a vast, coherent structure many different movements and sharply contrasting moods. In that sense, the C♯-Minor Quartet truly stands astride what we have identified as Classicism and Romanticism. The impulse toward rational order is challenged by forces that often fragment the musical and expressive discourse and push it toward what Hoffmann identified as "the monstrous and the immeasurable."

FRANZ SCHUBERT

Although Schubert lived at the same time and in the same city as Beethoven, the generation gap between them made for a big difference in their careers and their place in musical culture. Beethoven, born in 1770, was for much of his life a child of the Enlightenment; his ethical, social, and political values were largely shaped by figures like Kant and Schiller and by the ideals of the French Revolution. Beethoven's works often embody these values in ways that would have been unlikely for Schubert, who was born in 1797 and emerged as a young man and artist contemporaneously with the Congress of Vienna and the advent of the repressive Metternich regime.

Beethoven and Schubert moved in different circles. It is not clear that they ever met, although in the years 1815–18 they seem to have frequented the same music publishing house in Vienna, where composers gathered and exchanged ideas. One story, impossible to confirm but often repeated, says that Schubert visited Beethoven on his deathbed March 1827. We do know that Schubert came to revere Beethoven's music and sought to emulate his achievements in the larger instrumental forms.

Schubert was the son of a bourgeois schoolmaster working in a Viennese suburb. His musical talent was apparent from a young age, and in 1808 he was accepted as a boy soprano into the Imperial Court Choir, which had the special advantage of providing tuition and board at the finest school in Vienna, the Imperial and Royal City College. Schubert played violin in and also occasionally conducted the student orchestra, which performed works by Haydn, Mozart, and Beethoven. Schubert also had composition lessons with Antonio Salieri, one of the most admired composers in Vienna, though today best known as Mozart's archrival, thanks to the fictionalized play and film *Amadeus*.

Early on, Schubert developed a passion for the lied, which was still a relatively new musical genre in the Austro-German world. The lied (plural: lieder) is a setting of a poem for a singer with the accompaniment of a piano. The growing popularity of the lied around 1800 had much to do with the interest in German folk traditions spurred on by Johann Gottfried Herder in the later eighteenth century, as discussed in Chapter 2. There were two basic types of lieder written in the generation before Schubert. Composers in southern Germany like Johann Zumsteeg tended to favor lengthy, multisectional, narrative ballads that were through-composed, that is, in which there is little repetition of musical material in the setting in the poem. Composers from northern Germany, especially Berlin, including Johann Reichardt (whom we met earlier in this chapter as a critic) and Friedrich Zelter, wrote shorter songs that were mostly strophic, in which the same unit of music is repeated for each stanza of a poem. In the latter songs, the ideal was the *Volkston* or folklike feeling.

As early as 1811 Schubert began experimenting with both styles of lieder, the ballad and the folklike. By the time of his death in 1828, he had written over 600 lieder. Despite their small scale (relative to symphonies or operas), the greatest of these constitute lyrical masterpieces of the Romantic era, especially because of two distinctive features. First, unlike many of his predecessors and contemporaries, Schubert was often attracted to high-quality texts by leading German poets, including Johann Wolfgang von Goethe, Friedrich Schiller, Matthias Claudius, and Friedrich von Matthisson. Second, Schubert took an "interventionist" approach to the setting of a text. He was not content to underpin a melody with simple, discreet accompaniment, as other composers often did; he made the piano part an integral element of the work. Schubert's principal technique was to reach inside a poem for a vivid image, out of which he created a pattern for a piano accompaniment. That pattern then runs throughout the song as a unifying device, but at any moment it can be transformed according to the mood or content of the text.

Schubert's *Gretchen am Spinnrade* (Gretchen at the Spinning Wheel), his Op. 2 (D. 118), composed in November 1814, is a splendid example of this technique (see Anthology 2). The song is a setting of a text from Part 1 of Goethe's drama

Faust. One of the most famous works of German literature, *Faust* depicts how a man sells his soul to the devil in his desire to achieve perfect knowledge and happiness. Faust seduces Margarete (Gretchen is the familiar form of the name), who has fallen deeply in love with him.

In the scene that so captivated Schubert, Gretchen sits alone in her room, at her spinning wheel, and fantasizes about Faust. She is some ways a perfect Biedermeier portrait: the well-bred middle-class girl engaged in a domestic activity. But in Goethe's hands, and then Schubert's, any hint of Biedermeier coziness is eliminated by Gretchen's palpable agitation and her infatuation with a man she has met not through normal social interaction, but through demonic intervention. Instead of a cheerful folklike tune of the kind we might expect a girl to sing while spinning, she sings a theme that hovers nervously around the pitch A, the song's unstable dominant. The theme and its accompaniment capture perfectly the sense of Gretchen's words, "Meine Ruh' ist hin" (My peace is gone) (Ex. 3.3).

Example 3.3: *Schubert,* Gretchen am Spinnrade, *Op. 2 (D. 118), mm. 1–6*

My peace is gone, my heart is heavy.

Underneath the vocal part, Schubert's spinning wheel is rendered with an almost pictorial realism. Spinning wheels have a number of moving parts: the wheel is driven by a spindle, which in turn is activated by the motion of the spinner's foot on the treadle near the floor. In Schubert's accompaniment, the right hand of the piano captures the circular motion of the wheel. The bass (the bottom notes in the left hand), with longer rhythmic values, represents Gretchen's foot on the treadle, which keeps the wheel turning. The rhythmic pattern in the middle part (also played by the left hand), moving more quickly, represents the click of the spindle as it whirs.

Schubert's great achievement in *Gretchen am Spinnrade* is to make the piano part not only a representation of the spinning wheel, but also a more abstract reflection of Gretchen's turbulent emotions. Like the motion of the spinning wheel, her thoughts are at once circular and progressive, or, we might say, centripetal and centrifugal—focused on one thing but also pushing outward in many directions. To capture this situation, Schubert fuses elements of two kinds of musical song form discussed above: strophic and through-composed. The result is an innovative and effective "wave" structure: Gretchen's "Meine Ruh' ist hin" is a refrain that returns, obsessively and inevitably, but each time leads off into new musical material.

In later years Schubert composed several song cycles, in which a number of lieder are grouped together into a single work that follows a narrative thread or a coherent psychological trajectory and is intended to be performed in its entirety. Schubert completed two large song cycles, *Die schöne Müllerin* (The Lovely Maid of the Mill, D. 795, 1823), with 20 songs, and *Winterreise* (Winter's Journey, D. 911, 1827), with 24, both settings of the poetry of Wilhelm Müller. Each traces the emotions and actions of a young male protagonist who is rejected by his beloved.

In Schubert's day, song cycles were often created as Biedermeier party games. Young people would sit around the parlor and make up a story in poems, which composers would set to simple folklike music. The poems of Müller's *Schöne Müllerin* grew out of just such a collective endeavor that took place at the Berlin salon of a wealthy banker. But Schubert's song cycles, like so much of his other work, transcend that Biedermeier context, even while acknowledging it. The main characters of both Schubert cycles long for the quiet, domestic life that is the Biedermeier ideal, but it is beyond their reach. In *Winterreise* the poet-singer is literally outside any home; he wanders in a frozen landscape and looks longingly at various symbols of Biedermeier life—villages, houses, country inns, weathervanes, and even pet dogs.

In his larger-scale instrumental works of the 1820s Schubert sought a place alongside his great contemporary Beethoven. Schubert devoted much attention to four-hand piano music, for two players at one instrument. This was a Biedermeier genre into which Beethoven rarely ventured, but which Schubert transfigured with several masterpieces, including the Fantasy in F Minor (D. 940), written in the last year of his life, 1828. Here Schubert recasts the four traditional movement types into a continuous work of immense tragic power, joining the sections of the Fantasy together in a way different from the movements in Beethoven's Op. 131 Quartet. In what has been called "cyclic" form, the main theme of Schubert's first movement reappears at several important points across the Fantasy and then returns at the very end to close the circle. This structural technique would have great appeal for later Romantic composers like Liszt and Chopin.

Schubert did not neglect the traditional large-scale instrumental forms. In the years from 1821 on, he produced ambitious and original piano sonatas (especially the last three, in C minor, A major, and B♭ major [D. 958–60]), string quartets (in A minor, D minor, and G major [D. 804, 810, and 887]), a string quintet (D. 956 in C major), and symphonies (the *Unfinished* and *Great* C-Major [D. 759 and 944]). Schubert builds expansive forms not from short motives, as in Beethoven, but from lyrical melodies that seem to have come naturally to him as a great composer of lieder. The association between song and instrumental music is especially strong in Schubert. Several works, like the A-Major Piano Quintet (D. 667, *The Trout*) and the D-Minor String Quartet (D. 810, *Death and the Maiden*), use themes from his own lieder as the basis for variation movements.

Schubert's harmonic procedures are no less adventurous than, but very different from, Beethoven's. Where Beethoven might move to a remote key in an abrupt, quirky manner (as between the first two movements of the Op. 131 Quartet discussed above), Schubert will often pause and then pivot on a note common to two keys, thereby lifting us as if by magic from one to the other. In the first movement of the C-Major String Quintet, the exposition comes to a halt on a dominant chord, G major, whose main note is sustained by two cellos playing high in their range (Ex. 3.4). We expect that a second theme will unfold in that key, as in a conventional sonata form. Instead, as one of the cellos traces a chromatic descent, the G held by the other is recast as the third degree of an E♭-major harmony. The two cellos linger in this exotic, unexpected key, singing a duet in parallel thirds and sixths, before turning back to the dominant. With such harmonic shifts and seductive melodies, Schubert transports us momentarily to a distant land—or perhaps to a happier, more remote past. In the String Quintet and other late works of Schubert, the beauty and comfort of the Biedermeier world, as embodied in the E♭ theme, become tinged with bittersweet nostalgia.

Example 3.4: *Schubert, String Quintet in C Major, Op. 163 (D. 956), movement 1, mm. 59–65*

VIRTUOSITY, VIRTUOSOS

Schubert's career and reputation developed primarily through the publication of his songs and piano pieces, and through the private network of the Schubertiads.

Schubert was the exception among the prominent composers of the era after the Congress of Vienna, most of whom followed the professional path of the performing virtuoso, to which Schubert himself was neither technically nor emotionally suited. Virtuoso performers had been prominent on the European musical scene since the Baroque period, which is indelibly marked by figures like the singer Farinelli and the violinist Pietro Locatelli. The composer-virtuoso flourished anew in the first decades of the nineteenth century, with the growing middle-class appetite for music, the spread of public concerts, and the increasing prominence of instrumental genres.

As noted above, Beethoven began his career in Vienna in the 1790s as a keyboard virtuoso, performing first in private salons and then in more public venues. His playing was fiery and powerful, as revealed in the story of his renowned piano duel with Josef Wölffl at the home of a Viennese aristocrat in 1797. An eyewitness described the very different styles of the two virtuosos—which we might describe as Romantic and Classical, respectively—as they improvised in alternation:

> [Beethoven] was transported . . . above all earthly things;—his spirit had burst all restricting bonds, shaken off the yoke of servitude, and soared triumphantly and jubilantly into the luminous spaces of the higher aether. Now his playing tore along like a wildly foaming cataract, and the conjurer constrained his instrument to an utterance so forceful that the stoutest structure was scarcely able to withstand it; and anon he sank down, exhausted, exhaling gentle plaints, dissolving in melancholy.

His rival was much more restrained in his gestures and musical ideas:

> Wölffl, on the contrary, trained in the school of Mozart, was always equable; never superficial but always clear and thus more accessible to the multitude. He used art only as a means to an end, never to exhibit his acquirements. He always enlisted the interest of his hearers and inevitably compelled them to follow the progression of his well-ordered ideas. Whoever has heard Hummel will know what is meant by this.

The mention of Johann Nepomuk Hummel (1778–1837) is significant because his style as pianist and composer also contrasted strongly with that of Beethoven. Hummel deserves a place in this chapter as one of the leading figures in musical culture of the Metternich era. A child prodigy, he was a prized pupil of Mozart, who so admired his talent that he taught Hummel for free. Hummel's prominent career as composer and pianist in Vienna was in part eclipsed by Beethoven's arrival on the scene. Schubert greatly admired Hummel's music and planned to dedicate his final three piano sonatas to him, but died before arranging for their publication. Robert Schumann wanted to study with Hummel, another project that remained unrealized.

Hummel's music joins elements of what we think of as Classicism and Romanticism. He makes connections between musical structure and virtuosity in very different ways from Beethoven and Schubert. His two greatest piano sonatas, in F♯ minor, Op. 81 (1819) and D major, Op. 106 (1825), show a mastery of large-scale structure and of counterpoint, and at the same time a new style of piano writing combining florid virtuosity and chromaticism. The D-Major Sonata features a range of keyboard styles that look back to Bach and Mozart and forward to Chopin and Liszt. The closing group of the first movement, with its demanding right-hand pattern in thirds, shows how the newer virtuosic style could be incorporated into traditional formal structures (Ex. 3.5a). The right hand of the slow movement dissolves into filigree ornamentation that sometimes surpasses even the most elaborate passages in Chopin (Ex. 3.5b).

Example 3.5: *Hummel, Piano Sonata in D Major, Op. 106*

(a) First movement, mm. 83–84

(b) Third movement, m. 49

Nowhere are the role and stature of the virtuoso in the Metternich era more vivid than in the career of Nicolò Paganini (1782–1840). Born in Genoa, Paganini became first violinist of the court orchestra in Lucca in 1801 (Lucca was then under French control as part of Napoleon's empire). By 1808 the Lucca orchestra had been disbanded and Paganini turned his attention and his talents to public concerts. He transformed himself quickly from court musician to public virtuoso, a shift symptomatic of the changing musical culture of the period from one based on patronage to one based on a musician's need to make a living independently. Paganini's reputation spread quickly, especially because of the almost hypnotic power he held over his audiences. A reviewer in Milan in 1813 commented:

Herr P. is without a doubt, in a certain respect, the foremost and greatest violinist in the world. His playing is genuinely *incomprehensible*. He performs certain runs, leaps, and double stops that have never been heard before from *any* violinist . . . in short, he is . . . one of the most artful violinists that the world has ever known.

Paganini's image grew larger than life. Stories about him began to circulate: he had sold his soul to the devil in exchange for supernatural virtuosity; he had murdered a rival in love and had strung his violin with the intestines of the victim; he had spent eight years in prison, practicing the violin. Clearly appreciating the publicity they created, Paganini sought to neither deny nor confirm the stories. He began to act the part of the mad virtuoso, somewhat like Hoffmann's Kreisler discussed in Chapter 2 (see Fig. 3.4). In a restaurant in the city of Trieste, according to a contemporary report, Paganini once

> stood up suddenly, shouting desperately: "Save me, save me, from that ghost that has followed me here. Look at it there, threatening me with the same bloody dagger that I used to take her life . . . and she loved me . . . and she was innocent. . . . Oh no, two years of prison are not enough; my blood should run to the last drop . . ." and he picked up a knife that was lying on the table. It is easy to imagine how quickly someone seized his hand. Meanwhile everyone was left stupefied and astonished; but they soon recovered from their amazement. . . . Most of them understood that he had intended to ridicule those who were spreading falsehoods about him. The fact is that on the following evening the theater proved too small to hold everyone who wanted to get in, and more than a thousand people had to wait for the next concert.

Figure 3.4: *Silhouette of Paganini playing the violin. The disheveled hair and broken strings exaggerate the frenetic virtuosity for which he was famous.*

As the commentator notes, scenes like this one sell tickets.

Paganini's compositions, primarily for solo violin and for violin and orchestra, were written for his own performance and are among the most demanding ever conceived for the instrument. Early on he was renowned for composing pieces using only the lowest string (the G string) of the violin. The 24 Caprices for Solo Violin, which became a technical encyclopedia (or bible) for generations of violinists, were largely composed in Paganini's Lucca period, in 1805, then published in Milan in 1820 as his Op. 1. The performer is required to play—often in quick succession— rapid passages in octaves and in double and triple stops, wide-ranging arpeggios, and extended runs in small note values. Among other special effects called for by Paganini are a ricochet bowing across four strings (No. 1) and tremolos played underneath a melody (No. 6, Example 3.6a). Paganini sometimes turns the violin into a one-man orchestra: in Caprice No. 9, nicknamed *The Hunt*, the composer directs the violin's top two strings to imitate flutes, while the bottom two imitate horns (Ex. 3.6b).

Perhaps the greatest testimony to Paganini's influence is how the final caprice, No. 24, a set of variations on a theme in A minor, inspired piano variations by Liszt, Schumann, Brahms, Sergei Rachmaninoff, and other composers well into the twentieth century. What motivated them was not the quality of the theme itself, which they adapted note for note, but the virtuosity called for in Paganini's own variations. The later composers sought not to imitate Paganini's style but—in what is an even more flattering form of homage—to re-create his virtuoso effects in terms of their own instrument, the piano.

Example 3.6: *Paganini, Caprices for Solo Violin, Op. 1*

(a) No. 6

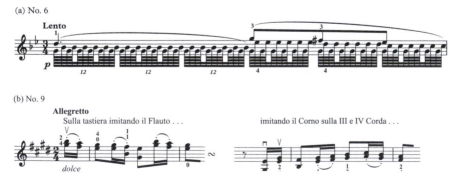

(b) No. 9

Paganini represents the musical culture of the Metternich era as much as Beethoven, Schubert, Hummel, or Diabelli. It was a culture that embodied, even embraced, contradictions. Middle-class residents of Vienna, Paris, London, and other major cities thronged concerts at which Paganini would play as if possessed by a demon; it was a kind of illicit thrill. But they also enjoyed performing duets at their parlor piano. They loved dancing at great balls and sewing quietly at home. They could admire the complexity of Beethoven's late quartets, the tunefulness of Schubert's folklike lieder, and the elaborate style of Hummel's sonatas. Public versus private, large versus small, highbrow versus popular—these were just some of the polarities that sustained the musical world in the years after 1815. Opera, as we will see in the next chapter, manifests many of these same values and priorities.

FOR FURTHER READING

The Cambridge Companion to Schubert, ed. Christopher Gibbs (Cambridge and New York: Cambridge University Press, 1997)

Hanson, Alice M., *Musical Life in Biedermeier Vienna* (Cambridge and New York: Cambridge University Press, 1985)

Metzner, Paul, *Crescendo of the Virtuoso: Spectacle, Skill, and Self-Promotion in Paris during the Age of Revolution* (Berkeley and Los Angeles: University of California Press, 1998)

Rumph, Stephen, *Beethoven after Napoleon: Political Romanticism in the Late Works* (Berkeley and Los Angeles: University of California Press, 2004)

Schubert's Vienna, ed. Raymond Erickson (New Haven and London: Yale University Press, 1997)

Scott, Derek B., *Sounds of the Metropolis: The 19th-Century Popular Music Revolution in London, New York, Paris, and Vienna* (Oxford and New York: Oxford University Press, 2008)

Solie, Ruth, *Music in Other Words: Victorian Conversations* (Berkeley and Los Angeles, University of California Press, 2004)

Solomon, Maynard, *Late Beethoven: Music, Thought, Imagination* (Berkeley and Los Angeles: University of California Press, 2003)

ⓢ Additional resources available at wwnorton.com/studyspace

CHAPTER FOUR

The Opera Industry

In 1827, the Paris Opéra was referred to as a "complicated machine." Two decades later, the Italian statesman Camillo Cavour called opera "a great industry with ramifications all over the world." "Machine" and "industry" might not be the first terms that come to mind when we think of the lyrical and dramatic art of opera. But from the moment the first public opera house opened in Venice in 1637, opera was big business. It depended on large sums of money and on the combined efforts of many different people—composers, librettists, singers, dancers, choristers, instrumentalists, costume and set designers, directors, stage crew, impresarios, and, of course, audiences.

Opera was also the first truly international musical commodity. By the early nineteenth century there were opera houses—or at least theaters that regularly presented opera—all over the Western world, from St. Petersburg to London, from New York to Buenos Aires. Indigenous cultures of opera written in the local language, already nascent in the eighteenth century, flourished in many different countries, including France, England, Germany, Spain, and Russia. Any consideration of opera in the early Romantic period must take account of these national traditions, each of which operated as a different kind of "industry." In this chapter we can only touch on a few, beginning in Italy, then turning to France, Germany, and Russia.

ITALIAN OPERA

At the start of the nineteenth century, Italy was the source of the most prestigious and influential operatic traditions, as it had been during the previous century. *Opera buffa*, fast-paced comic opera with a mix of character types from different classes of society, remained immensely popular. In addition to the three great Mozart operas of 1786–90—*Le nozze di Figaro* (The Marriage of Figaro), *Don Giovanni* (Don Juan), and *Così fan tutte* (Thus Do All Women)—audiences flocked to works by Giovanni Paisiello (1740–1816) and Domenico Cimarosa (1749–1801). Rossini and other Italian composers continued the buffa tradition after 1800. Meanwhile, especially since the French Revolution, there had been a decline of *opera seria*—serious opera with tragic or heroic plots based on history or myth, and filled with characters of noble rank. But the genre would experience a profound transformation in the first three decades of the nineteenth century in the work of Gioachino Rossini, Gaetano Donizetti, and Vincenzo Bellini.

THE IMPRESARIOS

Successful businesses depend on capable CEOs, and Italian opera was no exception. The all-powerful impresario was at once the manager of a theater (or more than one) and an entrepreneur. (The name *impresario* derives from the Italian *impresa*, "enterprise.") It was the impresario who would select the subject of an opera and engage the poet to create the libretto. He would then hire the composer, who would be under contract to supervise the preparation of the opera and would have to be present for the first three performances. Thereafter the composer would have no obligations and few rights. The impresario would retain ownership of the opera and normally of the original manuscript score. If the opera was successful, the impresario could lend or rent the music to opera houses in other cities; the profits were all his.

An Italian impresario of the early nineteenth century might be a singer or choreographer from the local opera house, but was just as likely to have little or no musical training. One of the most colorful and successful impresarios of the period was a former café waiter, Domenico Barbaia (1778–1841). Barbaia was barely literate and wrote his letters phonetically in Milanese dialect. Yet by the end of his life he was a millionaire who owned diamonds, racehorses, and a vast collection of paintings. Barbaia began his operatic career as a contractor for gambling operations at the prestigious Teatro alla Scala in Milan. (This was an era when more than just opera was offered to patrons at opera houses!) He promoted the new game of roulette and went on to create a gambling syndicate with a monopoly throughout much of Italy. In 1809 Barbaia became manager of the royal opera houses in Naples. He also produced Italian opera at the Kärntnertortheater in Vienna during much of the 1820s.

Barbaia's main gift was in spotting and nurturing talent. He was among the first to recognize the genius of Rossini, whom he signed to a six-year contract in Naples in 1815, with the obligation to compose two operas a year and to direct revivals of older works. Rossini's take would be 200 ducats a month (something like $4,000 in today's monetary values) and part of the proceeds from the lucrative gambling tables—not a bad deal for a young composer of 23. Rossini also managed to steal away Barbaia's mistress, the star soprano Isabella Colbran, who became the composer's wife in 1822. (Even so, Rossini and Barbaia remained on good terms.) Barbaia also nurtured the careers of the two most famous opera composers in the generation after Rossini: in the mid-1820s he helped Bellini gain a foothold in both Naples and Milan, and he signed Donizetti to a three-year contract at Naples.

THE SINGERS

Singers had always wielded enormous power in the world of opera. In the eighteenth century the stars were *castrati*, male vocalists who had undergone operations as young boys to allow them to retain their high vocal register. But by 1800 this barbaric practice had pretty much died out, and most castrati had passed from the scene. A typical Italian opera had three or four principal roles for *primi* or lead singers, and a group of secondary parts for *comprimarii*. The real star was now the lead soprano, the *prima donna,* who commanded astronomical fees and would not hesitate to demand that a score be modified to suit her voice. She might insist on the substitution of an aria from another opera, even one by a different composer. Famous singers would have ready several such numbers, called *arie di baule* or suitcase arias, that showed off their voices to best advantage. Singers would also improvise ornamentation over which the composer had little control.

The great singers of the early nineteenth century came and went long before recording technology permitted their voices to be captured (see Chapter 13). But we do have some vivid earwitness descriptions, including one of Giuditta Pasta (1797–1865; Fig. 4.1), who merited an entire chapter in the 1824 biography of Rossini by the famous French writer Stendhal. Stendhal described Pasta as an "an actress who is young and beautiful; who is both intelligent and sensitive; whose gestures never deteriorate from the plainest and most natural modes of simplicity, and yet manage to keep faith with the purest ideals of formal beauty." She possessed "a voice which never fails to thrill our souls with the passionate exaltation which we used, long ago, to capture from the great masters of the Golden Age; a voice which can weave a spell of magic about the plainest word in the plainest recitative; a voice whose compelling inflexions can subdue the most recalcitrant and obdurate hearts, and oblige them to share in the emotions which radiate from some great aria."

More specifically, Stendhal pointed to Pasta's exceptional vocal range, extending from the contralto up through the soprano register, and her ability to move from one "voice" or type of vocal production to another:

Figure 4.1: *The soprano Giuditta Pasta in the title role of Rossini's* Tancredi, *1822*

Madame Pasta's incredible mastery of technique is revealed in the amazing facility with which she alternates head-notes with chest-notes; she possesses to a superlative degree the art of producing an immense variety of charming and thrilling effects from the use of *both* voices. To heighten the tonal colouring of a melodic phrase, or to pass in a flash from one *ambiance* to another infinitely removed from it, she is accustomed to use a *falsetto* technique covering notes right down to the middle of her normal range; or else she may unconcernedly alternate *falsetto* notes with ordinary chest-notes. In all such displays of virtuosity, she apparently finds as little difficulty in securing a smooth transition between the two voices when she is employing notes in the *middle* of her normal chest-range, as she does when she is using the highest notes which she can produce.

From this description, we can understand why audiences flocked to hear a prima donna like Pasta and why composers like Rossini were eager to have their music sung by her. At the height of her career, in 1830, Pasta could command a salary in Milan of 40,000 francs (equivalent to about $140,000 in today's dollars) for singing twelve performances in a season.

Of course, the ultimate control of opera lay in the hands of the public, who bought seats and came to the opera houses to listen, gamble, and socialize. In Italy the opera house was a microcosm of society, its audiences ranging from the aristocracy and upper middle classes to the working classes, the so-called *popolo minuto* (little people), for whom only standing room was available. In order to get the maximum approval from this mixed crowd, singers would hire claques to cheer their performances. Rival impresarios or singers and their supporters might also organize an anticlaque to hiss and bring about the failure of an opera. After a successful first performance of a new opera, an enthusiastic audience might participate in a torchlight procession that would end beneath the composer's window. This kind of behavior will seem strange to the more restrained audiences for classical music in the twenty-first century. But it was part and parcel of the world of opera in the nineteenth century.

THE COMPOSERS

Composers were at the bottom of the pecking order in the Italian opera industry of the early nineteenth century; only gradually did they begin to gain greater authority. Rossini was the first to assert ownership of his music, a claim that led to a confrontation with Barbaia. In 1823 Rossini declared, "I own all my original manuscripts, it being custom and law that a year after an opera is given, authors have the right to have their autographs back. Did I perhaps steal my originals from Barbaia's archive? I asked him for them, and he granted them to me; then why now does he reclaim them?"

In order to establish definitive texts, Rossini arranged for some of his scores to be printed—a practice rare in opera up to that point. He took up the battle not only with impresarios but also with singers, by writing out his own ornaments and insisting that the music be performed as notated. Stendhal objected to this practice, feeling that it sapped opera of Romantic spontaneity. "The revolution inaugurated by Rossini has killed the gift of *originality* in the singer," he wrote. "The mere habit of expecting to find everything already worked out, already noted down in black and white in the music from which he has to sing, is enough to kill his own inventiveness, to quench the last spark of initiative within him." This statement acknowledges an important turning point in operatic history, the increasing control by the composer over his own creation. (Not until the mid-twentieth century did opera singers rediscover the art of improvising ornamentation, an ability that was taken for granted in Rossini's day.)

In the following decade, Bellini would insist on writing only one opera per year, a condition that would have been unheard of earlier; he also demanded that he be paid enough to live comfortably off the proceeds from that single opera. By the early 1840s, Giuseppe Verdi could virtually write his own contracts and set his own conditions. He would choose the librettist and topic; he would select the singers; he would orchestrate the score at his own pace, finishing it just before the dress rehearsal if necessary. In the 1850s Verdi went even further. He refused to deal directly with the impresario; instead, he sold his operas to his publisher, Giulio Ricordi of Milan, who then handled negotiations and enforced the composer's copyright. Verdi refused to allow any changes to his opera scores, and he held Ricordi responsible: "It is prohibited to subject the score in question to any addition, any mutilation, transposition . . . under threat of 1000 francs fine which I will extract through you from any theater where alterations are made to the score." Verdi was a great composer, as we will see in Chapter 9, but he was also a very shrewd businessman within the opera industry.

GIOACHINO ROSSINI

Of the many Italian composers striving for success in this competitive environment, Gioachino Rossini (1792–1868) stood out (Fig. 4.2). He dominated the world of Italian opera in the way Beethoven did that of German instrumental music. Rossini's musico-dramatic style appealed to the entire spectrum of the audience. He was able to fuse the comic pacing of Mozart's buffa operas with a more Romantic sense of harmony and orchestration.

It is again Stendhal who gives us perhaps the best description of the essential Rossini: "The most striking quality in Rossini's music is a peculiar *verve*, a certain stirring rapidity which lightens the spirit. . . . And close upon the heels of this first quality comes a second, a kind of *freshness,* which evokes a smile of pleasure at every bar. As a result, almost any score seems dull and heavy beside one of Rossini." For Stendhal, these qualities were not an unmixed blessing. "Rossinian scores, full of arias and duets which, all too often, are no more than brilliant firework-displays for the concert-platform, demand no more than the slightest, the most *careless* effort of attention, for the listener to harvest all the pleasure which they may afford." In other words, Stendhal considered Rossini's music to be primarily a form of aural gratification.

Figure 4.2: *Gioachino Rossini, composer of Italian bel canto opera, in 1819, after a drawing by Louis Dupré*

Yet one can turn Stendhal's valuation on its head, because the "firework-displays" are a key part of Rossini's aesthetic and originality. For him, melody and harmony contain their own expressive qualities apart from any specific dramatic representation. In that sense Rossini is a true Romantic, in light of the ideas discussed in Chapter 2. He wrote, "Music is a sublime art precisely because, not possessing ways and means of imitating the truth, it rises above and beyond everyday life into an ideal world."

The Italian term *bel canto*, or beautiful singing, has often been applied to the repertory of Rossini and his immediate successors. Although the phrase did not appear until about 1840, well after Rossini had stopped composing operas, bel canto had been in fact an ideal since the seventeenth and eighteenth centuries, when opera composers and star singers collaborated to create compelling new vocal styles. By generating the musico-dramatic content of his operas mainly out of lyrical melody or "fireworks," Rossini is in an important sense the heir to that earlier tradition of bel canto.

Rossini, who worked in both comic and serious styles, revitalized Italian opera in the early nineteenth century, when many contemporaries perceived a decline in the great tradition of Mozart, Cimarosa, and Paisiello. His first two operas to win international attention were written in 1813 for Venice: the opera seria *Tancredi* and the opera buffa *L'italiana in Algeri* (The Italian Girl in Algiers). Rossini began to close the gap between comic and serious opera in ways that would be critical for later composers. Pacing in the ensemble numbers of opera seria became more dynamic and fluid, as in buffa, while his comic operas took on the richly decorated melodic language of opera seria.

In 1815, Rossini was brought to Naples by Barbaia, and here he would reign until 1822, creating some of his finest works, including serious operas adapted from important literary sources, including *Otello*, based on Shakespeare (1816), and *La donna del lago* (The Lady of the Lake, 1819), based on a novel by the contemporary Sir Walter Scott. In the early 1820s Rossini arrived in Paris, where he would eventually relocate, in large part because the conditions for opera composers were much preferable to Italy, thanks to large state subsidies, better contracts, and carefully prepared productions. Rossini adapted some of his earlier operas for the French stage and—most significantly—wrote several new operas to French librettos. The most famous of these was also his last opera, *Guillaume Tell* (William Tell, 1829), a historical work on a grand scale that pointed the way to a new style of French opera, to be discussed below.

After *William Tell*, Rossini gave up operatic composition entirely. Although he was only 37 and would live nearly forty years longer, he produced no more works for the musical stage. The reasons for Rossini's premature retirement remain unclear, but factors include chronic illness and a changed political and cultural climate in France after the July Revolution of 1830, which overthrew the Bourbon monarchy.

Rossini's most enduring and popular opera, created for Rome in 1816, is *Il barbiere di Siviglia* (The Barber of Seville). This libretto by Cesare Sterbini was based on the first play in a trilogy by the French playwright Beaumarchais; the second play of the trilogy had been the basis of the libretto by Lorenzo Da Ponte for Mozart's *Marriage of Figaro* in 1786. In *Barber*, the young Count Almaviva, with the help of the barber Figaro, is wooing the future countess, Rosina; Rosina is being carefully supervised by her guardian, Don Bartolo. *The Barber of Seville* had already become an operatic hit before Rossini, in a version composed by Paisiello in 1782 (discussed by John Rice in *Music in the Eighteenth Century*).

Rossini's *Barber* follows the basic structure of the comic operas of Mozart and other late-eighteenth-century composers. Each act consists of a succession of solo numbers, duets, and ensembles, separated by recitative that was accompanied by harpsichord or, more likely in Rossini's day, pianoforte. In a famous aria from Act 1, *Una voce poco fà* (A voice just now; Opera Sampler), Rosina reacts to hearing the offstage voice of her admirer, the Count, who is disguised as a student named Lindoro. The aria falls into two parts, slower (Andante) and faster (Moderato), a form that would become popular with Italian composers. The "verve" and "freshness" to which Stendhal refers are amply evident in the Moderato, where a simple accompaniment, consisting of block harmonies or broken chords, underpins a lithe, wide-ranging vocal melody that features elegant ornamentation. Rosina is a role for which Giuditta Pasta was well known, and in the portion of *Una voce* shown in Example 4.1, we can well imagine how (as described by Stendhal) her "falsetto" would have rung out on the high, sustained G♯ in the first measure and how, five measures later, her rich chest voice would have tackled the G♯ two octaves below.

Example 4.1: *Rossini,* Il barbiere di Siviglia, *Act 1, aria,* Una voce poco fà

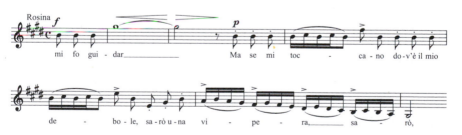

[I let] myself be led. But if they touch my weaker side, I will be a viper

As in Mozart, each act of a Rossini comic opera ends with an ensemble finale, a string of musical numbers lasting about twenty minutes and bringing various characters into complex and often hilarious interactions. The first-act finale in *Barber* is a classic of its type, with disguises, deception, and general confusion. The Count, pretending to be a drunken soldier, slips Rosina a love letter. When her guardian Bartolo demands to see it, she substitutes a laundry list. An argument begins and the police arrive to investigate. As an officer is about to arrest him, the Count whispers his identity and is released. The other characters are frozen in astonishment at this turn of events. Rossini moves suddenly from the prevailing key of C major to a remote A♭ major (a Romantic type of harmonic shift) and begins a slow, imitative sextet. Rosina sings a melody that is taken up in succession by the Count and Bartolo, and to which three other characters add counterpoint. The result is a polyphonic snapshot of everyone's consternation (Ex. 4.2; Bartolo has the melody), one that would influence later composers (as we will see in Verdi's *Rigoletto* in Chapter 9). After the sextet, Rossini breaks the spell with a return to C major and a headlong *stretta* or rapid conclusion in which all the characters onstage confess that their brains are "reduced to madness."

Example 4.2: *Rossini,* Il barbiere di Siviglia, *Act 1 finale*

I/They hardly have breath to breathe.
Cold and motionless like a statue.

GAETANO DONIZETTI AND VINCENZO BELLINI

In serious operas, which dominate his output from about 1817 on, Rossini creates large, coherent musical-dramatic units around the pairing of recitative-aria or recitative-duet. These innovations were carried forward in the next generation by Gaetano Donizetti (1797–1848) and Vincenzo Bellini (1801–1835), both of whom focused most of their efforts on serious opera. Donizetti, a prolific composer, wrote about 75 operas. As with opera seria of the previous century, some had historical plots, most notably his trilogy of operas that chronicle the English royal court from Henry VIII to Elizabeth I: *Anna Bolena* (Anne Boleyn, 1830), *Maria Stuarda* (Mary Stuart, 1835), and *Roberto Devereux* (Robert Devereaux, 1837).

Donizetti's best-known opera, *Lucia di Lammermoor* (Lucy of Lammermoor, 1835), places him firmly in the culture of Romanticism. Its libretto by Salvadore Cammarano was adapted from a novel, *The Bride of Lammermoor*, published in 1819 by Sir Walter Scott. Scott's novels, involving family or heroic dramas played out in his native Scotland, were enormously popular and were translated into many languages. *The Bride of Lammermoor*, supposedly based on a historical incident, recounts the tragic love of Edgar, master of Ravenswood, and Lucy Ashton, the sister of Ravenswood's enemy, Sir Henry Ashton. When Lucy is forced by her family to reject Edgar and marry another man, she goes mad and stabs the bridegroom on their wedding night. The most famous number in Donizetti's opera—indeed, one of the most famous in all nineteenth-century opera—is Lucia's Mad Scene in Act 3, in which the elaborate musical techniques of bel canto, including virtuosic vocal writing, are used to depict a mind out of control. The basic design of Lucia's Mad Scene is characteristic of Rossinian and post-Rossinian numbers, deriving from the two-part, slow-fast design we encountered in *Una voce poco fà* from *The Barber of Seville*, now greatly expanded.

Bellini, far less productive than Donizetti, completed only ten operas in his career—not just because he died young but also because, as discussed above, he belonged to the newer generation of composers who could exert more control over the conditions of production and could spend more time on each work. Bellini was paid an unprecedented 12,000 lire (close to $40,000 in today's values) for *Norma*, composed in 1831 to a libretto by his favorite collaborator Felice Romani. The plot, characteristic of many serious Italian operas of the nineteenth century, sets a personal, romantic drama against a political backdrop. In occupied Gaul, the Druid priestess Norma has had a secret, forbidden relationship with the Roman consul Pollione, whom she has borne two children. Pollione is now in love with a temple virgin, Adalgisa. When that relationship is discovered, Pollione is arrested and condemned to death. Norma says she will free him if he renounces Adalgisa, but he refuses. At the end, he and a repentant Norma together ascend a funeral pyre.

The role of Norma, one of the most demanding in Italian opera, was written for Giuditta Pasta. In it we can see the great range of style and emotion that so captivated Stendhal and other admirers of Pasta. Norma demands not only theatrical presence, but agility in executing the many high florid passages, as well as depth of tone for the lower-lying parts. These are the qualities for which Pasta was renowned, and we encounter them in Norma's invocation to the Druid goddess of the moon in Act 1, *Casta diva* (Chaste goddess), a multipart musical and dramatic structure that lasts over fifteen minutes.

As in Lucia's Mad Scene, the structure of *Casta diva* is anchored by two lyrical segments arranged in the tempo relation slow–fast, but now expanded and containing interpolations (see Anthology 3). As in many such numbers, there are four parts: (1) an opening segment, sometimes called the *tempo d'attacco* (beginning movement), that combines recitative and more rounded musical phrases; (2) the main slow, lyrical portion, commonly referred to as the *cantabile* (see Ex. 4.3); (3) a freer-form section with some recitative like the first one, called *tempo di mezzo* (middle movement); and (4) a fast concluding *cabaletta*, which is usually repeated. In (1) Norma cautions her followers to be patient and not rush into battle with the Romans; in (2) she prays to the moon goddess and is echoed by the chorus. Typically, something happens in the *tempo di mezzo* to

Example 4.3: *Bellini,* Norma, *Act 1, aria,* Casta diva

Pure Goddess, who silvers . . .

alter the dramatic situation; in part (3) of *Casta diva*, the Druids become defiant and demand that Pollione be sacrificed. In the virtuosic cabaletta, (4), Norma confesses she cannot sacrifice her former lover.

Bellini's music was especially admired for what Verdi would call "long, long, long melodies." Bellini continues the Rossinian aesthetic, in which what formerly might have been considered "ornaments" or nonessential notes become integral parts of the musical line. But he also restores a closer relationship between music and text. The words are declaimed with clarity; musical and verbal accents coincide, and the music carefully maps the intellectual-emotional content of a scene. The cantabile section of *Casta diva* is a splendid example of this integrated style.

FRENCH OPERA

The political, economic, and cultural structures of France made for an operatic world very different from Italy. In Italy, operatic activity was dispersed among several cities, principally Milan, Venice, Naples, and Rome; in France, almost all opera was centralized at the source of power and money, Paris. In Italy, opera was essentially a private enterprise; in France, a decree by Napoleon of 1806 had put all theatrical activity under state control. There were four opera houses in Paris: the Opéra, Théâtre-Italien, Comédie-Française, and Opéra Comique. Each had a specific repertory for which it was responsible.

The connection between French opera and politics was close not only administratively and financially, but thematically as well. At the turn of the nineteenth century, many operas reflected the liberal humanitarian values of the French Revolution. Especially characteristic were "rescue" operas, which involved the daring rescue of a political prisoner. Jean-Nicolas Bouilly wrote just such a libretto, which was set to music by Pierre Gaveaux in 1798, but is better known as the source for Beethoven's opera *Fidelio* (1805; rev. 1806 and 1814), in which the heroine Leonore, disguised as a prison guard named Fidelio, helps liberate her husband Florestan.

In the post-Napoleonic era a new kind of musical theater called grand opera developed in France. Grand opera came to mean a specific kind of work created for the Opéra in Paris: a large-scale historical drama in five acts that was sung throughout and involved "a subject with variety and offering opportunities for music, ceremonies, dance, spectacle, scenery and a grand setting," in the words of the principal librettist of the genre, Eugène Scribe (1791–1861).

French grand opera reflects the political values that culminated in the so-called July Revolution of 1830, when the middle class overthrew the autocratic Bourbon king Charles X and replaced him with the liberal Louis-Philippe (also called the Citizen King) and a constitutional monarchy. Plots of grand opera frequently involve groups of people challenging their oppressors. In Daniel Auber's *La muette de Portici* (The Mute Girl of Portici) of 1828, with a libretto by Scribe, the citizens of Naples rise up against their Spanish rulers. It was followed in 1829 by Rossini's *Guillaume Tell*, in which the Swiss fight Austrian occupiers.

The principal administrative force behind grand opera was Louis Véron (1798–1867), who as director of the Paris Opéra from 1831 to 1835 presents a strong contrast with Barbaia, the Italian impresario we encountered earlier. A doctor who had proven himself an entrepreneur by patenting medicines, Véron reflects the true ascendance of the bourgeoisie in France. His contract specified that he was to run the house "at his own risk, peril, and expenses." Véron received a large subsidy from the state, 810,000 francs in his first year (something like $3 million today), but he had to balance the demands for luxury and spectacle against a budget for which he was personally liable.

Véron believed that visual and theatrical effects were as important as musical ones. He explained:

> An opera in five acts can come to life only if it has a very dramatic plot, involving the great passions of the human heart and powerful historical factors. This dramatic plot must, however, be capable of being taken in through the eyes, like the action of a ballet. The choruses must play an impassioned role and be, so to speak, one of the interesting characters in the action. Each act must offer a contrast in scenery and costume and, above all, in carefully prepared situations.

The emphasis placed by both Scribe and Véron on visual spectacle in French grand opera marks a key moment in the nineteenth century when music began actively to participate in visual culture—that is, forms of media taken in primarily by the eyes. In our day, film and YouTube are obvious sites of vibrant visual culture; in the nineteenth century, the most prominent were theater, painting, the newly emerging technique of photography, and opera. The rise of French grand opera coincided with the birth of photography (to be discussed in Chapter 7). In fact, Louis Daguerre (1787–1851), who pioneered the new technology, began as a set designer at

Figure 4.3: *Stage set for Meyerbeer,* Robert le diable, *by Charles Séchan (Paris Opéra, 1831), inspired by the cloister of St. Trophime in Arles*

the Opéra in the 1820s. Sets at the Opéra were often strikingly realistic, re-creating in precise detail actual places that the audience would recognize (see Fig. 4.3).

The visual element of French grand opera tended to dwarf the literary one. Before the 1820s, opera libretti ("little books" in Italian) had usually been printed in advance and were often followed along by spectators as they watched the opera. That practice fell away during the nineteenth century, as audiences increasingly relied on their eyes to comprehend the action. One commentator on a French grand opera by Giacomo Meyerbeer actually suggested that "the libretto is not necessary for understanding the dramatic situation."

Giacomo Meyerbeer (1791–1864) was the third main pillar in the enterprise of grand opera, with Véron and the "house" librettist Scribe. Born as Jakob Liebmann Meyer Beer to a wealthy German Jewish family in Berlin, Meyerbeer settled in Italy in 1816, Italianized his first name, and over the next decade composed a number of Italian operas. Like many composers, he longed to work in Paris, where conditions for composers were so much better. Meyerbeer arrived there in 1827 and got a contract for what would become his first grand opera, with a libretto by Scribe, *Robert le diable* (Robert the Devil), produced in 1831.

Although Meyerbeer would write only three more grand operas for Paris, all with Scribe as librettist, his works define the genre like no others. *Les Huguenots* (The Huguenots) of 1836 exemplifies the goals and qualities of grand opera. It has a colorful historical setting, constructed around the large-scale massacre of Huguenots (French Protestants) by Catholics in Paris on the eve of the feast of St. Bartholomew in 1572. Embedded in the political conflict, and giving it a more personal dimension, is a romantic relationship between Raoul, a Huguenot, and Valentine, daughter of a Catholic nobleman, the Count de Saint-Bris. In the tragic final scene of the opera, during the massacre, the Count orders the execution of Raoul and Valentine, only later realizing that he has killed his own daughter.

The struggle between Protestants and Catholics dominates the opera visually, musically, and dramatically. In Act 3, one side of the stage is an inn frequented by Catholic students, the other a tavern where Huguenot soldiers are drinking. A sacred melody for the Virgin Mary is sung by the Catholic women against the military song (or "rataplan," representing a drum roll) and a drinking song of the Huguenot soldiers (Example 4.4). The famous Lutheran chorale *A Mighty Fortress Is Our God* also appears in the opera as a musical symbol for the Protestant cause.

The scene that most powerfully embodies the association between sound and image—the musical and the visual—that lies at the heart of French grand opera is the Benediction of the Swords in Act 4, where Saint-Bris and the Catholic noblemen plan the massacre of the Protestants (see Anthology 4). Monks arrive with white scarves to be worn by the Catholics. An oath is taken over the swords to the accompaniment of solemn chords, and the scene ends with the stirring hymnlike tune *Pour cette cause sainte* (For this sacred cause), sung in unison by the entire ensemble.

The liberal political values embedded in *Les Huguenots* did not sit well with government authorities. The ending of the opera was perceived as subversive by the official French censors and had to be modified so as to avoid the implication that royalty was directly responsible for the massacre. (In nineteenth-century France as elsewhere in Europe, political censorship was a fact of life for composers and playwrights.) As a genre, French grand opera did not long outlast the "bourgeois monarchy" of Louis-Philippe, who had come to the throne as a popular figure with wide support among the middle class, but whose policies became increasingly conservative and absolutist. Louis-Philippe abdicated during the revolutions of 1848, after the declaration of the Second Republic. As we will see in Chapter 9, other operatic genres would dominate the French scene in the latter half of the nineteenth century. Yet the legacy of French grand opera was enormous, not only within France but also outside of France in the works of Verdi and Wagner (see Chapters 8 and 9).

GERMAN OPERA

In 1769 Johann Gottfried Herder, philosopher, critic, and leading advocate for German culture, sent out a plea: "Oh for a newly created German opera! On a human basis and foundation; with human music and declamation and décor,

Example 4.4: *Meyerbeer,* Les Huguenots, *Act 3*

Virgin Mary. Long live the war! Drink, my friends,
    to our father, to Coligny.
Profane ones! Faithless ones!

but with feeling, with feeling! Oh mighty purpose! Mighty task!" Opera had
been produced in German-speaking lands since the early seventeenth century
but had struggled to find a true national identity because of the domination of
Italian and French traditions, and because Germany was a loose conglomeration
of states and principalities with no centralized government. One of the greatest
German composers of the eighteenth century, Johann Adolph Hasse (1699–1783),
wrote exclusively Italian operas for the court of Friedrich August II in Dresden.
In Vienna, capital of the Habsburg Empire, Italian opera also remained the

most prestigious genre in the hands of figures like Christoph Willibald von Gluck (1714–1787) and Mozart's famous rival Antonio Salieri (1750–1825), both of whom had appointments at court.

German opera emerged less from court and royal patronage than from private entrepreneurship. In the eighteenth century, an impresario or *Prinzipal* would organize a group of actors and singers at his own risk and profit. They would travel from city to city and present *Singspiele* (singular, *Singspiel*) or sung plays, in which musical numbers alternated with spoken dialogue—all delivered in German. Over the course of the later eighteenth century, such *Singspiele* caught on, and in German-speaking lands some cultural resources began to shift from Italian to German opera (as discussed by John Rice in Chapter 14 of *Music in the Eighteenth Century*).

In Vienna in 1776, Emperor Joseph II created a German National Theater to present plays in German; two years later came a new troupe, the National Singspiel, specifically devoted to sung plays in German. The most famous and beloved *Singspiel* of all time would be created just over ten years later by a different Viennese troupe: Mozart's *Die Zauberflöte* (The Magic Flute), produced in 1791 at the Theater auf der Wieden. Beethoven offered his sole contribution to the genre with *Fidelio*. But only with the Berlin premiere of Carl Maria von Weber's (1786–1826) *Der Freischütz* (The Free-Shooter) in 1821 did the real promise of a musically and dramatically integrated German opera begin to be realized. *Der Freischütz* paved the way for German Romantic opera, including that of Wagner.

With a libretto by Johann Friedrich Kind, *Freischütz* has all the essential elements to appeal to German listeners: a plot about everyday people (the *Volk*); an emphasis on the land, especially the forest (the *Wald*); basic values of simplicity, piety, and fidelity; and at the same time, a strong belief in the powers of the supernatural that lurk just beyond the everyday world (as in the stories of E.T.A. Hoffmann discussed in Chapter 2). In *Freischütz*, a good-hearted hunter named Max is eager to win a shooting contest and get the prize, his beloved Agathe. He makes a pact with demonic forces in the person of the "Black Hunter" Samiel, a character who is invisible and speaks, but does not sing. With the help of Caspar, a hunter under Samiel's influence, Max casts magic bullets that are guaranteed to hit their target and win him Agathe, but only on the condition that one bullet remain under the control of Samiel. At the contest, that bullet goes amiss and appears to strike Agathe. But all ends happily as Max confesses his ill-advised pact with the devil, and the forgiving Prince agrees to join Max and Agathe in marriage.

Der Freischütz was the first work to be performed in the newly renovated Schauspielhaus (Playhouse) in Berlin. Within a few years of its premiere in 1821, it had appeared on most of the major stages of Europe. By 1830 *Freischütz* had been produced in many other languages, including Danish, Swedish, Czech, Russian, English, French, Hungarian, Polish, and Dutch. One of the biggest fans of the opera was the French composer Hector Berlioz. When in 1841 the Paris Opéra decided to stage a French version of *Freischütz*, Berlioz wrote recitatives for it, since the regulations of the Opéra prohibited the use of spoken dialogue.

Audiences loved how in Weber's opera the world of the *Volk* was projected by hunters' and bridesmaids' choruses, by melodies that evoke folksongs or hymns, and by dances. Weber also deploys tonalities and tone colors in a strategic fashion. In *Freischütz* the keys of C major and E♭ major, and the timbre of brass and horns, come to represent the world of Max, the forest, and the folk. The darker powers and the demonic world are represented by C minor and F♯ minor, by the interval of the tritone the separates those two keys, and by the low strings and clarinets. Weber's practice is the germ from which Wagner would later develop the technique of the leitmotif, by which a certain harmony, timbre, or theme would become associated with a character or concept.

Der Freischütz remains essentially in the tradition of the *Singspiel* in that musical numbers tend to be self-contained and separated by spoken dialogue. But there is also recitative, as well as more than a hint of Italianate melodies and structures alongside the German style. Agathe's aria from Act 2, *Leise, leise, fromme Weise* (Gently, gently, pious melody), is a bedtime prayer that adapts Rossini's two-part, slow-fast model (see Anthology 5). After an opening recitative, Agathe sings a simple tune that embodies the German Romantic ideals of the folklike and the pious (Ex. 4.5a). The latter part of the aria, as she imagines the joy of her

Example 4.5: *Weber,* Der Freischütz, *Act 2, aria,* Leise, leise

(a)

Softly, softly, my pious melody . . .

(b)

Sweetly enchanted by him . . .

Figure 4.4: *Casting of the magic bullets in the Wolf's Glen scene from Weber,* Der Freischutz, *Act 2, showing (from left to right) Caspar, Max, and Samiel*

wedding, is a rapid and more athletically Rossinian melody accompanied by a thumping bass-and-chord pattern (Ex. 4.5b).

In the renowned finale of Act 2 of *Freischütz* the magic bullets are cast in a dark, forbidding part of the forest called the Wolf's Glen. Here Weber creates a larger, continuous musico-dramatic unit that lasts approximately seventeen minutes. In one sense this scene relates back to the complex finales of Mozart's and Rossini's operas, where characters enter successively and the plot gets ever more complicated. But there is an important difference: the only real "action" in the Wolf's Glen scene is the casting of the magic bullets, around which Weber creates a unique sonic-visual world (see Fig. 4.4).

The scene begins in the opera's demonic key of F♯ minor, with a chorus of invisible spirits chanting "Uhui" above the spookiest harmony available to Weber, the diminished seventh chord (Ex. 4.6). Later, Weber summons a series of terrifying supernatural visions between the castings of the seven bullets: flapping night birds; a raging black boar; a hurricane; cracking whips, charging horses, and wheels of fire; a wild hunt, including stags, hounds, and an invisible male chorus; and finally, thunder, lightning, hail, meteors, and fire. Some of these special effects were created in imitation of magic lantern shows, popular during the

Example 4.6: *Weber,* Der Freischütz, *Act 2 finale*

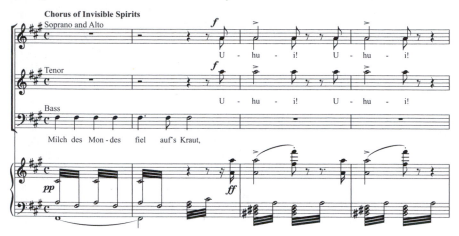

The milk of the moon fell upon the herbs.

early nineteenth century, in which the precursor of the modern projector would flash a series of images across a screen.

German operatic singing in the early nineteenth century was as different from Italian singing as the operas themselves. Value was placed more on acting and gesture than on pure vocalism, as is pointed up by the career of the greatest German soprano of her era, Wilhelmine Schröder-Devrient (1804–1860), a kind of German counterpart to Pasta. Schröder-Devrient was regarded as the greatest interpreter of the heroine of Beethoven's *Fidelio*, Leonore. Weber thought her the very best Agathe in his *Freischütz*. She was admired for her powerful acting, which outweighed her vocal equipment.

Vivid description of Schröder-Devrient comes from the British writer Henry Chorley, who described her arresting appearance and compelling stage presence:

> She was a pale woman.—Her face—a thoroughly German one—though plain, was pleasing, from the intensity of expression which her large features and deep tender eyes conveyed.—She had profuse fair hair, the value of which she thoroughly understood—delighting, in moments of great emotion, to fling it loose with the wild vehemence of a Moenad.

Chorley emphasized how Schröder-Devrient's singing, which was far from technically perfect and represented the antithesis of the Italian bel canto style, captivated audiences by its dramatic intensity: "She cared not whether she broke the flow of the composition, by some cry hardly on any note, or in any scale—by even *speaking* some word, for which she would not trouble herself to study the right musical emphasis or inflexion—provided, only, she succeeded in continuing to arrest the attention." One fan of Schröder-Devrient was the aspiring composer Richard Wagner, who was overwhelmed by her performances in the roles of Leonore and Agathe, and whose story we will pick up in Chapter 8.

RUSSIAN OPERA

Although it is not possible within a limited space to survey the other operatic traditions in the first part of the nineteenth century, we can look briefly at the situation in Russia, which was similar to Germany and parts of eastern Europe and Scandinavia in that a distinctly national operatic identity began to overtake the long-standing Italian influence. In the eighteenth and early nineteenth centuries, western European culture carried enormous prestige in Russia. During her long reign (1762–96), Empress Catherine the Great and the nobility often looked to the West to animate the empire's musical life. Foreign musicians were well paid and took up long residencies—sometimes entire careers—at the imperial court in St. Petersburg. Two of the greatest Italian opera composers worked there, Paisiello from 1776 to 1784, and Cimarosa from 1787 to 1791. For much of the eighteenth century opera was a private affair among the royalty and nobles, but by the 1780s there were several public opera houses in Moscow and St. Petersburg.

Operas in foreign languages dominated the Russian scene until well into the nineteenth century. A milestone was reached in 1836 with *A Life for the Tsar* by Mikhail Glinka (1804–1857). This was the first large-scale opera with continuous music (thus, no spoken dialogue) ever written by a Russian to a Russian text. Labeled a "patriotic heroic-tragic opera" by its creators, *A Life for the Tsar* is based on a historical event of 1613, when a Russian peasant named Ivan Susanin died while resisting the invading Polish army in order to defend the newly elected tsar, the 16-year-old Mikhail, founder of the Romanov dynasty.

Glinka treats the conflict between Russians and Poles somewhat as Meyerbeer does the Catholics and Protestants in *Les Huguenots*: each group is characterized by distinctive music. (The operas were written at more or less the same time, so there is no question of influence one way or the other.) Glinka deploys the national styles with a fairly pointed political-cultural agenda. Poles are represented stereotypically by national dances mostly in triple meter, including the polonaise and the mazurka, which dominate Act 2. The Russians are depicted more sympathetically by Italianized (and thus "civilized") folk or folklike melodies in duple meter. As in Meyerbeer, the two styles are directly juxtaposed at the climax of Act 3, where the Poles seize Susanin and he cries out, "God, save the Tsar!" The overture also brings the Polish and Russian idioms into direct conflict.

The opera industry in the nineteenth century involved many types of professionals—impresarios, composers, librettists, designers, choreographers, dancers, and singers. Although opera was an international phenomenon, operatic cultures were usually specific to a region or city. The creators knew their local audiences and wanted the works to be meaningful to them. Opera plots were diverse, involving individual, religious, or national identity; love, loyalty, and betrayal; cowardice and bravery; or madness, evil, and genius. But everyone involved in the making of opera had the same goal: to fill their houses with audiences who would pay to weep and laugh, cheer and boo, and to experience great singing and vivid productions. In the following chapter, we will explore how outside the opera house there was an equally strong desire on the part of creative artists and their audiences and critics to make music matter.

FOR FURTHER READING

The Cambridge Companion to Grand Opera, ed. David Charlton (Cambridge and New York: Cambridge University Press, 2003)

Gerhard, Anselm, *The Urbanization of Opera: Music Theater in Paris in the Nineteenth Century*, trans. Mary Whittall (Chicago and London: University of Chicago Press, 1998)

Gossett, Philip, *Divas and Scholars: Performing Italian Opera* (Chicago and London: University of Chicago Press, 2006)

Rosselli, John, *The Opera Industry in Italy from Cimarosa to Verdi: The Role of the Impresario* (Cambridge and New York: Cambridge University Press, 1984)

Stendhal, *Life of Rossini*, translated and annotated by Richard N. Coe (Seattle: University of Washington Press, 1972)

Taruskin, Richard, *Defining Russia Musically* (Princeton: Princeton University Press, 1997)

Warrack, John, *German Opera: From the Beginnings to Wagner* (Cambridge and New York: Cambridge University Press, 2001)

Ⓢ Additional resources available at wwnorton.com/studyspace

CHAPTER FIVE

Making Music Matter
Criticism and Performance

In Chapters 5 and 6 we turn from the world of opera to consider musicians, most born in the first dozen years of the nineteenth century, who made their reputations primarily in the world of concert and domestic music. This was the "generation of the 1830s," as the pianist and writer Charles Rosen has called them, referring to the decade when they reached artistic maturity. Many knew each other—indeed, some were siblings or were related by marriage—but they were not a "school" or coherent group. The generation of the 1830s included both men and women: Robert Schumann and his wife Clara Wieck Schumann, Felix Mendelssohn and his sister Fanny Mendelssohn Hensel, Franz Liszt, and Frédéric Chopin. Three other important figures from this generation, Hector Berlioz, Richard Wagner, and Giuseppe Verdi, were closely involved with opera. As reformers, they had a contrarian relationship to some aspects of the "opera industry" explored in the last chapter. (Berlioz will be discussed in Chapter 6, Wagner in Chapter 8, and Verdi in Chapter 9.)

The generation of the 1830s shared a strong sense of mission: to make music matter. Of course, all musicians want their music to "matter" in the sense of being heard by and having an effect upon audiences. But this generation felt a special obligation to communicate through and about music to a middle-class public that was increasingly numerous and musically literate. Most of these musicians were small children during the Congress of Vienna. By the time they entered adulthood, the pre-Napoleonic world was a fading memory. Aristocratic patronage of music, enjoyed by Beethoven and still sought by Schubert, had almost completely vanished. The Schumanns, Mendelssohns, Berlioz, and Chopin developed new strategies to make a career in music, and to bring music to the public. We will explore some of the activities they pursued—and the obstacles they encountered. In the present chapter we will look mainly at their activities as critics and performers; in Chapter 6 we will focus on their musical compositions.

MUSIC JOURNALISM

Today most people rely on the Internet and on television for news and commentary. This role was filled in the later eighteenth and early nineteenth centuries by a huge expansion of what has been called print culture, the ways in which print media—including books, newspapers, and magazines—affect the lives and thought of people. One of the most popular and powerful forms of journalism in the nineteenth century was the *feuilleton*, a short polemical or provocative commentary that appeared in newspapers and was usually separated from more straightforward news reports. (The term is a diminutive of the French word *feuillet*, or leaf of a book.) Although it began in France, the feuilleton, which could be on any subject—political, cultural, artistic, or social—spread rapidly throughout Europe. It was in this context that the music review as we know it blossomed in the decades after 1800. Composers with literary gifts were especially well suited for this platform of communication.

As we saw in Chapter 3, periodicals devoted to music proliferated in the first decades of the nineteenth century. Their subjects ranged from the very specialized (piano manufacturing, music pedagogy, and church music) to broader coverage of musical life, composers, performances, and scores. These periodicals were read by an increasingly literate middle class, who attended concerts and opera, and purchased music to play and sing at home. Between 1800 and 1848, some 80 new music periodicals appeared in Germany alone; in France, 49; in Austria, 30.

HECTOR BERLIOZ

One of the first Romantic composers to take advantage of print media was the Frenchman Hector Berlioz (1803–1869). Despite an early interest in music, Berlioz at first pursued a career in medicine, following reluctantly in the steps of his physician father. In his autobiography Berlioz recalled his aversion to this course of study: "Become a doctor! Study anatomy! Dissect! Take part in horrible operations—instead of giving myself body and soul to music, sublime art whose grandeur I was beginning to perceive! . . . No, no! It seemed to me the reversal of the whole natural order of my existence. It was monstrous. It could not happen. Yet it did." But not for long. By the early 1820s Berlioz was turning his attention back to music, and in 1826 he entered the Conservatoire in Paris.

Berlioz's compositions, which we will consider in the next chapter, were only part of his activities. From 1823 until well into the 1860s, he wrote criticism for a wide range of French periodicals, employing the same vivid prose style evident in the above excerpt. He set out to educate the public and elevate their taste by writing passionately about the music and musicians he most admired and by criticizing those of whom he disapproved. Berlioz championed composers he felt were underappreciated, like Gluck, as well as composers whose works were still little understood in France, especially Beethoven and Weber. Although Berlioz had a blind spot for Wagner, whose music he found incomprehensible, he was an early, prescient advocate for Georges Bizet (1838–1875).

Berlioz traveled and performed widely in Europe. He first went to Italy in 1831, as a winner of the prestigious Prix de Rome (Rome Prize) for composition, awarded by the Paris Conservatoire. In the 1840s he visited Germany, Austria, Czech lands, Hungary, and Russia. He thus had an international frame of reference, and it was all grist for his critical mill. Berlioz wrote penetratingly about musical institutions at home and abroad, including opera houses and orchestral societies. He was fascinated with new instruments like the saxophone and musical gadgets like the "electric metronome," a kind of remote baton activated by a conductor to facilitate the coordination of large choruses, offstage bands, and the like. Berlioz described this contraption enthusiastically and in great detail in the second edition of his orchestration treatise, *Traité d'instrumentation* (1855): "a set of copper wires connecting a battery underneath the stage to the conductor's stand and then on to a moving baton pivoted at one end on a board *at any distance* from the conductor."

Later in his life Berlioz published collections of his articles that have become classics of music criticism. The best known are *Voyage musical en Allemagne et en Italie* (Musical Voyage in Germany and Italy, 1844), *Les soirées de l'orchestre* (Evenings with the Orchestra, 1852), and *A travers chants* (literally, "across song," translated as *The Art of Music*, 1862). Some of Berlioz's journalistic writings were also incorporated into his autobiography, completed in 1865 and published posthumously in 1870 as *Mémoires* (Memoirs).

Berlioz's rich and entertaining writing captures the musical life of his day, clearly projects his musical values, and aims to reform musical taste. In one article in *Evenings with the Orchestra* called "How a Tenor Revolves around the Public," he pokes fun at arrogant tenors and at the audiences that revere them. Berlioz compares a tenor's career to the arc of the sun during a day: "Before Dawn," "Sunrise," "The Tenor at His Zenith," "The Sun Sets," and so on. Here is the tenor at his zenith:

His salary is one hundred thousand francs, with a month's leave annually. . . . Art for him is nothing but gold coin and laurel wreaths, and the most likely means to obtain both quickly are the only ones he cares to use. . . .

Ten years on the stage south of the Alps have made him an addict to hackneyed themes with pauses during which he can hear himself applauded, or can mop his brow, fix his hair, cough, and swallow a lozenge. Or again he insists on senseless vocalizes, interspersed with threatening, angry, or tender accents, and laced with low notes, shrill cries, buzzings of hummingbirds, screechings of guinea-fowl, runs, arpeggios, and trills.

Amid the humor of these paragraphs is a very serious critique of the state of operatic singing and also of what Berlioz and others felt was the inordinate status possessed by singers, at a time when (as we saw in Chapter 4) composers were beginning to assert their authorial rights.

Berlioz could retire the sarcasm when it came to appreciating foreign and even exotic sounds. On his trip to St. Petersburg, Berlioz marveled at hearing the singers of the imperial Russian Chapel perform harmonizations of plainchant by the composer Dmitry Bortniansky "with a perfection of ensemble, delicacy of shading, and a beauty of tone of which you cannot form any idea." Berlioz's description captures the setting, the atmosphere, the music, and the performance with compelling immediacy. He describes how the 80 singers, ranging from basses to child sopranos, stood facing each other on either side of the altar:

Motionless, with downcast eyes, they all waited in profound silence for the time to begin, and at a sign doubtless made by one of the leading singers—imperceptible, however, to the spectator—and without anyone's having given the pitch or indicated the tempo, they intoned one of Bortniansky's biggest eight-part concertos. In this harmonic web there were complications of part-writing that seemed impossible, there were sighs, vague murmurs such as one sometimes hears in dreams, and from time to time accents that in their intensity resembled cries, gripping the heart unawares, oppressing the breast, and catching the breath. Then it all died away in an incommensurable, misty, celestial decrescendo; one would have said it was a choir of angels rising from the earth and gradually vanishing into the empyrean.

In a paragraph like this Berlioz sets a high standard for how to communicate musical experiences in prose. Although we have no recording or visual image of the Russian singers, this vivid description brings us directly inside the imperial Chapel.

ROBERT SCHUMANN

Another composer of the 1830s generation who showed an affinity for writing about music was Robert Schumann (1810–1856). At an early age he became passionate about literature, in part, perhaps, because his father was a leading publisher who had also written several popular novels. At thirteen Schumann began writing poems and dramatic fragments, and in 1825 he got together with other like-minded teenagers to form a literary society where they shared their works and read the works of great German authors.

Already at age 7 Schumann had begun to learn piano and to compose. Like Berlioz, he was steered away from artistic activities by his mother and guardian (his father died in 1826), who pushed him to study law. Schumann enrolled at the University of Leipzig in March 1828. But within a year, he abandoned law to devote himself exclusively to music, especially (like Berlioz) composition and criticism, where his musical and literary gifts, respectively, could find expression.

In the early 1830s Schumann became increasingly dissatisfied with what he saw as the shallowness of contemporary musical life, especially those aspects we have mentioned in the previous two chapters: showy virtuosity in the concert hall and the appealing but (to him) frivolous melodies of Italian opera. Schumann, as we saw briefly in Chapter 2, invented a group of like-minded figures—some imaginary, some based on real people—whom he called the Band of David, or *Davidsbund*, named after the Bible's King David; its goal was to fight against the Philistines, the perpetrators and consumers of bad music.

The Band of David first appeared in 1833 in the pages of a periodical called *Der Komet* (The Comet), to which Schumann contributed prose pieces and aphorisms that were attributed variously to "Florestan," "Eusebius," and "Master Raro." These imaginary characters reappear in much of his music and his writings. Each represents a different aspect of Schumann's personality. Florestan was impulsive and passionate; Eusebius, dreamy and sensitive; Master Raro displayed a balance of the two temperaments.

In 1834 Schumann took his campaign further by helping to found a music journal for the Band of David, the *Neue Zeitschrift für Musik* (New Journal for Music; Fig. 5.1). In an editorial for the *Neue Zeitschrift* in January 1835, Schumann set out its credo clearly: "Our fundamental attitude . . . is simple, and runs as follows: to acknowledge the past and its creations, and to draw attention to the fact that new artistic beauties can only be strengthened by such a pure source; next, to oppose the recent past as an inartistic period, which has only a notable increase in mechanical dexterity to show for itself; and finally, to prepare for and facilitate the advent of a fresh, poetic future."

Schumann continued to edit the *Neue Zeitschrift* for a decade, during which time it published articles, reviews, and commentary about contemporary music and

Neue
Zeitschrift für Musik.

Im Vereine
mit mehren Künstlern und Kunstfreunden
herausgegeben unter Verantwortlichkeit von R. Schumann.

| Dritter Band. | № 1. | Den 3. Juli 1835. |

Welcher Unsterblichen
Soll der höchste Preis sein?
Mit Niemand streit' ich, —
Aber ich geb' ihn
Der ewig beweglichen,
Immer neuen,
Seltsamen Tochter Jovis,
Seinem Schooßkinde,
Der Phantasie.   Goethe.

„Aus dem Leben eines Künstlers."
Phantastische Symphonie
in 5 Abtheilungen von Hector Berlioz.
I. *)

Nicht mit wüstem Geschrei, wie unsre altdeutschen Vorfahren, laßt uns in die Schlacht ziehen, sondern wie die Spartaner unter lustigen Flöten. Zwar braucht der, dem diese Zeilen gewidmet sind, keinen Schildträger und wird hoffentlich das Widerspiel des homerischen Hector, der das zerstörte Troja der alten Zeit endlich siegend hinter sich herzieht als Gefangene, — aber wenn seine Kunst das flammende Schwert ist, so sei dies Wort die verwahrende Scheide.

Wundersam war mir zu Muthe, wie ich den ersten Blick in die Symphonie warf. Als Kind schon legt' ich oft Notenstücke verkehrt auf das Pult, um mich (wie später an den im Wasser umgestürzten Pallästen Venedigs) an den sonderbar verschlungenen Notengebäuden zu ergötzen. Die Symphonie sieht aufrecht stehend einer solchen umgestürzten Musik ähnlich. Sodann fielen dem Schreiber dieser Zeilen andre Scenen aus seiner frühesten Kindheit ein, z. B. als er sich im Spätmitternacht, wo schon Alles im Hause schlief, im Traum und mit verschlossenen Augen an sein altes, jetzt zerbrochenes Clavier

*) Ein zweites Urtheil folgt demnächst.   D. Red.

geschlichen und Accorde angeschlagen und viel dazu geweint. Wie man es ihm am Morgen darauf erzählte, so erinnerte er sich nur eines seltsam klingenden Traumes und vieler fremden Dinge, die er gehört und gesehen und er unterschied deutlich drei mächtige Namen, einen in Süden, einen in Osten und den letzten in Westen — Paganini, Chopin, Berlioz. — Mit Adlerkraft und Schnelligkeit machten sich die beiden ersten Platz; sie hatten leichter Spiel, da sie in ihrer Person Dichter und Schauspieler zusammen vereinten. Mit dem Orchestervirtuosen Berlioz wird es schwerer halten und härtern Kampf geben, aber vielleicht auch vollere Siegeskränze. Laßt uns den Augenblick der Entscheidung beschleunigen! Die Zeiten streben immer und ewig: dem Urtheile der Künstigen sei es überlassen, ob vor- oder rückwärts, ob gut oder übel. Das letztere mit Bestimmtheit von unsrer Gegenwart vorauszusagen, hat indeß für mich noch Niemand vermocht.

Nachdem ich die Berliozsche Symphonie unzähligemal durchgegangen, erst verblüfft, dann entsetzt und zuletzt erstaunend und bewundernd, werde ich es versuchen, sie mit kurzen Strichen nachzuzeichnen. Wie ich den Componisten kennen gelernt habe, will ich ihn darstellen, in seinen Schwächen und Tugenden, in seiner Gemeinheit und Gesteshoheit, in seinem Zerstörungsingrimm und in seiner Liebe. Denn ich weiß, daß das, was er gegeben hat, kein Kunstwerk zu nennen ist, eben so wenig wie die große Natur ohne die Veredlung durch Menschenhand, eben so

Figure 5.1: *First page of an early issue of Robert Schumann's journal* Neue Zeitschrift für Musik, *1835, containing his review of Berlioz's* Symphonie fantastique

musical life, much of it written by Schumann himself. Schumann crusaded for the appreciation of past or little-known masters like Bach, Handel, and Schubert. He also championed composers of a newer generation. As early as 1831, in the *Allegemeine musikalische Zeitung*, Schumann praised the second published work (Op.2) of a little-known Polish composer named Frédéric Chopin (1810–1849). He did so in the form of an entertaining conversation among some of the members of his Band of David about the appearance of a set of variations for piano and orchestra written by Chopin on *Là ci darem la mano*, the beloved duet for Don Giovanni and Zerlina from Mozart's *Don Giovanni*:

> Eusebius came in quietly the other day. You know the ironic smile on his pale face with which he seeks to create suspense. I was sitting at the piano with Florestan. Florestan is, as you know, one of those rare musical minds which anticipate, as it were, that which is new and extraordinary. Today however, he was surprised. With the words, "Hats off, gentleman—a genius!" Eusebius laid a piece of music on the piano rack. We were not allowed to see the title page. Vacantly I turned over its leaves, the secret enjoyment of music which one does not hear has something magic in it. . . . Turning to the title page, [Florestan] read the following: "*Là ci darem la mano, varié pour le pianoforte par Frederic Chopin, Oeuvre 2.*"

This is a dialogue very much in the spirit of Romantic fiction. Schumann also includes closer analysis of the music itself, especially Chopin's evocation of Mozart's opera. Schumann always felt journalistic music criticism should give readers an idea of the sound and structure of a score. No critic has ever done this better than he:

> Don Juan, Zerlina, Leporello, and Masetto are the *dramatis personae*; Zerlina's answer in the theme has a sufficiently amorous character; the first variation might be called distinguished and coquettish—the Spanish grandee flirting amiably with the peasant girl. The flirtation develops in the most natural way in the second, which is much more intimate, comic, and quarrelsome, as though two lovers were laughingly chasing each other. How all this is changed in the third, which is again filled with moonlight and enchantment.

One of Schumann's most famous articles—also his longest—was his 1835 review of Berlioz's *Symphonie fantastique* (Fantastic Symphony); the beginning is shown in Fig. 5.1. This work was at that time unknown to the German public (see Chapter 6). Here Schumann analyzes each of the movements in considerable detail; he uses formal charts and makes reference to page and measure numbers in the score (he worked from Liszt's piano transcription). That Schumann wrote at such a high level is testimony both to his highly educated readership and to his goal to further raise the standards of his audience.

Schumann's last article for the *Neue Zeitschrift*, published in October 1853, is also one of his best known. It served to introduce another young talent to the public: Johannes Brahms (1833–1897), to whom we return in Chapter 10. Schumann wrote this article after only having just met the young man and heard his music; the 20-year-old Brahms had appeared suddenly on the doorstep of the Schumanns' house on September 30. In the article, called "Neue Bahnen" (New Paths), Schumann depicted Brahms as a kind of messiah of music:

> There inevitably must appear a musician called to give expression to his times in ideal fashion; a musician who would reveal his mastery not in a gradual evolution, but like Athene would spring fully armed from Zeus's head. And such a one *has* appeared; a young man over whose cradle Graces and Heroes have stood watch. His name is *Johannes Brahms*, and he comes from Hamburg, where he has been working in quiet obscurity. . . . Even outwardly he bore the marks proclaiming: "This is a chosen one." Sitting at the piano he began to disclose wonderful regions to us. We were drawn into even more enchanting spheres.

Schumann's article effectively launched Brahms's career; it brought him to the attention of publishers and concert organizers. This process is a testimony to the power that musical journalism, especially as practiced by a prominent figure like Schumann, could have in the nineteenth century.

FRANZ LISZT

The musical and cultural values of Berlioz and Schumann were fully shared by Franz Liszt (1811–1886), who promoted them through both performance and writing. Born in a German-speaking area of Hungary and trained in Vienna by two of its leading musical figures, Carl Czerny and Antonio Salieri, Liszt was by his mid-twenties one of the most celebrated pianists in Europe. He often used that status, as Berlioz and Schumann used print media, to advocate for high-quality music. He was one of the first pianists to play Beethoven's sonatas in recitals. In addition to the customary virtuoso showpieces, he also programmed his own transcriptions of works he felt were too little known by the general public, including Bach's preludes and fugues for organ, Beethoven's symphonies, and Schubert's lieder. Liszt also gave many charity concerts—for example, one to benefit victims of a devastating flood of the Danube River in March 1838.

In the 1830s Liszt settled in Paris, where he participated in a lively intellectual and musical community. He came under the sway of a group of Christian socialist thinkers called the Saint-Simonians (named after their founder, Count Saint-Simon), who advocated a new role for artists in society. They believed that with the end of the aristocratic age brought about by the French Revolution, a new cooperative social order could come into being, based on a three-pronged organization of people involved in industry, learning, and the arts. Artists, far from being isolated or second-class citizens, should play a leading role.

These ideas appealed strongly to Liszt, who promoted them in a series of extended letters published in the Parisian press between 1835 and 1841. His

motivation was in part personal, arising from his resentment that as a pianist playing for wealthy patrons he was too often "nothing but a rather pleasant 'means of amusement.'" Liszt also bemoaned the loneliness and isolation of the modern artist:

> Isn't he always a stranger among men? Isn't his homeland somewhere else? Whatever he does, wherever he goes, he always feels himself an exile. . . . Today's artist exists outside the social community because the poetic component, that is, the religious component, of mankind has disappeared from modern governments. . . . What do they care about these men, *useless* to the mechanics of government, who travel the world reviving the sacred flame of noble sentiments and sublime exaltations?

Rather than exaggerate or celebrate the distance between artists and society, as had earlier writers like Hoffmann and Wackenroder (Chapter 2), Liszt looked to the past to help close the gap. As Wagner would do some years later (see Chapter 8), Liszt professed admiration for ancient Greece, where sculpture, architecture, and drama brought together people of many different types:

> The happy times have passed when art spread its flowering branches over all of Greece, intoxicating the land with its perfume. In those days every citizen was an artist, because all the people—legislators, warriors, or philosophers—were concerned with the idea of moral, intellectual, and physical beauty. No one was astonished by the sublime, and great deeds were as common as the great works that simultaneously inspired and celebrated them.

Liszt also praised medieval society and bemoaned the passing of "the forceful, austere art of the Middle Ages, which erected cathedrals and summoned the enthralled populace to them with the sound of the organ."

Liszt's image is anachronistic: booming cathedral organs came only in the high Baroque period. And his characterization of an ancient Greece united in harmony by common artistic ideals is undoubtedly exaggerated. But Liszt tried to adapt his ideals to the present day. He advocated that the French government be pressured to create no fewer than eight musical projects. These included competitions for new musical works; music education in schools; reform of church music; state-sponsored festivals of symphonic music; encouragement of opera, recitals, and chamber music; music schools with branches in the provinces; courses in music history and aesthetics; and inexpensive editions of the great works of the past. Needless to say, this ambitious plan was never realized. But it reflects, in a way that is important for the theme of this chapter, how strongly Liszt's generation wanted music to become an integral part of everyday life.

CIVIC ENGAGEMENT: THE CASE OF FELIX MENDELSSOHN

Nowhere was the goal of making music matter more evident than in the life of another member of this generation, Felix Mendelssohn (1809–1847). He and his sister Fanny (whom we discuss below) were scions of an upper-middle-class family from Berlin and grandchildren of the well-known German-Jewish philosopher Moses Mendelssohn. Their father Abraham, a prominent banker, converted to Protestantism, adding the Christian "Bartholdy" to the family name, and he had his children baptized in order to assimilate them more fully into German society.

Felix Mendelssohn was wealthy enough not to have to work for a living, yet he maintained an active, even exhausting dual career focused simultaneously on creation (as a composer) and re-creation (as conductor, performer, and administrator). In the latter capacity he worked to make high-quality music of the past and present available to a large public in the urban centers of Europe, especially his native Germany. The most famous example of such an activity occurred in Berlin in March 1829, when Mendelssohn, just over 20 years old, conducted the first modern revival of J. S. Bach's *St. Matthew Passion*, a work that had not been heard outside its original venue, Leipzig, since Bach's death in 1750. This concert was recognized as one of the most important musical events of the nineteenth century, because it brought a new awareness and appreciation of Bach to the general public.

For the next two decades Mendelssohn would remain active in the musical life of several cities. He became municipal musical director in Düsseldorf for two years, from 1833 to 1835, during which time he assumed a wide range of responsibilities, including conducting the choral and orchestral societies and the sacred music for Catholic services. (Schumann would later hold this same post.) In 1835 Mendelssohn received offers of directorships from two prestigious German musical institutions, the Munich Opera and the Gewandhaus Orchestra in Leipzig. The former might have proved a higher-profile and more glamorous job. But Mendelssohn chose the latter and began a 12-year relationship that lasted until his death. During his time in Leipzig, he transformed and raised the standards of musical life in the city, using the Gewandhaus hall, built in the former Clothier's Exchange, as his base (see Fig. 5.2). Each year he conducted a series of 20 orchestral subscription concerts, as well as charity concerts; he also organized performances of chamber music and visits by virtuosos. Mendelssohn took on professional responsibilities in Berlin as well.

As a composer, Mendelssohn added important works to the standard concert repertory of piano, chamber, and orchestral music. His magnificent Octet, Op. 20, for double string quartet (four violins, two violas, two cellos), was composed when he was only 16. The Overture to Shakespeare's *Midsummer Night's Dream*, Op. 21, followed a year later. These and later works, including five

Figure 5.2: *The Leipzig Gewandhaus in 1840, when Mendelssohn served as music director of the orchestra. Its original use as the hall of a clothmaker's guild accounts for the unusual seating arrangement.*

symphonies and the Violin Concerto, Op. 64, show Mendelssohn's ability to inflect large Classical forms with a Romantic sense of harmonic and orchestral color that could be at once vivid and intimate.

Mendelssohn's most heartfelt—and perhaps his most significant—musical contributions to civic culture were his two oratorios for vocal soloists, chorus, and orchestra, *St. Paul*, Op. 36, and *Elijah*, Op. 70. The genre of the dramatic oratorio had been developed by Handel in England in the eighteenth century for a public that enjoyed hearing the famous Bible stories in their own language. It was a natural vehicle for Mendelssohn's goal of community outreach. *St. Paul* was premiered in 1836 at the Lower Rhine Music Festival in Düsseldorf by a chorus of over 350 amateur singers and an orchestra of almost 200 mostly amateur players. The German text traces the Christian awakening of Paul and his subsequent missionary work. As in Handel's oratorios, and as in Bach's passions, the story is told by a succession of soloists, ensembles, and choruses.

For Mendelssohn, *St. Paul* seems to have reflected not only a confirmation of his own Protestant identity but also his secular, civic role as a musical "missionary." The work is permeated by five chorales; all would have been familiar to the composer's north German public and were emblematic of the ideal of communal Protestant worship stemming from the sixteenth and seventeenth centuries. The best-known chorale used by Mendelssohn is *Wachet auf*

(Sleepers Awake), also prominently employed by Bach in one of his most famous cantatas (BWV 140). The chorale appears twice in *St. Paul*, played sumptuously by the orchestra in the overture, then sung by the chorus with bold brass interludes between the phrases (Ex. 5.1).

Example 5.1: *Mendelssohn,* St. Paul, *No. 16, mm. 1–7*

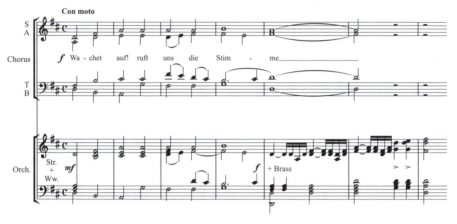

Sleepers wake, the voice calls to us

The oratorio *Elijah*, concieved just after *St. Paul* but completed only in 1846 upon a commission from England, tells the main events in the life of the prophet in a series of intensely dramatic scenes. In his setting of this story, Mendelssohn was not necessarily reconnecting with his Jewish roots, but rather, like Handel in *Messiah*, was casting an Old Testament prophet within a Christian framework. As a figure who wanders in the wilderness, is vilified by nonbelievers, suffers, and at the end ascends to heaven, Elijah becomes a precursor of Jesus. Yet *Elijah* is ultimately a work that bridges Jewish and Christian concerns and, like *St. Paul*, was aimed at a broad public. Its premiere in Birmingham in August 1846 was viewed as a musical milestone. A prominent British critic claimed *Elijah* was "not only the sacred work of our time, we dare fearlessly to assert, but it is a work 'for our children and our children's children.'"

The best-known number in *Elijah*, often performed separately, is "He, watching over Israel." This chorus from Part 2 shows Mendelssohn's mastery of choral writing, counterpoint, and large-scale pacing, as well as a simplicity that could appeal to a broader public (see Anthology 6). The unpretentious main theme (Ex. 5.2) stays very close to the tonic D major, and is accompanied by a rocking triplet figure that imparts the feeling of a lullaby. Mendelssohn is imparting a subtle message: as the text tells us that God "slumbers not, nor sleeps," the firm, gentle pattern hewing to the tonic assures us of His constancy. This triplet pattern remains as

Example 5.2: *Mendelssohn,* Elijah, *No. 29, mm. 2–5*

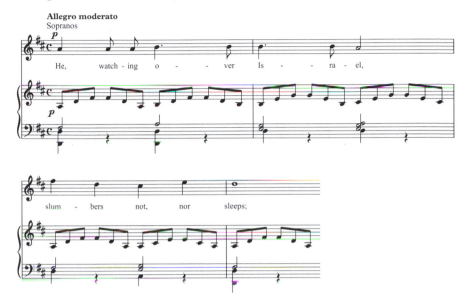

an ostinato throughout the movement, even when the chorus rises to a powerful and more chromatic climax in the middle, singing of "grief" that God can console.

Paul and Elijah are sympathetic rather than heroic figures; they care deeply for their "flock." Mendelssohn was himself such a person, tending to and seeking to widen his audience of music lovers. Indeed, it may be that in his final years, with all his administrative duties, performing, as well as composing, he literally worked himself to death. He died just over a year after the premiere of *Elijah*, in November 1847, at the age of 38.

FANNY MENDELSSOHN HENSEL AND THE MUSICAL SALON

Felix Mendelssohn's older sister Fanny Mendelssohn Hensel (1805–1847) was one of the most accomplished female musicians of the nineteenth century. She received virtually the same musical education as her brother, including composition and theory lessons with Carl Friedrich Zelter, and was recognized by many as his equal in talent. She played piano and composed excellent solo pieces, chamber works, and lieder. But in adolescence the paths of Felix and Fanny diverged in ways that reflect the cultural and social patterns of the period, and also point up the challenges faced by women in pursuing professional careers at the time. Mendelssohn went on, as we have seen, to a busy and highly visible public life as a musician. That avenue was not open to—or even necessarily desired by—Hensel and other women. She was restricted by her social status as part of the upper middle class, which rarely produced professional female musicians. (Clara Wieck Schumann, to whom we turn below, was from the working class and pursued her career largely out of financial need.)

In 1829 she married Wilhelm Hensel, a prominent painter, with whom she had a son. For the rest of her relatively short life—she died of a stroke just six months before Felix—she remained a devoted daughter, sister, wife, and mother. Yet Hensel had no less a desire than Mendelssohn to make music matter. Although surely frustrated in some respects by the limitations placed on her by her social situation, she remained very active in the musical life of Berlin. Hensel thrived in what has been called the "semiprivate life" characteristic of accomplished and cultivated upper-middle-class women of the era. As we saw earlier in this book, in the first decades of the nineteenth century the boundaries between "public" and "private" in the arts were not as clear as they are today, and it is in the context of this still little-understood world that we should view Hensel's achievements.

This semiprivate world of culture was one to which Hensel was in many ways destined. On her mother's side she was descended from one of the wealthiest Jewish families in Berlin, the Itzigs. Her great-grandfather Isaac Daniel Itzig had been banker to the royal court in the eighteenth century and had a palace opposite the king's. He was one of the first of a small number of Jews who were granted citizenship and whose descendants were allowed to inherit land and houses in the city. Most women of the Itzig family were involved with Berlin's cultural life as leaders of salons, and as patrons of libraries and the arts.

Hensel became involved in music through the establishment of a weekly musical gathering or salon in her home in the 1830s and 1840s. The salon, in which a private home was opened to musical events attended by both aristocracy and the bourgeoisie, was an important element of Berlin musical life. As a *salonière* Hensel was far more than a mere hostess. She planned the programs, and she conducted and performed many compositions, including her own and those of her brother. As with some of Mendelssohn's concerts, the performers were often a mix of amateurs and professionals. Like him—and like other members of the generation of the 1830s we discussed earlier—Hensel sought to introduce audiences to composers still largely unfamiliar, including Bach and Gluck. At the salon she also programmed portions of Handel's oratorios, Mozart's *La clemenza di Tito* (The Clemency of Titus), and Beethoven's *Fidelio*. Hensel's dynamic style of conducting was described by a contemporary:

> She seized upon the spirit of the composition and its innermost fibers, which then radiated out most forcefully into the souls of the singers and audience. A *sforzando* from her small finger affected us like an electric shock, transporting us much further than the wooden tapping of a baton on a music stand.

Felix Mendelssohn and their father Abraham encouraged Hensel in musical composition—Mendelssohn in fact had enormous admiration for her creative talent—but strongly advised against publication of her works. Early on, Hensel herself was decidedly ambivalent. In 1837 Mendelssohn wrote to his mother that he would be willing to step in and help only if his sister decided to pursue publication actively:

> But *persuade* her to publish something I cannot, for it is against my view and conviction. . . . I consider publication to be something serious . . . and believe that one should only do it if one wants to present oneself and continue one's whole life as an author. For this a series of works is required, one after the other; one or two alone is only an annoyance to the public, or it becomes a so-called vanity publication.

As paradoxical as it may seem, the stances of both siblings reveal their firm belief in the overall theme of this chapter, making music matter. For Mendelssohn, and at least initially for Hensel, the only purpose in publishing one's music should be to make a long-term and "serious" impact on musical life. Anything less would be a superficial and dilettantish gesture that could lower rather than elevate the status of music in society. Social status was also a factor in Hensel's case. It was considered by many unseemly or immodest for a woman of the high bourgeoisie to appear in print. (Many female novelists, like Chopin's mistress George Sand and the British writer George Eliot, published under male pseudonyms.)

Toward the end of her life Hensel began to shake off these taboos. Her husband encouraged her to publish her works, as did a young German musician and critic, Robert von Keudell. Yet during Hensel's lifetime only a small amount of her music appeared in print, comprising eleven opus numbers and some additional pieces. Hensel's qualities as a composer are evident in *Das Jahr* (The Year) of 1841, an ambitious cycle of twelve piano pieces (plus a postlude), each representing a month of the calendar. The manuscript was illustrated by her husband, and each piece is accompanied by a poem. The work did not appear in print until 1989. *Das Jahr* encompasses a wide range of pianistic styles and is tightly organized by a broad key plan and by recurring thematic elements, including chorale melodies. It can stand without apology alongside other great piano cycles of the period such as those of Schumann and Liszt (to be examined in the next chapter).

CLARA WIECK SCHUMANN AND THE KEYBOARD

A very different picture is presented by the life and career of the other most prominent female musician of the nineteenth century, Clara Wieck Schumann

Figure 5.3: *Clara Wieck Schumann at the piano in her later years*

(1819–1896; Fig. 5.3). She had none of the privileges or opportunities provided to the wealthy upper middle class. Her father, Friedrich Wieck, was a Leipzig piano teacher who was also in the business of selling, lending, and repairing pianos. Her mother was a pianist who taught and helped out with the family business. The couple divorced in 1824 and Friedrich retained custody of the five children.

Instead of the extended and highly educated family of Hensel, Wieck Schumann had her tyrannically efficient father, who taught her piano and supervised her musical training, which included instruction in violin, theory, orchestration, counterpoint, fugue, and composition. She was a child prodigy, pushed by her father as Mozart had been by his. She first played at the Leipzig Gewandhaus at age nine and went on to impress audiences over much of Europe. At about the same time, she got to know a young law student in Leipzig named Robert Schumann, nine years her senior, who began to study piano with her father in 1828. By 1830 he was living in Wieck's home. Thus began one of the most famous musical love affairs of all time. Despite Wieck's legal battle to prevent it, the marriage of Clara and Robert took place in 1840.

We have already seen that during the 1830s Schumann's crusade to make music matter took the form of a new kind of music criticism, which advocated the highest standards of performance and composition, and sought to bring to the public's attention neglected composers old and new. As she matured, Wieck Schumann came to share that sense of mission, which she would carry out through her concerts and later through her teaching.

In the Robert Schumann archives in Zwickau, Germany, are almost 1,300 programs of concerts in which Wieck Schumann participated during her career. The 1830s was an era of the piano virtuoso, as we have seen, and of concerts given by composer-performers, many of whom tended to feature splashy works by themselves or others. Early in her career, before 1835, she followed this fashion, playing the virtuoso music of the day, including some of her own compositions. But as time went on—and as her association with Schumann deepened—that kind of music receded behind works of the Baroque, Classical, and Romantic masters, including J. S. Bach, Domenico Scarlatti, Beethoven, Schubert, Mendelssohn, and, of course, Schumann. Between 1840 and 1850, her recital repertory included three works by Mozart, eight sonatas by Beethoven, seven works by Mendelssohn, and over a dozen pieces by Schumann. With this kind of programming, unusual for the period, Wieck Schumann pioneered changes in the piano recital. Like her husband, she was seeking to elevate the taste of her listeners, to wean them away from contemporary works of superficial appeal.

Wieck Schumann was to have a great impact on the shape and structure of piano recitals. Like Liszt, she used her prestige as a performer to change the habits and tastes of the public. Her goal was to focus solely on the music, with as few distractions as possible. As a young woman she became one of the first pianists to give solo piano concerts without any assisting artists, thus departing from the tradition of mixed programs with a variety of performers. She made her concerts shorter, and offered fewer compositions. She paid close attention to the composer's written text, and avoided any additions or embellishments.

Wieck Schumann's life and career, like Hensel's, point up the burdens that having a family could place on female musicians in the nineteenth century. At the time of her marriage, Clara Wieck was the better-known member of the couple: Robert Schumann was a relatively obscure composer, while she already had a wide reputation as a piano virtuoso. Between 1841 and 1854, the Schumanns had eight children. The family moved several times, essentially following the husband's career opportunities. Throughout, Wieck Schumann carried on performing, composing, and teaching, although the pressures of family limited her ability to tour widely. As a composer, she was not prolific, issuing just 23 opuses between 1831 and 1856. Schumann encouraged her in composition and made contacts with publishers on her behalf, but his composing took priority over her musical activities: she could only practice and compose during hours when he was not working. Wieck Schumann's earlier compositions for solo piano tended to be either virtuoso showpieces or shorter lyrical character pieces (like the *Soirées musicales*, or Musical Evenings, Opp. 5 and 6). After her marriage, she turned to larger-scale instrumental genres, the same ones in which she encouraged Schumann to compose. She wrote a Piano Sonata in G Minor, some preludes and fugues, and perhaps her greatest work, the Piano Trio in G Minor, Op. 17 (1846). After Schumann's death, she published no more works, but resumed an active concert career, in part to support herself and her family, but also to continue her reform of concert life.

In 1878 Wieck Schumann began another phase in her quest to make music matter: she became professor of piano in Frankfurt and would go on to teach many important pianists. It is clear that her values as a teacher were the same as those she held as a performer. One of her pupils, Adelina de Lara, recalled:

> She taught us to play with truth, sincerity and love, to choose music we could love and reverence, not just music which merely displayed our technique in fast passages and allowed us to sentimentalize the slow ones. We were exhorted to be truthful to the composer's meaning, to emphasize every beauty in the composition and to see pictures as we played—"a real artist *must* have vision," she would say. If the music were to mean anything to our listeners, she told us, it must mean even more to us, and in giving pleasure to our hearers we had a great purpose to fulfil.

In 1884 a reviewer of a recital in London summarized Wieck Schumann's status and her impact as a performer upon the musical life of the nineteenth century:

> We think we are correct in saying that no pianist ever before retained so powerful a hold upon the public mind for so long a period. . . . Madame Schumann's character, intellect and training saved her from becoming a mere partisan: though for years she has been acknowledged unequal as an exponent of Schumann's music, yet one always hears of her wonderful interpretations of Bach, Mozart and Beethoven. By her modesty, prudence and talents she has gradually achieved a veritable triumph.

———————————

Here, near the end of the nineteenth century, in the figure of this diminutive, elderly woman at the keyboard, critics could still perceive the passion that inflamed her and other members of the generation of the 1830s many decades earlier. Through their many activities—including performance, criticism, teaching, concert organization, salons, and the composition of large-scale oratorios—these musicians worked tirelessly to share with the broader public their tastes, their standards, their values, and their aspirations. They wanted to make music matter.

FOR FURTHER READING

Berlioz, Hector, *Evenings with the Orchestra,* trans. Jacques Barzun (Chicago and London: University of Chicago Press, 1973)

Gooley, Dana, *The Virtuoso Liszt* (Cambridge and New York: Cambridge University Press, 2004)

Liszt, Franz, *An Artist's Journey: Lettres d'un bachelier ès musique, 1835–1841,* trans. Charles Suttoni (Chicago and London: University of Chicago Press, 1989)

Reich, Nancy B., *Clara Schumann: The Artist and the Woman,* rev. ed. (Ithaca and London: Cornell University Press, 2001)

Rosen, Charles, *The Romantic Generation* (Cambridge, MA: Harvard University Press, 1995)

Schumann, Robert, *On Music and Musicians*, ed. Konrad Wolff, trans. Paul Rosenfeld (New York: W. W. Norton & Company, 1969)

Todd, R. Larry, *Fanny Hensel: The Other Mendelssohn* (Oxford and New York: Oxford University Press, 2010)

ⓢ Additional resources available at wwnorton.com/studyspace

CHAPTER SIX

Making Music Speak
Program Music and the Character Piece

The generation of the 1830s sought to make music "matter" through their roles as critics, performers, and organizers of musical events. There was another, equally important side to their artistic mission: composition, ultimately their most powerful form of communication. We examined Mendelssohn's contribution to the high-profile genre of the oratorio as critical to his goal of civic outreach. In this chapter we will look at music written by some of the other figures introduced in Chapter 5, to whom we add Frédéric Chopin.

The question that most preoccupied composers and writers on music between about 1830 and 1860 was not *whether* music could communicate, but *how* and *what* it communicated. Such discussions, growing from the concerns we identified in Chapter 2 as part of Romantic thought, provide the principal cultural-intellectual context in which to understand this music. We recall that music played a central role in early Romantic aesthetics in part because of its apparent purity and abstractness. For Arthur Schopenhauer music was the unmediated expression of the Will; for E.T.A. Hoffmann instrumental music, especially Beethoven's, was the most Romantic of the arts because its subject was indeterminate and immeasurable. Many composers believed in these ideas. Yet at the same time those with strong literary leanings actively sought to wed word and tone in newer Romantic genres like the lied. They were also drawn to program music and the character piece for piano, genres we will examine in this chapter.

ABSOLUTE AND PROGRAM MUSIC

Often understood to represent fixed categories, "absolute music" and "program music" are better viewed as points on a broad spectrum of ways in which music was believed capable of communication. From the middle of the nineteenth century until our own day, the terms have been used to describe basic musical values and practices. The term *absolute music* was coined by Richard Wagner in the 1840s to characterize—and criticize—instrumental music that was "endless and imprecise" in expression, as well as vocal music that had no real expressive relation to the words being sung (such as Rossini's, in his view). For others who picked up the term, absolute music had less of a pejorative connotation; it served as a more or less neutral description of music that had no overt literary, pictorial, or philosophical content. Wagner, as we will see in Chapter 8, believed that absolute music had to yield to music drama, where instrumental and vocal music were fully integrated.

Franz Liszt and others preferred to escape from absolute music along the path indicated by program music. The term was used in the middle of the nineteenth century to refer to an instrumental work in which the composer seeks to represent some kind of narrative, poetic, or emotional content, usually with the aid of a written document (a "program") that is meant to be read by the listener before or during the performance. Although in a strict sense "extramusical" or lying outside the sonic realm of the music, the program becomes an important part of the listener's experience of the work. Program music does not necessarily involve imitation of natural or familiar sounds, although such effects—like birdcalls and hunting horns—are sometimes encountered. The goal is less to paint in tones than to communicate ideas or feelings.

The basic idea of program music had been around for well over a century. Each work in Vivaldi's *The Four Seasons*, a group of violin concertos published in 1725, is prefaced by a sonnet, probably written by Vivaldi, which describes a particular season. The concertos engage in mimetic effects (the birds, the thunderstorm, and the barking dog in *Spring*), but Vivaldi also attempts to evoke more broadly the qualities and moods of the different seasons of the year.

In the later eighteenth and early nineteenth centuries, composers and critics often used the term "characteristic" to describe instrumental music whose subject was specified by sentences or paragraphs. Beethoven's Sixth (*Pastoral*) Symphony (1808), which the composer called a "sinfonia caracteristica" in an early draft, is the most renowned example of this kind of music. Beethoven added descriptive rubrics to each of the five movements: "Awakening of Cheerful Feelings on Arriving in the Country," "Scene by the Brook," "Merry Gathering of Country Folk," "Thunderstorm," and "Shepherd's Song—Happy and Thankful Feelings after the Storm." As with Vivaldi, the *Pastoral* Symphony employs imitative effects, most notably of birds in the second movement and thunder in the fourth. Yet in a note distributed at the premiere of the Sixth, Beethoven expressly observed that his goal was "more an expression of feeling than painting."

Both Vivaldi and Beethoven anticipate many later works of program music in fitting the literary or poetic component to a largely traditional formal structure. Each of the *Four Seasons* has the standard three-movement, fast-slow-fast design of the Baroque concerto. Beethoven's *Pastoral* has the outward shape of a standard Classical symphony: a first movement in sonata form, a broad slow movement, a scherzo with trio, and a rondo-like finale. The exception—and here the program is the primary motivation—is that after the scherzo Beethoven inserts a short movement of about three and a half minutes that represents the thunderstorm. Even this passage, however, has a function that a listener of Beethoven's day might recognize as that of an extended transition or introduction to the finale.

BERLIOZ AND THE *SYMPHONIE FANTASTIQUE*

In these respects Beethoven's *Pastoral* clearly provided a model for the most famous piece of program music of the nineteenth century, the *Symphonie fantastique* (Fantastic Symphony), composed in 1830 by Hector Berlioz. Like the *Pastoral*, the *Symphonie fantastique* is in five movements; in this case the central slow movement is flanked by two dancelike ones, a waltz on one side and a march on the other. But far more than in either the *Pastoral* Symphony or *The Four Seasons*, the musical shape of the *Symphonie fantastique* is driven by the composer's program.

Berlioz's original title for the symphony is more elaborately descriptive than Beethoven's: *Episode in the Life of an Artist, Fantastic Symphony in Five Parts*. Significantly, the word *symphony* is a subtitle, and Berlioz uses the term *part* instead of *movement*. He thereby distances himself from the Beethoven symphonic tradition. The "episode" that is the subject of the symphony is narrated in what Berlioz specifically called a "program," distributed to the audience at the premiere and published with the score in 1845 and, in revised form, in subsequent editions. Berlioz preceded the narrative with the following note: "The composer's intention has been to develop, insofar as they contain musical possibilities, various situations in the life of an artist. The outline of the instrumental drama, which lacks the help of words, needs to be explained in advance. . . . The distribution of this program to the audience . . . is indispensable for a complete understanding of the dramatic outline of the work." Thus, the program is not supplemental; it is an integral aspect of the symphony.

In Berlioz's program, each "part" of the symphony is given a title and an explanatory paragraph, of which we can provide excerpts here:

Part One: Reveries—Passions. The author imagines that a young musician . . . sees for the first time a woman who embodies all the charms of the ideal being he has imagined in his dreams, and he falls desperately in love with her. Through an odd whim, whenever the beloved image appears before the mind's eye of the artist, it is linked with a musical thought whose character, passionate but at the same time noble and shy, he finds similar to the one he attributes to his beloved.

The melodic image and the model it reflects pursue him incessantly like a double *idée fixe.* . . .

Part Two: A Ball. The artist finds himself in the most varied situations—in the midst of the *tumult of a party*, in the peaceful contemplation of the beauties of nature; . . . but everywhere . . . the beloved image appears before him. . . .

Part Three: Scene in the Country. Finding himself one evening in the country, he hears in the distance two shepherds piping a *ranz des vaches* [cow-calling tune] in dialogue. . . . [The artist] reflects upon his isolation; he hopes that his loneliness will soon be over.—But what if she were deceiving him!—This mingling of hope and fear, these ideas of happiness disturbed by black presentiments, form the subject of the Adagio.

Part Four: March to the Scaffold. Convinced that his love is unappreciated, the artist poisons himself with opium. . . . He dreams that he has killed his beloved, that he is condemned and led to the scaffold, and that he is witnessing *his own execution.*

Part Five: Dream of a Witches' Sabbath. He sees himself at the sabbath, in the midst of a frightful troop of ghosts, sorcerers, monsters of every kind come together for his funeral. Strange noises, groans, bursts of laughter. . . . She [the beloved] takes part in the devilish orgy.—Funeral knell, burlesque parody of the *Dies irae.*

Berlioz's program about the obsession of the "young musician" with his beloved was inspired by his own experiences. In 1827 Berlioz had fallen in love with Harriet Smithson, an Irish actress performing as Shakespeare's Juliet in Paris. He was thrown into despair by her initial rejection—hence the symphony's program. But they soon began a romantic relationship, and married in 1833, only to become miserable and to separate by 1840. Since its premiere, the *Symphonie fantastique* has been associated with the composer's personal life by

Figure 6.1: *Henri Fantin-Latour, lithograph illustration for second movement* (Un bal) *of Berlioz's* Symphonie fantastique, *showing the composer and the beloved, 1888.*

audiences, critics, and even artists. In 1888 the French painter Henri Fantin-Latour created a series of illustrations of the work. The one for the second movement shows Berlioz with his beloved in an intimate encounter apart from the busy dancers at the ball (Fig. 6.1).

However much inspired by Berlioz's experiences, the *Symphonie fantastique* is more than musical autobiography. It is a bold experiment in symphonic music undertaken just three years after Beethoven's death. Berlioz seeks to unify the symphony by means of a theme he calls the *idée fixe* (roughly, obsessive idea), which appears in all five movements and represents the musician's image of the beloved in her different guises. As a theme, the *idée fixe* is not taken apart into its motivic components and developed, as it would be by Beethoven and his predecessors. Rather, it is modified by means of thematic transformation, an important principle pioneered by Berlioz and later adopted by composers like Liszt, Tchaikovsky, and Wagner. The *idée fixe* remains largely intact but changes character dramatically. By an alteration of instrumentation, tempo, rhythm, meter, and harmony, the plaintive theme of longing played by the strings in the first movement becomes many different things in subsequent movements (Ex. 6.1). In the second movement, when the musician sees his beloved at a ball, her theme is a lilting waltz in triple meter (Ex. 6.1b; see also Anthology 7). In the finale, it becomes a squeaky tune played by an E♭ clarinet, a transformation that represents the degraded image of the beloved as a mocking witch (Ex. 6.1c).

Example 6.1: *Berlioz,* Symphonie fantastique, *transformations of the* idée fixe

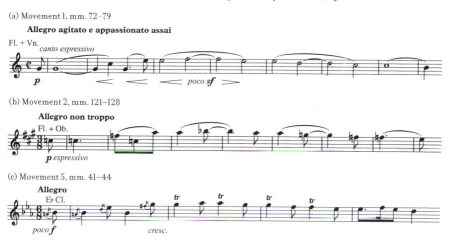

(a) Movement 1, mm. 72–79

Allegro agitato e appassionato assai

(b) Movement 2, mm. 121–128

Allegro non troppo

(c) Movement 5, mm. 41–44

Allegro

Despite Berlioz's stated goal to convey the passions and emotions aroused by the story, rather than the actual events or settings, the relationship of the program to the music caused confusion and controversy. Some critics objected that Berlioz was telling the same story simultaneously in music and in words. In response Berlioz felt the need to clarify his work even further. In a footnote appended to the program he wrote:

> The aim of the program is by no means to copy faithfully what the com-
> poser has tried to present in orchestral terms, as some people seem to
> think; on the contrary, it is precisely in order to fill in the gaps which the
> use of musical language unavoidably leaves in the development of dra-
> matic thought, that the composer has had to avail himself of written prose
> to explain and justify the outline of the symphony. He knows very well that
> music can take the place of neither word nor picture.

The program therefore does not duplicate the music but serves to express, Berlioz says, the "passions and feelings" aroused by the dramatic situation of the program.

Berlioz also addresses head on the question of imitation, of which there are numerous examples in the *Symphonie fantastique*, such as the "distant sound of thunder" represented by the timpani in the third movement and the beheading of the protagonist in the fourth movement, conveyed by a fortissimo chord with percussion and pizzicato "bounces" in the strings. Berlioz writes that

> since the composer of this symphony is convinced that the abuse of such
> imitation is quite dangerous . . . he has never considered this branch of
> the art as an end, but as a means. And when, for example, in the Scene

in the Country [third movement], he tries to render the rumbling of distant thunder in the midst of a peaceful atmosphere, it is by no means for the puerile pleasure of imitating this majestic sound, but rather to make silence more perceptible, and thus to increase the impression of uneasy sadness and painful isolation that he wants to produce on his audience by the conclusion of this movement.

Berlioz makes two important points here. First, the timpani's "thunder" is designed not to "imitate," but to make silence perceptible. Berlioz is one of the earliest composers to explore how silence can become a "sound," a concept that composers like John Cage would explicitly develop in the twentieth century. Second, Berlioz notes that the depiction of thunder is not an end but a means to stimulate the emotion of sadness and isolation in his listeners. The emphasis is not on imitation per se, but on the conveying of emotions.

Berlioz's comments, as well as the *Symphonie fantastique* itself, reveal how wide was the range of expressive qualities that could be claimed for instrumental music in the years around 1830—and how controversial the subject was. His remarks also help to reinforce what was suggested at the outset of this chapter: that program music is really a moving target, shifting back and forth along a spectrum of music's perceived ability to paint or communicate.

FRANZ LISZT AND EDUARD HANSLICK

After Berlioz, Liszt played the most important role in defining and defending program music at midcentury. Liszt's most extended discussion appears in an article published in 1855 in the *Neue Zeitschrift für Musik*, the journal founded over twenty years earlier by Robert Schumann (see Chapter 5). In the 1840s editorship of the journal had been assumed by Franz Brendel, a strong promoter of what he would in 1859 call the "New German School" of composers, a group including Liszt that strongly supported program music and the operas of Wagner, and disdained the traditional forms of instrumental music.

Liszt's 1855 essay (likely cowritten by his mistress Carolyne von Sayn-Wittgenstein) was nominally about Berlioz's symphonic work *Harold en Italie* (Harold in Italy), based on a poem by Lord Byron. But Liszt also uses Berlioz's work as a stick to beat the traditional symphony—to shatter, as he puts it, "the hallowed frame which has devolved upon the symphony." He argues that like science and other aspects of culture, the arts need to progress, and that program music is "one of the various steps forward which art has still to take." Liszt contrasts what he calls the "specifically musical" symphonist, who is a "formalist" and writes without resort to program or anything extramusical, with the "painter-symphonist," who has the task of "developing a series of

emotional states which are unequivocally and definitely latent in his consciousness." For Liszt, the genre of the symphony has been "hitherto wholly impersonal" and now needs to be advanced by the kind of programmatic content Berlioz
brings to it. Liszt argues that such music will bring about a genuine union of music
and literature. Up to now, the genre of song has provided "*combinations* of music
with literary or quasi-literary works." But program music can offer "a *union* of the
two which promises to become a more intimate one than any that have offered
themselves so far." (All quotations are from SR 158; 6/11.) Liszt thus distinguishes
between mere "combinations" of the arts and a genuine "union." Liszt's thought
was strongly influenced by the midcentury writings of Richard Wagner, to
whom we return in Chapter 8.

During the 1850s Liszt produced a series of what he called "symphonic poems," orchestral works mostly in one movement that were accompanied by a
program usually based on a literary or poetic source. Among Liszt's symphonic
poems are *Prometheus* and *Orpheus* (Greek myth), *Hamlet* (Shakespeare), *Tasso*
(Byron), and *Les Préludes* (Lamartine). There are many progressive aspects to
these works in terms of harmonic and melodic language, but as with Vivaldi,
Beethoven, and Berlioz, the forms of Liszt's symphonic poems are often traditional in outline—normally some variant of sonata form.

Liszt's 1855 article about Berlioz and program music was a response to one
of the strongest and most famous arguments against program music, made in a
short book called *Vom Musikalisch-Schönen* (The Beautiful in Music), published a
year earlier by the Viennese writer on music Eduard Hanslick (1825–1904). This
book would go through eight more editions by the end of the nineteenth century,
all prepared by Hanslick, who became the most powerful critic in the German-
speaking world and also the first professor of music history at the University of
Vienna.

In *The Beautiful in Music* Hanslick argues against Berlioz and Liszt, asserting
that although music can arouse feelings and emotions, it cannot represent them.
Music may try to imitate natural sounds, like birdcalls, but it can never capture
the feelings aroused by them. In one passage Hanslick specifically takes on the
composers of program music:

> The composer of instrumental music never thinks of representing a
> definite subject; otherwise he would be placed in a false position, rath-
> er outside than within the domain of music. His composition in such a
> case would be programmusic, unintelligible without the program. If this
> brings the name of Berlioz to our mind, we do not hereby call into ques-
> tion or underrate his brilliant talent. In his steps followed Liszt, with his
> much weaker "Symphonic Poems."

To be sure, Hanslick argues, composers have long associated music with
great stories or ideas—he mentions the concert overtures and incidental music

by Beethoven, such as *Egmont* and *Coriolan*. But there is nothing *intrinsic* to music that allows it to narrate or to represent concepts. Those concepts can never be the "content" of music. Hanslick explains:

> No instrumental composition can describe the ideas of love, wrath, or fear, since there is no causal nexus between these ideas and certain combinations of sound. Which of the elements inherent in these ideas, then, does music turn to account so effectually? Only the element of motion. . . . This is the element which music has in common with our emotions, and which, with creative power, it contrives to exhibit in an endless variety of forms and contrasts.

By "motion" Hanslick is referring to the entire temporal or horizontal dimension of music—its rhythmic, metrical, and even dynamic properties. Ultimately, for Hanslick, the ideas expressed by a composer are "purely musical." He thus comes down firmly on the side of "absolute" music, although he does not use that term. In his most renowned formulation Hanslick says, "The essence of music is *sound and motion*" (literally, in the original German, "forms moved in sounding").

Thus, as we learn from these discussions, Liszt and his circle saw program music as a way to move beyond styles and forms that in their view had dried up after Beethoven. For the other side, programs were crutches used by composers who could not master what (in Hanslick's mind) were self-standing musical techniques and structures.

ROMANTIC PIANO MUSIC: THE CHARACTER PIECE

Like orchestral music, piano music composed by the generation of the 1830s ranged widely along the spectrum between the absolute and the referential or programmatic. It was often linked to poetic or literary sources, or had associations that went well beyond what Hanslick would call the "purely musical." After about 1830, the multimovement piano sonata—until then the most prestigious genre for the instrument, as exemplified in Beethoven's 32 sonatas—tended to retreat behind what was called the "character" piece, a term likely related to the eighteenth-century designation of "characteristic" music discussed above. Character pieces are shorter works for piano that, normally without any accompanying text, seek to convey a mood, atmosphere, or scene. The association is accomplished by means of the title, and perhaps a short inscription.

As with program music, the trend toward character pieces had begun well before the 1830s. Contemporary with Vivaldi, the French composer François Couperin (1668–1733) published many short harpsichord pieces with evocative titles like "The Little Windmills" or "The Nightingale in Love." Baroque dance movements by Couperin and Bach, such as the gigue or allemande, were "character" pieces in the sense of capturing a single mood. The idea of associating keyboard pieces with specific dance types would carry forward into the nineteenth century. As we saw in Chapters 1 and 3, composers and publishers began to make handsome profits with collections of waltzes, ländler, écossaises, and other dances. Character pieces also began to appear with a variety of titles, including impromptu, nocturne, romance, bagatelle, and eclogue. Such pieces were often in a simple ternary form and playable by amateurs. More important for the present chapter, these character pieces also served to "poeticize" music, to help make it speak.

Václav Tomášek (1774–1850), a Czech composer working in Prague, noted in his autobiography that he had long felt "an inexplicable indifference towards the piano sonata" and that he began to "take refuge in poetics and to try to render different poetic forms in music." With his character pieces called "Eclogues" (in the tradition of pastoral poetry by Theocritus and Virgil), which began to appear in 1807, Tomášek said he "imagined shepherds who live a simple life that, as with all humans, is subject to fate. The attempt to render in music their moods during the different phases of their lives was the task I set myself." In emphasizing the expression of feeling rather than tone painting or imitation, Tomášek's comment shows the underlying affinity between character pieces and program music.

The character piece became elevated to the status of a major compositional genre by the generation of the 1830s. Schumann, Liszt, Chopin, and Mendelssohn, who published barely a dozen piano sonatas among them, each wrote many character pieces, often arranged into collections or cycles that rival sonatas in large-scale structural complexity. Each of these composers had a different approach to the character piece. Broadly speaking, we might say that Liszt's musical imagination was more visual, Schumann's more literary, and Chopin's and Mendelssohn's more purely musical in the sense articulated by Hanslick.

FRANZ LISZT

Among Liszt's greatest collections of piano pieces were the three volumes of *Années de pèlerinage* (Years of Pilgrimage), inspired by places, literary works, and ideas he had encountered in his wide travels as a virtuoso. Composed, revised, and published over a period of almost fifty years, from 1835 to 1883, they form a musical counterpart to some of the letters discussed in the Chapter 5. Many of the pieces in the *Années de pèlerinage* are landscape images translated into musical terms. As such they partake in the appeal to visual culture that we examined in connection with French grand opera in Chapter 4. They also show Liszt engaging with music's sister arts of landscape poetry and painting.

As early as 1794 the German poet and writer Friedrich Schiller had suggested that landscape painting and music were similar in their abstract qualities, their lack of fixed content. What the composer and landscape painter have in common, he wrote, is the "form of their representation." They "simply dispose the spirit to a certain kind of feeling and to the reception of certain ideas; as for the content of these ideas and feelings, they leave that to be found by listener and spectator."

In the first volume of Liszt's *Années* (1855), subtitled *Suisse* (Switzerland), each piece is preceded by a handsome full-page engraving of the place in Switzerland (real or imagined) evoked. Figure 6.2 reproduces the engraving for the fourth piece, *Au bord d'une source* (Beside a Spring), showing a goatherd and his flock resting and refreshing themselves near a mountain stream. A short excerpt of landscape poetry by Schiller himself appears in the lower left: "In murmuring coolness begin the games of young nature."

Liszt's *Au bord d'une source*, which lasts about four minutes, is indeed a sonic image of the bubbling, flowing aspect of the spring as it bursts forth from the mountain (Ex. 6.2; see Anthology 8 for the complete work). But, as with the orchestral program music of Liszt and Berlioz—and as is suggested by Schiller's

Figure 6.2: *Title page engraving of Liszt's* Au bord d'une source *from the* Années de pèlerinage I: Suisse, *1855*

Example 6.2: *Liszt,* Années de pèlerinage, *Vol. 1* (Suisse), *No. 4,* Au bord d'une source, *mm. 1–4*

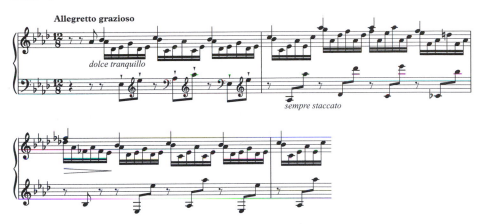

comment about landscape images stimulating a "feeling" rather than capturing a specific subject—the aim is less to paint a natural phenomenon than to convey the emotions that would be evoked by it. For Liszt, the fusion of the literary, visual, and musical could help music to communicate but not to narrate. Above all, Liszt treats the piano as a huge musical canvas on which to spread extraordinary figurations and effects. His treatment of the instrument directly anticipates the kind of musical Impressionism developed by Debussy at the end of the nineteenth century. But the immediate relevance of a work like *Au bord d'une source* to musical culture of the middle of the century lies in the way Liszt directly allies virtuosity with expression, with making music speak.

ROBERT SCHUMANN

The character pieces of Robert Schumann are shaped by a different sensibility from Liszt's. Rather than natural phenomena or foreign locales, Schumann's cycles tend to be inspired by the literature of German Romanticism in which, as we saw in Chapter 5, the composer had steeped himself. Schumann's principal cycles of character pieces, all composed between 1831 and 1838, include *Papillons* (Butterflies), Op. 2; *Davidsbündlertänze* (Dances of the Band of David), Op. 6; *Carnaval* (Carnival), Op. 9; *Fantasiestücke* (Fantasy Pieces), Op. 12; *Kinderszenen* (Scenes from Childhood), Op. 15; and *Kreisleriana*, Op. 16.

Schumann himself noted privately that *Papillons* is based on a chapter about a masked ball from the novel *Flegeljahre* (roughly, Years of Awkward Youth) by his favorite German Romantic writer, Jean Paul. The title of *Kreisleriana* (as discussed in Chapter 2) refers to the character Johannes Kreisler created by another Romantic writer beloved by Schumann, E.T.A. Hoffmann. *Davidsbündlertänze* and *Carnaval* are populated by characters from Schumann's own life, real and imagined. In the original edition of *Davidsbündlertänze*, most of the 18 pieces are ascribed by means of initials to either Florestan or Eusebius, the two sides of Schumann's musical personality (see Chapter 5). Florestan and Eusebius also appear in *Carnaval*, along with a host of other figures including Chiarina (a diminutive form of Clara's name), Paganini, Chopin, and characters from the commedia dell'arte (Columbine, Pantalon), a tradition of improvised theater dating back to the Renaissance. The pieces labeled *Eusebius* and *Florestan* in *Carnaval* are true character studies in conveying the essential emotional qualities of their protagonists. In *Eusebius*, the right hand floats as if in a dream, playing irregular groupings of seven notes above a relatively simple harmonic progression (I–IV–V–I; Ex. 6.3a). In *Florestan,* the melody is disjointed and frenetic, unfolding over a dissonant diminished seventh chord that is repeated obsessively (Ex. 6.3b).

Example 6.3: *Schumann,* Carnaval, *Op. 9,* Eusebius *and* Florestan

(a) *Eusebius,* mm. 1-4

(b) *Florestan,* mm. 1-4

Although Schumann did not refer to his piano works as "program" music, they clearly fall toward that end of the broad continuum of expression—of making music speak—that we have described in this chapter. Schumann understood his own compositions as falling into two categories: "characteristic music," which captures more intimate "states of the soul" (*Seelenzustände*), and "pictorial music," which portrays more external, real-life events (*Lebenszustände*). His cycles seem to comprise an imaginative mixture of the two types. In *Papillons* and *Carnaval*, Schumann is evoking dancers and dances at a masked ball. He is creating a series of moods or "states," yet at the same time there are representations of real-life characters like Clara or Liszt. Like Berlioz, Schumann also indulges in clear mimetic effects, such as the evocation of the chimes of the grandfather clock at the end of *Papillons*.

While both Liszt and Schumann organize their piano pieces into groups, Schumann's pieces tend to be briefer, more fragmentary in nature than Liszt's. They are intended to be played not on their own, but as a sequence. Schumann's sets are cycles rather than collections, in that, as with the cyclic form of Berlioz's *Symphonie fantastique* discussed earlier, and as in Schumann's song cycle *Dichterliebe* (to be discussed below), musical material from the beginning can return at the end, and there are other motivic or thematic connections among the pieces. Throughout the piano cycles, especially the earlier ones, Schumann makes much use of the shorter binary forms characteristic of the waltzes and other dances of Schubert, a composer he much admired. All but one of the pieces in *Papillons* are in triple time.

FELIX MENDELSSOHN AND FRÉDÉRIC CHOPIN

Of the piano music of the generation of the 1830s, that of Mendelssohn and Chopin is falls closest to the "absolute" end of the spectrum. Mendelssohn's efforts in the character piece were focused on what he called *Lieder ohne Worte* (Songs without Words). Throughout his career, from 1830 to 1845, he composed 48 such pieces, which were published in eight volumes. Only five of the *Songs without Words* carry original titles provided by Mendelssohn. Three of them are called *Venetianisches Gondellied* (Venetian Gondolier's Song), and are in a rocking $\frac{6}{8}$ meter characteristic of the genre associated with such songs, the barcarolle. The other two are called simply *Duet* and *Folk Song*. The rest of the pieces have no inscriptions, and Mendelssohn seems to have conceived them without extramusical associations. When a friend wrote to Mendelssohn in 1842 wanting to know the specific meanings of pieces in the *Songs without Words* (and suggesting his own interpretations), Mendelssohn refused to provide any. He responded:

> What the music I love expresses to me are thoughts not too *indefinite* for words, but rather too *definite*. . . . And if I happen to have had a specific word or specific words in mind for one or another of these songs, I can never divulge them to anyone, because the same word means one thing to one person and something else to another, because only the song alone can say the same thing, can arouse the same feelings in one person as in another—a feeling which is not, however, expressed by the same words. (SR 161:1201; SR 6/14:159)

For Mendelssohn, music can communicate feelings more successfully without words or any extramusical assistance. It has a kind of universality that verbal language lacks. Mendelssohn's position might seem to put him in line with Hanslick, whom we discussed above. But Hanslick felt music was not capable of expressing feelings, only of arousing them in individual listeners. Nor are those feelings necessarily the same in each case. Mendelssohn believed that music can actually manage to arouse the same feeling in each listener, which suggests that he believed there is something intrinsic in the music—definite but not capable of being put into words—that can accomplish that goal.

Chopin was, like Mendelssohn, reticent about associating words with his music. Chopin is distinctive among the generation of the 1830s in that almost his entire output as a composer is for solo piano, and mostly in the realm of the character piece. Arranged roughly in order from the briefest to the most expansive, Chopin's major solo piano works include 26 preludes, 58 mazurkas, 20 waltzes, 21 nocturnes, 27 études, 12 polonaises, four impromptus, four scherzos, four ballades, one fantasy, one berceuse, and one barcarolle, as well as two mature piano sonatas. A short list can scarcely begin to suggest the variety of technique, structure, and expression across this body of over 200 pieces in Chopin's oeuvre. The shortest preludes last less than thirty seconds, the longest Polonaise or the Fantasy about twelve minutes. Chopin uniquely captures the "character" of each genre. The mazurkas evoke a Polish dance in triple meter, in which the accent is shifted from the downbeat to the weaker second and third beats of the measure. The polonaises each feature in some way the specific rhythmic pattern of this other Polish dance. Chopin's waltzes often share the elegant rhythm and swirling figuration associated with that Viennese dance from earlier in the century.

Chopin composed his Preludes, Op. 24, as a kind of homage to J. S. Bach's *Well-Tempered Clavier* (1722, 1742). As in Bach, there are pieces in each of the 12 major and 12 minor keys. But Chopin transformed the model in important ways that reflect his Romantic imagination. Bach pairs every prelude with a fugue in the same key; in Chopin, each prelude stands alone and leads only to the next prelude. The twentieth-century writer André Gide claimed to be puzzled by this design:

> I admit that I do not understand the title that Chopin liked to give to these short *pieces*: Preludes. Preludes to what? Each of Bach's preludes is followed by its fugue; it is an integral part of it. But I find it hardly easier to imagine any one of these Preludes of Chopin followed by any other piece in the same key, be it by the same author, than all of these Preludes of Chopin played immediately one after the other. Each one of them is a prelude to a meditation.

Indeed, Chopin's preludes unfold as a series of fragments in a constant state of becoming. The set is thus genuinely Romantic in the sense discussed in Chapter 2.

Chopin provided no program or inscription for his works, only a generic name. This is true even for the four ballades, whose titles might imply the narrative form of the poetic ballad, like Goethe's renowned *Erlkönig* (Erlking), set to music by Schubert in 1815. Chopin was the first composer to write instrumental ballades. In his lifetime it was often claimed—by no less a critic than Schumann—that his ballades were directly inspired by the poetry of Adam Mickiewicz, a Polish compatriot and fellow exile in Paris. Chopin's Second Ballade, for example, was said to depict Mickiewicz's ballad *Switez*, in which Lithuanian women, whose village is being attacked by Russian soldiers of the tsar, are saved by being transformed into water lilies. There is no evidence from Chopin to support this association with the poem. Even though Chopin's ballade could be fitted to the larger plot outline of *Switez*, there are more "purely musical" ways (to use Hanslick's phrase) to explain the piece's broad narrative design of confrontation–mediation–transformation. These musical features involve strong contrasts of musical style and an opposition between two key areas, somewhat as in a sonata form. Like Mendelssohn, Chopin seemed to believe that instrumental music can be most expressive, and can even narrate, without any words or stories.

Many of Chopin's pieces are "songs without words," but in a sense different from Mendelssohn's. In the case of his nocturnes, the music often sings in the manner of Italian opera. Chopin was passionate about Bellini, especially the limpid, long-breathed, and highly ornamented melodies like that of the aria *Casta diva* from the opera *Norma* (see Chapter 4 and Anthology 3). One can almost imagine the theme of Chopin's early Nocturne in B♭ Minor, Op. 9, No. 1 (1830–32), emanating from the throat of a Bellini heroine. As in Bellini, the elaborate ornamentation is not incidental, but central to the melodic shape and dramatic effect (Ex. 6.4; see Anthology 9). This work has the basic nocturne texture of a theme draped over an arpeggiated accompaniment. Like most of Chopin's nocturnes, and like so many character pieces of the nineteenth century, the B♭-Minor Nocturne has a broad ABA' form. The contrasting middle section abandons the decorative melodic style for a simpler, more direct theme played in octaves.

Example 6.4: *Chopin, Nocturne in B♭ Minor, Op. 9, No. 1, mm. 1–4*

In Chopin's later works the chromaticism is more pervasive, occurring at
several structural levels (theme, individual chord, larger tonal areas). The
piano writing is often highly contrapuntal. We can consider briefly one example of Chopin's late style in the Fourth Ballade in F Minor, Op. 52, composed
in 1842. A sonata-form model is recognizable (exposition with two contrasting themes, development, and recapitulation) but radically transformed by the
unusual proportional relationships among the segments, blurred structural
boundaries, and harmonic ambiguities. The piece has a distinctive "modular"
structure in which musical components are reshuffled and juxtaposed rather
than linked by logical progression. Despite thematic-formal returns, there is a
continuous forward trajectory, as manifested in the increasingly contrapuntal
texture of the main theme at each appearance (Ex. 6.5). When it is first heard
the theme is given a simple bass-and-chord accompaniment (Ex. 6.5a). At the
next presentation Chopin adds an inner voice moving urgently in sixteenth
notes (Ex. 6.5b). The third appearance, at the beginning of the recapitulation,
is still more radical. The theme begins away from the tonic key. Emerging almost imperceptibly out of the end of a cadenza-like passage, it is presented in
spare imitative counterpoint, with no chordal accompaniment at all (Ex. 6.5c).

Example 6.5: *Chopin, Ballade No. 4 in F Minor, Op. 52*

(a) mm. 8–10

(b) mm. 58–59

(c) mm. 135–137

There is no explicit story behind Chopin's Fourth Ballade, and the transformations of his main theme are very different from the explicitly program-driven modifications to which Berlioz subjects his *idée fixe* in the *Symphonie fantastique*. Yet Chopin's music "speaks" as powerfully as that of any of his contemporaries. It is as if with the increasingly polyphonic versions of the main theme Chopin is telling us that musical structures can become as complex as life itself, without ever losing their appeal or comprehensibility.

ROBERT SCHUMANN AND THE LIED

Finally in this chapter we turn to another way in which the generation of the 1830s made music speak—through song. As we saw in Chapters 2 and 3, the lied emerged as an important genre in Romanticism because of the strong affinity of some composers for high-quality lyric poetry. In the hands of Schubert, the lied developed into something more than the sum of its parts, words and music. The poet set most often by Schubert was Goethe, the leading figure of late Classicism. At the very end of his life Schubert turned to poems by the early Romantic Heinrich Heine, who would become the preferred poet of Schumann and also popular among other composers. As suggested in Chapter 2, Heine's poetry captured a new subjectivity, a more personal style that appealed to a younger generation.

Many Romantic composers contributed to the lied. Mendelssohn wrote about 70 solo songs, drawing on a wide range of poets including Goethe, Schiller, and Heine. Liszt composed about the same number, in a variety of languages including German, French, Italian, and Hungarian. Chopin did not show much interest in the genre, leaving only about 15 songs, set to Polish texts. In France, Berlioz created a small number of important *mélodies* (the analogue to lieder), including the first orchestral song cycle, *Les nuits d'été* (The Nights of Summer, 1841).

Among his contemporaries, Schumann emerged as the greatest and most prolific composer of lieder, one who lifted the genre to new levels. Schumann wrote almost 250 solo songs, over half of them within his so-called *Liederjahr* (Year of Song), 1840. This was the year in which he was finally able to marry Clara Wieck, overcoming a long process of obstruction by Clara's father. The happy event released a flood of creativity in Schumann, mainly in the form of songs.

Among the works of 1840 are several song cycles analogous in scope and ambition to Schumann's piano cycles of the 1830s, and also worthy as successors to Schubert's song cycles *Die schöne Müllerin* and *Winterreise*, discussed briefly in Chapter 3. Schumann wrote two cycles on poems of Heine: the *Liederkreis* (Song Cycle), Op. 24, and *Dichterliebe* (Poet's Love), Op. 48. Two other important song cycles of 1840 are the *Liederkreis*, Op. 39, set to the poetry of Joseph Eichendorff; and *Frauenliebe und -leben* (A Woman's Love and Life), Op. 42, which sets the poems of Adalbert von Chamisso.

In Chapter 2 we looked briefly at the first song of *Dichterliebe*, emphasizing how Schumann creates a musical language of longing and desire analogous to that of Heine's compact lyrics and Romantic in spirit (see Anthology 10). Schumann selected 16 poems from a much larger collection by Heine, *Lyrisches Intermezzo* (Lyrical Intermezzo). His song cycle traces a range of emotions in the protagonist, from tenderness, to excitement, to frustration and bitterness at rejection by his beloved—and finally to a kind of defiant acceptance, when in the last song he metaphorically puts his songs in a coffin and tosses them into the Rhine River, thus burying his "love and pain." Yet the listener learns that moving on is not so easy. For after the final words are sung comes a long, lyrical postlude for piano, bringing back material from an earlier song (No. 12) that communicates more longing and regret than angry resignation.

Dichterliebe has no clear narrative, nor even a linear progression of feelings. As with the piano cycles discussed above—and as with much of the music examined in this chapter—Schumann aims not to tell a story but to portray a series of "states of the soul." Nowhere has Romantic irony been better captured in music. As we saw in Chapter 2, Schumann is responsive to the frequent moments in Heine's verses where the poet is saying one thing but clearly meaning something else. Irony can take a form as in the song *Ein Jüngling liebt ein Mädchen* (A Boy Loves a Girl, No. 11), when the poet bitterly reports the story of a youth who loves a girl who loves another boy, who in turn marries a different girl. Schumann creates a melody and accompaniment that are on the surface simple and folklike, with mainly tonic and dominant harmonies (Ex. 6.6). The music seems thus to be in ironic contrast

Example 6.6: *Schumann,* Dichterliebe, *Op. 48, No. 11,* Ein Jüngling liebt ein Mädchen, *mm. 5–12*

A boy loves a girl, who has chosen another. The other loves another and has married her.

to the text. Yet at another level, the patterns of sharply syncopated accents, the fragmentary musical texture, and the thumping, angular bass line tell us that all is not right. The yearning postlude of the final song (No. 16) presents a still different instance of musical irony in that the composer reveals to us something that the protagonist may not even be aware of—the desire he still feels for his beloved.

That within one song cycle Schumann can create musical languages for so many emotional states shows his unparalleled ability to communicate through music. As we have seen in this chapter, he was one of a group of composers in the years after 1830 to achieve that goal in a wide array of forms, including program music, character pieces for piano, and lieder. Schumann, Berlioz, Liszt, Mendelssohn, and Chopin all were composing in a musical culture which, after the first flush of Romanticism in the early decades of the nineteenth century, became increasingly concerned with what music could express and how it could do so. In the next chapter we will see that concerns about music's relationship to the individual and to the world did not go away, but that new ways of explaining and negotiating it developed around the middle of the nineteenth century.

FOR FURTHER READING

The Age of Chopin: Interdisciplinary Inquiries, ed. Halina Goldberg (Bloomington: Indiana University Press, 2004)

Berlioz, Hector, *Fantastic Symphony*, ed. Edward T. Cone, Norton Critical Score (New York: W. W. Norton & Company, 1971)

Dahlhaus, Carl, *The Idea of Absolute Music*, trans. Roger Lustig (Chicago and London: University of Chicago Press, 1989)

Daverio, John, *Robert Schumann: Herald of a "New Poetic Age"* (Oxford and New York: Oxford University Press, 1997)

Franz Liszt and His World, ed. Christopher H. Gibbs and Dana Gooley (Princeton: Princeton University Press, 2006)

Hanslick, Eduard, *The Beautiful in Music*, trans. Gustav Cohen (New York: Liberal Arts Press, 1957)

Parakilas, James, *Songs without Words: Chopin and the Tradition of the Instrumental Ballade* (Portland, OR: Amadeus Press, 1992)

Will, Richard, *The Characteristic Symphony in the Age of Haydn and Beethoven* (Cambridge: Cambridge University Press, 2002)

Ⓢ Additional resources available at wwnorton.com/studyspace

about the evils of capitalism and the need for a constitutional monarchy. When the Prussian troops began to quell the Dresden uprising, Wagner fled the city, making his way to Switzerland. A warrant was issued for his arrest. Like Marx, he would live in exile for many years. As we will see in Chapter 8, these experiences left a lasting mark on Wagner's artistic theories.

The revolutions of 1848 are generally deemed to have failed. Most of the uprisings were put down, and some states established even stronger, more authoritarian rule than before. "We have been beaten and humiliated. We have been scattered, imprisoned, disarmed and gagged," lamented Pierre-Joseph Proudhon, a renowned French anarchist and revolutionary, in 1850. "The fate of European democracy has slipped from our hands—from the hands of the people." But the uprisings of 1848 also left positive political and social legacies, including universal male suffrage in France and Switzerland in 1848, the abolishment of serfdom in Russia in 1861, and the unifications of Italy and Germany in 1861 and 1871, respectively.

ANTI-ROMANTICISM AND PESSIMISM

Proudhon's statement reflects the sense of disillusionment that settled over many European citizens in the aftermath of 1848, an attitude that has been characterized as "anti-Romanticism." Romanticism was now widely seen as too subjective, too inward, and too self-indulgent; it was associated with passive or escapist behavior in an era that required active engagement. "The political gravity of the present situation has dealt a serious blow to Romanticism," wrote the music critic Karl Kahlert in 1848. "The time for dreams is past. . . . Romanticism has sapped the strength of the German nation."

Unlike the optimistic Liszt of the 1830s (see Chapter 5), many were now skeptical that political developments could have any positive effect on music or musical life. The German writer on music Eduard Krüger asked in 1848, with obvious irony: "Is there such a thing as a republican or monarchical harmony or melody? Will a republican always play his trombone better in a republic than an aristocrat would? . . . Neither instruments nor triads, let alone the talents or insights of artists, will be much affected by the Frankfurt Assembly." (Krüger refers here to the parliament that met in Frankfurt in 1848–49 and tried without success to create a unified German state.)

It is no surprise that discouragement fed a pessimistic worldview. We recall from Chapter 2 how Schopenhauer had articulated a philosophy of pessimism in his book *The World as Will and Representation*, first published in 1819. He argued that life consists of unfulfilled desire and suffering, from which there can be no relief except in death. Schopenhauer's work had relatively little impact at the time of its initial publication. In 1844 he issued a new expanded edition, and in the years after 1850 the book's ideas began to find much broader resonance.

Wagner discovered Schopenhauer's work in 1854, and it substantially influenced his opera *Tristan und Isolde*, completed in 1859, and the operatic cycle *The Ring of the Nibelung*, completed in 1874. In *Tristan*, the pessimism is personal, individual; the lovers' passion is doomed to remain unfulfilled in life. In the *Ring*, the pessimism is more collective and historical: we learn that with power comes greed and that the gods are destined to fall in a kind of global cataclysm.

A broader cultural pessimism was also characteristic of the years after 1850. Many felt that the Golden Age was in the past, and that creative artists were now "epigones," or second-rate imitators, doomed only to repeat the achievements of their predecessors. This attitude had already surfaced in 1836, when the German writer Karl Immermann published a three-volume novel called *Die Epigonen* (The Epigones), which takes a cynical view of rising industrialism and the worship of money by the middle class. In 1857 a music critic named Karl Debrois van Bruyck argued that music was in a period of decline, following a "sublime" phase of Bach, Handel, and Gluck; a "beautiful" phase of Haydn, Mozart, and Beethoven; then an "attractive" phase of Schubert, Mendelssohn, and Schumann. Van Bruyck noted glumly: "We are and remain, whatever names we have, epigones—large, small, talented, and untalented." Van Bruyck's dark view goes well beyond Schumann's earlier claim of 1835 (discussed in Chapter 5) that people were living through an "inartistic period."

The most brilliant cultural pessimist of the later nineteenth century was the philosopher Friedrich Nietzsche (1844–1900; Fig. 7.1). At first, as he argued

Figure 7.1: *Friedrich Nietzsche, a leading German philosopher and cultural critic of the later nineteenth century*

in *The Birth of Tragedy from the Spirit of Music* (1872), Nietzsche thought cultural regeneration would be achieved through the works of Wagner. As he became disillusioned with Wagner, however, he turned his gaze more broadly on European culture, which he felt had fallen into decline and "decadence." It had lost the vitality necessary for the creation of a truly great culture. In 1888 Nietzsche defined decadence as when "life no longer dwells in the whole . . . the vibration and exuberance of life is pushed back into the smallest forms. . . . The whole no longer lives at all: it is composite, calculated, artificial, and artifact." Decadent artists also lacked "authenticity"; they wore masks and disguises. Both criticism and celebration of decadence became widespread in the later nineteenth century. Perhaps the figure most famous—or infamous—for a lifestyle perceived as decadent was the flamboyant Irish writer Oscar Wilde [1854–1900], who in 1895, after a much-publicized trial, was imprisoned in London for sodomy and "gross indecency."

Nietzsche's influential writings took on many basic assumptions of Western culture. He called for a "revaluation of values," including those of morality and Christianity (he famously wrote that "God is dead"). Nietzsche rejected the idea that the distinction between good and evil is somehow absolute or that it should be imposed on an individual from above either by religion, by society, or by what the philosopher Immanuel Kant called the "categorical imperative." Nietzsche was not a pure pessimist, however. In his most famous work, *Also sprach Zarathustra* (Thus Spake Zarathustra, 1885), he envisioned a social and cultural order in which a new kind of "overman" or *Übermensch* would transcend nihilism and transfigure life.

IDEALISM VERSUS MATERIALISM

The darker worldview represented by anti-Romantic and pessimistic sentiment around 1850 is part of a broader change, a shift in attitude from idealism to materialism, which affected many realms, including the arts. Idealism, the prevailing philosophy of the late eighteenth and early nineteenth centuries, maintained that "reality" is in the mind, that the external world cannot be experienced directly because it cannot be separated from the mind, of which it is a projection. The classic formulation of idealism came from Immanuel Kant (1724–1804), who wrote in his *Critique of Pure Reason* (1781):

> We are justified in maintaining that only what is in ourselves can be perceived immediately, and that my own existence is the sole object of a mere perception. . . . I am not, therefore, in a position to *perceive* external things, but can only infer their existence from my inner perception, taking the inner perception as the effect of which something external is the proximate cause.

Kant's position led the early Romantics to place a great value on imagination and fantasy, on the "internal" senses. Imagination was the real source of art, and it could come into direct conflict with the everyday world. As we saw in Chapter 2, in the early nineteenth century music was often deemed the most Romantic of the arts precisely because of its supposed other-worldliness, its location in the realm of fantasy.

By midcentury, idealism began to yield to materialism, which tipped the balance toward the real world. Materialism holds—contra Kant—that we can only assume to exist that which can be observed or experienced directly through the senses. All phenomena in the material world must be explained in terms of natural causes or principles, which can be discovered through empirical observation and experimentation. This attitude helped propel some of the great advances in science in the later nineteenth century, such as the theory of evolution put forward in Charles Darwin's *Origin of Species* (1859), which was based in part on data collected from his own extensive travels on the HMS *Beagle*.

The intersection between the scientific worldview and the creative arts, especially music, showed itself in several ways. We recall from Chapter 6 that Eduard Hanslick, in his book *The Beautiful in Music* (1854), claimed that music cannot portray emotions, images, or anything deemed extramusical. Hanslick's position can be seen as anti-Romantic and as an attempt to ground the aesthetics of music in a materialistic viewpoint worthy of his day. Hanslick defined music as a physical object, as "sound and motion." "The crude material which the composer has to fashion," he claimed (and note his use of the word "material"), "is the entire scale of musical notes and their inherent adaptability to an endless variety of melodies, harmonies, and rhythms."

At around the same time as Hanslick—and not by chance—the acoustics and physics of music became topics of intense investigation, especially in the work of Hermann von Helmholtz (1821–1894), one of the most prominent materialists of the 1850s and 1860s. In 1863 Helmholtz published *On the Sensations of Tone as a Physiological Basis for the Theory of Music*, the first comprehensive modern investigation of the properties of sound. The book went through many editions in both German and (from 1885) English. His basic goal is to show the relationship—and bridge an apparent gap—between the physical properties of sounds and their aesthetic effects. Among the topics he investigates are sound as a spectrum ranging from noise to musical tone; the structure of the human ear that allows us to process sound; and the distinction between consonance and dissonance.

Outreach to the general public was an important part of Helmholtz's mission. He gave many popular lectures, which were also published and translated. In 1857 in Bonn, Germany, he delivered a talk called "On the Physiological Causes of Harmony in Music." His talk begins by warmly recognizing the birthplace of Beethoven as an appropriate venue for a lecture on music and for an attempt to bridge the gulf between science and the arts. Up to now music had "withdrawn itself from treatment more than any other art," Helmholtz said, because unlike poetry or painting, music does not attempt to "describe," and only rarely seeks "to imitate the outer world." In comparison with the other arts, music "seems in its action on the mind as the most immaterial, evanescent, and tender creator of incalculable and indescribable states of consciousness."

As we can recognize by now, Helmholtz is describing the Romantic view of music that prevailed before 1850. Against this he takes a materialist stance, arguing that the science of mathematics could be helpful in developing a theory of musical sounds and understanding the physical and technical foundations of music. Helmholtz goes patiently through the properties of sound, including how the vibrations of air or a string produce pitches, and how the human ear receives and processes musical tones. In his writings Helmholtz provides detailed, complex illustrations, as in his representation of part of the cochlea, the auditory portion of the inner ear (see Fig. 7.2).

For all his materialism and emphasis on the physical attributes of sound, Helmholtz appreciated the emotional qualities of music. At the end of his 1857 lecture he observes that ultimately "in a musical work of art the movement follows the outflow of the artist's own emotions." Such a statement makes Helmholtz in some sense more Romantic in outlook than Hanslick.

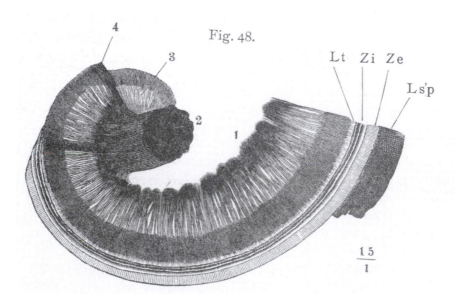

Figure 7.2: *Illustration of the cochlea, the auditory portion of the inner ear, by Hermann von Helmholtz, 1863*

REALISM

Helmholtz was no less interested in sight than in hearing, as is revealed by a lecture of 1871 called "On the Relation of Optics to Painting," which seeks to accomplish in the realm of visual arts what his work on acoustics had done in music. In the visual arts, science and aesthetics—or, to put it somewhat differently, technology and artistic expression—had already begun to draw closer together by midcentury in a way that would happen only later for music. The development of photography in France in the 1820s and 1830s allowed the direct reproduction of images in ways that had a profound effect on many aspects of culture. Only in the last decade of the nineteenth century and the first two of the twentieth, as we will see in Chapter 13, would sound recording begin to have a similar impact in music.

The advent of photography enhanced realism as an artistic value. Figure 7.3 shows one of the earliest photographs, a "daguerreotype" still life made in 1837 by one of the pioneers of photography, the French chemist Louis Daguerre (1787–1851), after whom the technique was named (and who, as we saw in Chapter 4, was active as a set designer at the Paris Opéra). Prominent painters embraced and sometimes practiced the new techniques of photography. In his studio the great French realist painter Gustave Courbet (1819–1877) kept photographs of

Figure 7.3: *One of the earliest known photographs, a still life, by Louis Daguerre, 1837*

female nudes that served as models for his painting. Some of Courbet's critics felt his paintings were too realistic and too graphic—too close to contemporary photography. Edouard Manet (1832–1883), another French realist painter, often took photographs of his own works to send to friends, critics, and curators. Once, when he was painting a portrait of a woman from real life, he requested a photograph of her, so that he could get a "better likeness."

Another aspect of realism, partly a result of the revolutions of 1848, was an interest in depicting the difficult life of the lower classes. Courbet, who was sympathetic to the revolutionaries, made a practice of painting peasants, farmers, and urban laborers like stonecutters in everyday situations. The French novelists Gustave Flaubert (1821–1880) and Emile Zola (1840–1902) attempted something similar in fiction, often focusing on the more salacious aspects of private lives. Flaubert's *Madame Bovary* (1856) is about a farmer's daughter whose boredom with her marriage to a doctor and with provincial life leads her into adulterous affairs. Zola's most famous novel, *Nana* (1880), is about a Parisian prostitute who destroys the lives of all the men with whom she is involved and in the end suffers a horrible death from smallpox. Zola claimed his goal as "first and foremost a scientific one" and likened his approach to "the analytical methods that surgeons apply to corpses." Indeed, his final description of Nana's body riddled by smallpox is shockingly graphic: "She was fruit of the charnel house, a heap of matter and blood, a shovelful of corrupted flesh thrown down on the pillow. The pustules had invaded the whole of the face, so that each touched its neighbor."

Realism had different implications for music than for painting or literature, at least in the era before recorded sound. In the world of opera, Verdi's *La traviata* (The Fallen Woman) of 1853 comes closest at midcentury to the Flaubert-Zola kind of realism. It was based on a recent novel of 1848 about a Parisian courtesan named Violetta, who dies from tuberculosis. In Violetta's music for the last scene of *La traviata* (Opera Sampler), Verdi conveys vividly the shortness of breath that accompanies the final stages of the illness. But where Zola maintains a strict "scientific" distance from Nana, Verdi clearly sympathizes with Violetta, for whom he creates some of the most moving music of the nineteenth century. In music, even in the anti-Romantic second half of the nineteenth century, Romantic expression often tempers realism.

REALISM IN INSTRUMENTAL MUSIC

As we have seen in earlier chapters, the early Romantics believed in music's expressive power but were skeptical of its ability to imitate directly anything in the real world. Even Beethoven, who had evoked birds and thunder in his *Pastoral* Symphony, described his goal as capturing emotions rather than "painting." And Berlioz, who sought in the third movement of his *Symphonie fantastique* to imitate shepherds piping in the (physical) distance, also maintained that music could not paint sounds directly (although he also employed realistic effects such as the bells tolling the funereal *Dies irae* chant in the finale).

In the later nineteenth and early twentieth centuries, the apparent limitations of music did not stop composers from striving for ever more realistic effects from orchestras. The most prominent examples come from Gustav Mahler (1860–1911) and Richard Strauss (1864–1949), to whom we return in Chapter 12. In his Sixth and Seventh Symphonies (1904–1905), Mahler calls for cowbells to play in the orchestra. Like Berlioz before him, however, Mahler explained that the intended effect was more symbolic or metaphorical than realistic: the cowbells were meant to suggest the loneliness of an alpine landscape. Strauss aims for more direct realism when in his tone poem *Don Quixote* (1897), based on the novel by Cervantes, he calls for a wind machine to depict the Don's and Sancho Panza's imagined ride through the air. The wind machine was developed in the nineteenth century for such special effects. It produces no real wind, but rather approximates the sound of wind by rotating a cylindrical drum against a piece of fabric (Fig. 7.4).

REALISM IN VOCAL MUSIC

A different kind of realism became important in both opera and song of the later nineteenth century. Singing became in many cases more like speech,

Figure 7.4: *Wind machine, an orchestral instrument for realistic effects*

with careful attention to declamation, often at the expense of more purely lyrical lines. In opera, what had previously been a distinction between speechlike "recitative" and melodic "aria" became ever more blurred. In Germany, largely under the influence of Richard Wagner, singers cultivated a declamatory style in which enunciation was as crisp and precise as in spoken language.

In Russia, composers had similar goals, as we will see in more detail below in our discussion of Modest Musorgsky (1839–1881). "My music must be an artistic reproduction of human speech in all its finest shades," Musorgsky wrote in a letter to a friend. "That is, the *sounds of human speech*, as the external manifestations of thought and feeling, must, without exaggeration or violence, become true, accurate *music*."

HUGO WOLF

Nowhere are the principles of naturalistic declamation reflected more clearly than in the lieder of Hugo Wolf (1860–1903). Wolf wrote one opera and a handful of instrumental works, but concentrated almost all his efforts on the genre of the lied, publishing some 250 songs between 1888 and 1897. He saw himself as carrying forward the achievements of Schubert and Schumann into the latter part of the nineteenth century.

Wolf generally chose poems by the greatest German Romantic poets, including Goethe and Eduard Mörike, as well as German translations of folk verses from Spanish and Italian. He was attracted to both comic and serious poems, as well as to ones with sacred or religious content. To emphasize the literary values of his songs, Wolf published some with the title *Gedichte* (poems) rather than the more normal *Lieder* or *Gesänge* (songs). In standard concert practice of the nineteenth century, lieder by various composers would appear on the same program, or would be mixed with instrumental or other vocal music. In a radical departure, Wolf organized entire recitals around his own settings of a single poet. Often the poems would be read aloud before the musical versions were performed.

In his settings, Wolf sought to capture every nuance of a poetic text. His lieder thus rarely have hummable melodies. As in Wagner's operas, the musical continuity tends to be created by the accompaniment. In the song *In der Frühe* (Early Morning, 1889; No. 24 of his *Mörike-Lieder*), the poet describes arising after a sleepless night. The piano creates a steady, rhythmic-thematic pattern, repeated in sequence, over which the voice declaims the text starkly (Ex. 7.1; see Anthology 11). The voice moves independently of the piano part; it begins in the middle of the first measure, almost as an afterthought, and ends on the second beat of the following one. There is a powerful naturalism at work here. We would not expect a rounded, lyrical melody from a tired, anxious speaker (or singer). Only at the end of the song, when he or she hears morning bells, does the mood turn optimistic and the vocal line become broader and more triadic.

Example 7.1: *Wolf,* Mörike-Lieder, *No. 24,* In der Frühe, *mm. 1–4*

No sleep has yet cooled my eyes,

Day is already beginning to appear at the window of my bedroom.

HISTORICISM

Realism of the later nineteenth century can be understood as substituting a continuum for what were formerly held to be absolute distinctions between art and nature. Composers for voice explored a range from song to speech; instrumental composers, from music to noise. Painters like Courbet blurred the boundaries between aesthetically pleasing images and realistic ones. The cultural critic Siegfried Kracauer, writing in 1927, suggested that photography created "spatial continuum" of objects and images, capturing their physical relationships at a single moment in time. Kracauer argued that historicism is a parallel development of the nineteenth century, placing discrete events in a temporal continuum.

Historicism originated among historians and philosophers who maintained that everything human beings create—meanings, values, language, institutions, and culture—is the product of history, the result of previous historical circumstances. Therefore, we must study history in order to understand ourselves. Historicism implies a knowledge of and respect for the past, but not necessarily a conservative stance. The historicist looks for ways in which the past can inform the present creatively.

Musical historicism follows a similar train of thought. If we are a product of the past, then we must come to appreciate the works of the great composers who preceded us. The increasing awareness of Bach in the nineteenth century is a perfect example of this process. In 1802, the German music historian Johann

Nikolaus Forkel published the first full biography of Bach—and the first real biography of any musician. In 1829, Felix Mendelssohn led the first modern performance of Bach's *St. Matthew Passion*. Just over two decades later—in fact, at the precise midpoint of the century, 1850—the Bach Gesellschaft (Bach Society) of Leipzig, in connection with the prominent publisher Breitkopf & Härtel, set out to issue a complete edition of Bach's works, many of which had never been published or had appeared only in limited editions. This monumental project, which would extend to the year 1900 and encompass 46 volumes, marked the real beginning of musicology, the scholarly study and editing of music.

Complete editions of other early composers were soon begun in other countries, including the works of Henry Purcell (1659–1695) in England, and Jean-Baptiste Lully (1632–1687) and Jean-Philippe Rameau (1683–1764) in France. Many of the compositions were brought to the attention of the public through special "historical" concerts or in programs of "ancient" music (see Chapter 10). Musicology and concert life, as they developed in the later nineteenth century, show how the systematic or large-scale application of a historicist frame of mind can lead to entirely new disciplines or activities.

Historicism was equally important among composers. Earlier in the nineteenth century, as we saw in Chapter 5, Mendelssohn had a strong relationship with the music of Bach and Handel, and his oratorios absorb their high Baroque style into his own early Romantic idiom. Such historicist practices become even more prominent later in the century, when more early music became available in collected editions. Johannes Brahms (1833–1897) passionately studied the music not only of the high Baroque, but also of the early Baroque and Renaissance masters, including Giovanni Pierluigi da Palestrina (1525/26–1594) and Heinrich Schütz (1585–1672). In Brahms's choral masterpiece *Ein deutsches Requiem* (A German Requiem, 1868), earlier techniques are joined almost seamlessly to a modern sense of harmony and form. In France in the 1880s, César Franck (1822–1890) wrote many powerful organ works inspired by Baroque composers. For piano he wrote a massive Prelude, Chorale, and Fugue (1884), a work fully of its era in harmonic and melodic style, but deeply historicist in form. There is a sweeping prelude meant to capture an improvisatory Baroque style; a fantasy on a "chorale" tune made up by Franck; and finally, a highly chromatic four-voice fugue. Like Mendelssohn and other historicists, Brahms and Franck (both of whom we return to in Chapter 10) fully acknowledged—and even celebrated—their links to the past. Earlier music was part of their identity as creative artists.

NATIONALISM

In the latter half of the nineteenth century, composers increasingly defined their identities with reference not only to the musical past but to the geopolitical present. Nationalism, an ideology or feeling based on strong identification with a people, land, or country, was not a new sentiment for artists. As we saw in Chapters 2 and 3, the German philosopher and critic Herder argued in the later eighteenth century that geographical, ethnic, and linguistic identity was essential in shaping the culture and art of a people. In the first decades of the nineteenth century Beethoven and other creative artists shared a nationalistic sensibility that opposed French domination and tried to frame German identity in part around musical achievement. In the 1830s the Italian philosopher and statesman Giuseppe Mazzini felt it appropriate to urge artists toward a more universal outlook transcending nationalism.

Nationalistic concerns and activities grew throughout the century. In Italy and Germany, struggles for independence culminated in the creation of unified states. In Italy, as we will see in Chapter 9, Verdi took an active part in the culture of the Risorgimento, the Italian movement for independence. In Germany Richard Wagner, to whom we return in Chapter 8, began to work actively on *Die Meistersinger von Nürnberg* (The Mastersingers of Nuremberg, completed 1868), an opera that embodies many of the ideals of German nationalism. Set in the Renaissance era, it celebrates the German *Volk* or people for their integrity, values, and support of "German art."

In the same year as *Meistersinger*, Brahms's *German Requiem* had its premiere. By rejecting the traditional Latin text in favor of the German version of the Bible, as translated by Martin Luther during the Reformation, Brahms was making a statement about German values. Both Brahms and Wagner, so different in most respects, were enthusiastic about the founding of the German Empire in 1871. On the wall of his music room Brahms kept a bronze relief of Otto von Bismarck, the "Iron Chancellor" and architect of German unification. In 1871 Brahms composed a stirring choral work, the *Triumphlied* (Song of Triumph), in direct response to the Prussian victory over France and the declaration of the empire. For the same occasion Wagner composed his *Kaiser-Marsch* (Emperor's March), an orchestral work premiered in the presence of the new emperor, Wilhelm I, and prominently featuring the Lutheran chorale *Ein feste Burg ist unser Gott* (A Mighty Fortress Is Our God).

Chorale tunes were a sonic emblem of German national consciousness. Folk or folklike melodies were another. Many Austrian and German composers, including Schubert, Weber, Brahms, and Mahler, used such melodies in their vocal and instrumental compositions. Folk tunes, which were usually diatonic and triadic, could be easily assimilated into the prevailing styles of German music in the nineteenth century (as they had been for Mozart and Haydn).

In the later nineteenth century, interest in using indigenous or "local" elements in art music became widespread among populations that would not have an independent state for many decades, like the Czechs, Slovaks, and Hungarians, as well as in Russia and other long-established nations that sought to assert their cultural independence from the West. Composers drew upon scales, rhythms, formal structures, melodies, and genres—as well as plays, novels, and poetry—characteristic of their linguistic or ethnic group.

RUSSIAN NATIONALISM

In the later nineteenth century Russian music developed a self-consciously nationalist attitude. A group of five composers dubbed by a critic the "Mighty Handful"—Mily Balakirev (1836/37–1910), Aleksandr Borodin (1833–1887), César Cui (1835–1918), Modest Musorgsky (1839–1881), and Nikolay Rimsky-Korsakov (1844–1908)—gathered in the city of St. Petersburg during the years 1865–70 with the goal of fostering a distinctly Russian art music. The Mighty Handful prided themselves on being largely self-taught and took a stance in opposition to conservatory-trained composers, especially the Moscow-based Pyotr Il'yich Tchaikovsky (1840–1893), whom they saw as too cosmopolitan (and to whom we return in Chapter 10). With the exception of Balakirev, the composers of the Mighty Five initially made their professional careers outside of music: Borodin was a chemist and doctor, Cui an army officer, Musorgsky a civil servant, and Rimsky-Korsakov a naval cadet.

Musorgsky is today recognized as one of the greatest composers of the nineteenth century, one who fused realistic and nationalistic impulses in an original way. For his magnum opus, the opera *Boris Godunov*, he fashioned his own libretto from a recent historical drama by Alexander Pushkin about a tsar who ruled Russia from 1598 to 1605. In Pushkin's and Musorgsky's version of the story, Boris has secretly arranged the murder of a nine-year-old heir and possible claimant to the Russian throne. (The real Boris's guilt has never been proven; some historians acquit him of the crime.) Although he rules wisely and generously, Boris is tormented by a guilty conscience, and his story takes on the dimensions of a Shakespearean tragedy.

Musorgsky composed *Boris Godunov* in 1869 in the naturalistic style of almost pure recitative favored by his circle. After the opera was rejected by the Russian Imperial Theaters, in part because it had no leading female characters or love interest, he reworked it. The revision, completed in 1872 and premiered in 1874, makes some concessions to operatic conventions, including an entirely new act that introduces a prima donna, the Polish noblewoman Marina (not in the Pushkin play), and features an extended love duet between her and Grigory, the pretender to the Russian throne. Throughout the opera Musorgsky also enhances the distinction between recitative and aria, while still maintaining a fluid vocal style of powerful psychological realism. This style is exemplified in Boris's great Act 2 soliloquy, where the libretto unfolds in a proselike fashion, following the twists and turns of Boris's thoughts as he expresses the conflict between maintaining his public role as tsar and his coping with private anguish. Musorgsky's music reflects this process, changing in meter and style of accompaniment as Boris shifts between more lyrical and declamatory expression (Ex. 7.2; see Anthology 12).

Example 7.2: *Musorgsky,* Boris Godunov, *Act 2, Boris's monologue*

In vain the soothsayers promise me a long life and many days of untroubled power. Neither life, nor power . . .

Musorgsky's special blend of realism and nationalism in *Boris Godunov* is also apparent in the colorful Coronation scene in the Prologue (Opera Sampler). Here the tolling of bells celebrating Boris's ascent to the throne is captured in a striking fashion by the alternation of two dominant seventh harmonies with roots that are a tritone apart, A♭ and D. When combined, the notes of these two chords, which have the tritone C–F♯ in common, yield six of the eight notes of the octatonic scale (the full scale is A♭, A♮, B♭, C♮, D♮, E♭, F♮, F♯). This scale, comprised of alternating half and whole steps, became a characteristic sonority in Russian music in the later nineteenth century and into the twentieth, in the works of Rimsky-Korsakov and Igor Stravinsky.

CZECH NATIONALISM

To the southwest of Russia, among the smaller ethnic and linguistic groups that make up central Europe, nationalism was a powerful ideological force, especially after midcentury. About eight million Czech people lived in the territories of Bohemia and Moravia, which were part of the sprawling, multiethnic Habsburg Empire (and today comprise the Czech Republic). (See Fig. 7.5; Bohemia and

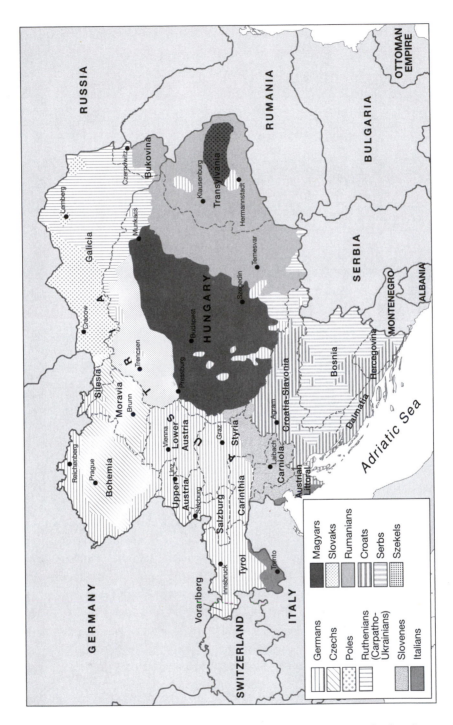

Figure 7.5: *Habsburg Empire in the later nineteenth century, showing the distribution of national and ethnic groups*

Moravia are represented in the upper left part of the map.) German was the official language of the empire and also of the educated upper classes. But in the aftermath of the revolutions of 1848, Czechs began to assert ever greater cultural and intellectual independence, and the Czech language became widespread in administrative, educational, and private realms.

Composers took an active part in helping to increase national consciousness. Bedřich Smetana (1824–1884), often called the father of Czech music, grew up in a small town east of Prague. German was the language of the middle-class household in which he grew up; Smetana would learn Czech only later in life, and would never fully master the language. Yet during his young adulthood he became an advocate for Czech independence and participated in the revolutions of 1848, manning barricades on the main bridge in Prague. (In a similar way, Liszt, who grew up in a German-speaking family and never learned Hungarian, became a strong supporter of Hungarian national self-determination.)

Smetana developed a vision for a genuinely Czech music. A fellow composer, Václav Novotný, reported about Smetana during a visit to Liszt in the 1850s: "I can see him now, eyes flashing as he told us how the idea of creating an independent Czech musical style began to mature in him for the first time." Other musicians present at the discussion were skeptical of the idea, claiming that Czech composers had always been dependent on German, French, and Italian styles. This only strengthened Smetana's determination:

> On the way home, Smetana turned his moist eyes to the starry heaven, raised his hand, and deeply moved swore in his heart the greatest oath: that he would dedicate his entire life to his nation, to the tireless service of his country's art. And he remained true to his oath even during the most trying periods of his life, to the last flickerings of his spirit, to the last breath.

In the 1860s a new opera house specifically for works written in Czech, the Provisional Theater (today called the National Theater), opened in Prague. For this theater Smetana completed *Prodaná nevěsta* (The Bartered Bride, 1866), which is considered the first real Czech opera. It features a bagpipe in the prelude, characteristic dances (polka, *skočná,* and *furiant*), and a libretto framed in poetic meters and prose that reflect the Czech language.

Smetana's most beloved orchestral piece, which became a national musical monument for Czechs, is the 12-minute *Vltava* (The Moldau), part of a cycle of six symphonic poems he composed between 1874 and 1879 under the collective title *Má Vlast* (My Country). The simple but powerful concept behind *The Moldau* is expressed by Smetana's brief program:

> The work tells of *the flow of the Moldau*, beginning from its first tiny sources—the *cold* and *warm* Moldau, the joining of the two little streams

into one, then the *sweep* of the Moldau through the groves and along meadows, through the countryside where harvest festivals are being celebrated; in the light of the moon, the dance of the water-nymphs; on the nearby rocks proud castles rear up, wide mansions and ruins; the Moldau swirls in the St. John's rapids, then flows in a broad sweeping current on to Prague, where the *Vyšehrad* [an ancient castle] comes into sight, and finally disappears in the distance with its majestic sweep into the Elbe [River].

The river, represented by a recurring lyrical theme (the piece has a rondo-like form), flows through and thus unites the country's diverse landscapes and activities. The Moldau theme becomes the musical symbol of the national identity championed by Smetana.

In the generation after Smetana, the most prominent Czech composer was Antonín Dvořák (1841–1904). Dvořák's career shows how a composer could balance national identity and an international reputation. For much of his twenties, Dvořák worked in relative obscurity, playing viola in the Provisional Theater Orchestra, which was conducted from 1866 by Smetana. In 1871 he gave up this position in order to compose full-time, focusing on chamber and symphonic music in the Austro-German mold, and on songs and operas that featured Czech texts. A major career break occurred in 1877 when Dvořák's music came to the attention of Brahms, who enthusiastically recommended the younger composer to his publisher, Simrock. Publications and performances followed, catapulting Dvořák to international prominence.

Although a firm Czech nationalist, Dvořák displayed cosmopolitan savvy about his career; he wanted his works to have maximum appeal both in his native land and abroad. He insisted that the title pages of his compositions be printed in both German and Czech, and that editions of his vocal works give the texts in both languages. He also asked for his first name to be printed simply as "Ant.," since this would be equally good in both languages, as an abbreviation for the German form "Anton" and the Czech "Antonín."

The fusion of Germanic and Czech features is evident in Dvořák's *Dumky* Piano Trio, Op. 90 (1891; see Anthology 13). Although in instrumentation (piano, violin, cello) the work falls squarely in the chamber music tradition of Haydn, Mozart, and Beethoven, it is not structured in the conventional four movements. Dvořák casts the trio as a suite of six short movements, each of which evokes the *dumka* (plural: *dumky*), a Slavic instrumental or vocal piece that is ruminative in character and proceeds in alternating sections of slow and fast tempos. The brooding quality of the *dumka* is exemplified by the opening theme of the last movement (Ex. 7.3). In the first measure the strings seem to imitate the strumming of a folk instrument; the piano part is almost improvisatory in nature, with two strongly contrasting phrases.

As befitted his international stature, Dvořák extended his beliefs and practices beyond the borders of his native land. From 1892 to 1895 he lived in the United

Example 7.3: *Dvořák, Piano Trio No. 4 in E Minor* (Dumky), *Op. 90, movement 6, mm. 1–4*

States as director of a conservatory in New York. During his stay he urged American composers to create their own national music using, as he and other Czech composers had done, indigenous materials—in this case the music of African Americans and Native Americans (see Chapter 11). In his own Ninth Symphony, Op. 95 (1893), subtitled *From the New World*, Dvořák set out to show how this could be done by basing some of the melodies on African American spirituals.

We might say that music "grew up" in the second half of the nineteenth century, losing some of the innocence of the 1820s and 1830s. Once deemed the most Romantic and idealistic of the arts, music began to engage more directly with the real world—the world of science, technology, politics, and national identity. As we have seen in this chapter, the terms of engagement often represented a departure from Romantic principles, with the pursuit of realism or materialism at the expense of traditional beauty or fantasy. But in many ways, the newer attitudes followed logically upon the activities of composers we examined in Chapters 5 and 6, who sought to make music "matter" and "speak" to a growing middle class. Now some composers wanted to communicate directly with their own nation or ethnic group. In the next five chapters we will look more closely at how some major figures and institutions continued to negotiate the realities of music and musical life in the later nineteenth century.

FOR FURTHER READING

Burrow, J. W., *The Crisis of Reason: European Thought, 1848–1914* (New Haven and London: Yale University Press, 2000)

Dahlhaus, Carl, *Realism in Nineteenth-Century Music*, trans. Mary Whittall (Cambridge and New York: Cambridge University Press, 1985)

Helmholtz, Hermann von, *Science and Culture: Popular and Philosophical Essays*, ed. David Cahan (Chicago and London: University of Chicago Press, 1995)

Nietzsche, Friedrich, *The Birth of Tragedy and The Case of Wagner*, trans. Walter Kaufmann (New York: Vintage, 1967)

The Revolutions in Europe, 1848–1849: From Reform to Reaction, ed. R.J.W. Evans and Hartmut Pogge von Strandmann (Oxford and New York: Oxford University Press, 2000)

Taruskin, Richard, *Musorgsky: Eight Essays and an Epilogue* (Princeton: Princeton University Press, 1993)

Taruskin, Richard, "Nationalism," In *Grove Music Online/Oxford Music Online;* or in *The Revised New Grove Dictionary of Music and Musicians*, ed. Stanley Sadie and John Tyrrell (London: Macmillan, 2001), vol. 17, pp. 689–706

Ⓢ **Additional resources available at wwnorton.com/studyspace**

CHAPTER EIGHT

Richard Wagner and Wagnerism

A significant "ism" of the later nineteenth century not discussed in the last chapter is also the only one that derives directly from the name of a composer: Wagnerism. The term reflects the enormous influence exerted by Richard Wagner (1813–1883; Fig. 8.1) in areas beyond music, including literature, drama, art, society, and even politics. Wagner demonstrated audaciously how a composer after 1850 could negotiate a more modern, complex, and materialistic world, a world "beyond Romanticism," yet at the same time promote earlier belief systems, especially a view of music as the most powerful and elemental of the arts.

Wagner's works, personality, career, and influence cannot be easily separated out. His principal domain was German opera, which he sought to reform from top to bottom: its musical structures, performance styles, institutions, and relationship to society. Some aspects of Wagner are extremely unpalatable and make his legacy hard to appreciate even today, over 125 years after his death. Most infamously, he was an outspoken anti-Semite whose ideas resonated with a culture already prone to racial and ethnic discrimination. In this chapter we will examine Wagner as man and artist and Wagnerism as a cultural and political phenomenon.

Figure 8.1: *Richard Wagner in a photo-graph by Franz Hanfstaengl, 1871*

WAGNER'S EARLY LIFE AND CAREER

Wagner came to artistic maturity somewhat later than the generation of the 1830s of which he was a part and which we examined in Chapters 5 and 6. He was no child prodigy like Mendelssohn and Liszt; nor was he destined for a performing career like Chopin, or Robert and Clara Schumann. Along with Berlioz, Wagner was one of the few major composers of the Romantic period not trained as a keyboard player. In a brief autobiography written in 1843, Wagner recalled how, despite having little early musical education, he developed a passion for German opera:

> In my ninth year I went to the Dresden Kreuzschule [a well-known Lutheran high school]: I wished to study, and music was not thought of. . . . Nothing pleased me so much as [Carl Maria von Weber's] *Der Freischütz*; I often saw Weber pass before our house, as he came from rehearsals; I always watched him with a reverent awe. A tutor . . . was at last engaged to give me pianoforte instruction; hardly had I got past the earliest finger-exercises, when I furtively practised, at first by ear, the Overture to *Der Freischütz*; my teacher heard this once, and said nothing would come of me.—He was right; in my whole life I have never learnt to play the piano properly.

Wagner returned to his native Leipzig, and it was there that he developed another lifelong passion: the Viennese Classical composers, especially Beethoven and Mozart. Wagner was given brief but intensive musical instruction by the music director of St. Thomas Church, Christian Weinlig, who occupied the position once held by J. S. Bach. Wagner began writing symphonic and operatic works inspired by his models.

Wagner learned his operatic craft in a more practical way from the early 1830s on, when he took a series of positions as a professional conductor or chorus master in opera houses in small German towns. He conducted or helped prepare much of the standard repertory of his day, including the German operas of Mozart, Weber, Heinrich Marschner; the French operas of Luigi Cherubini and Daniel Auber; and the Italian operas of Mozart, Rossini, and Bellini. Wagner could have had no better operatic education.

Through the 1830s, almost as if undergoing a series of self-imposed final examinations, Wagner composed one opera in each of the principal styles familiar to him. For each, he wrote his own libretto, as he would do throughout his life. First came *Die Feen* (The Fairies, 1833–34), a German setting of a fantasy by the Italian playwright Carlo Gozzi, influenced by Weber and Marschner. Wagner's next opera was *Das Liebesverbot* (The Ban on Love, 1835–36), adapted from Shakespeare's comedy *Measure for Measure*. Here the models were Bellini and Auber. At the end of the decade Wagner wrote *Rienzi* (1838–40), based on a story about a Roman tribune by Edward Bulwer-Lytton. Five acts long and replete with processions, ballets, and marches, *Rienzi* evokes the extravagant world of French grand opera, especially that of Giacomo Meyerbeer (discussed in Chapter 4).

It was Meyerbeer who late in 1839 recommended that Wagner go to Paris and offered him introductions to the leading administrators of the Paris Opéra. In Paris Wagner worked on what was to be his first fully mature work, *Der fliegende Holländer* (The Flying Dutchman, 1841). Much to Wagner's disappointment, the director of the Opéra bought only the story, in order to have it set to music by another composer. Wagner fell deeply into debt, and eventually in April 1842 made his way back to Germany in order to supervise the premiere of *Rienzi* in Dresden. There his situation improved when he was offered the position of assistant music director at the court of the king of Saxony. His responsibilities included conducting performances of operatic and orchestral music (including the premiere of his own *Flying Dutchman* in 1843), and also composing pieces on royal demand.

While in Dresden, Wagner composed two more operas, *Tannhäuser* (1845) and *Lohengrin* (1848). Together with *Dutchman*, they represent the summit of early Romantic opera in the traditions of Weber and Meyerbeer, and at the same time point the way to Wagner's later works. Both librettos are drawn from medieval stories that explore German themes. *Tannhäuser* concerns a song contest at the Wartburg, a castle in central Germany. In *Lohengrin* a knight of the Holy Grail helps Germany defend itself against a Hungarian invasion. *Lohengrin* would have its premiere under the baton of Liszt in Weimar in 1850, but Wagner was not to hear the work for many years. As we saw in Chapter 7, in May 1849 Wagner participated in the Dresden uprising and was forced to flee Germany for political exile in Switzerland.

WAGNER'S THEORIES OF OPERATIC REFORM

Wagner's exile lasted until 1860, when a partial amnesty was granted. During those 11 years, he carved a new path for German opera—in terms of both theory and practice—with an intensity and ambition that has never been equaled in the history of music. In the years around 1850, he devoted himself to a series of writings about opera and musical culture as a whole. The larger, most important essays included *Die Kunst und die Revolution* (Art and Revolution, 1849), *Das Kunstwerk der Zukunft* (The Artwork of the Future, 1849), *Oper und Drama* (Opera and Drama, 1850–51), and *Eine Mitteilung an meine Freunde* (A Communication to My Friends, 1851). He also wrote his notorious essay *Das Judentum in der Musik* (Judaism in Music, 1850), to which we return below.

In his quest to transform opera and culture, Wagner looked back to the art form he deemed the most important in Western civilization, ancient Greek tragedy. Wagner saw Greek tragedy as first and foremost a communal artwork: it arose from, and gave expression to, the feelings and concerns of a people. All true art, for Wagner, must have its origin in the "folk" (*das Volk* in German). He saw his own mature operas as embodying the spirit of the German people and as a much-needed restoration of the Greek ideal.

A second, related aspect of Greek tragedy that Wagner would seek to emulate was its reliance on myth. Myths were familiar to Greek audiences before they entered the theater and saw them interpreted by great playwrights like Sophocles and Euripides. Above all, for Wagner, a myth is timeless and universal; it "is true for all time, and its content . . . is inexhaustible throughout the ages." Myths were thus better suited for stage works, including operas, than were purely historical or epic subjects.

A third dimension of Greek tragedy that attracted Wagner was its union of various arts—music, spoken drama, and dance. Music was an integral part of ancient drama; both actors and the chorus sang many of their parts, and there was music-accompanied dance. Today we know little more than Wagner did about exactly how the different art forms were integrated in antiquity. But for Wagner—as for the members of the Florentine Camerata around 1600 and later operatic reformers—Greek tragedy represented an ideal toward which modern art should aspire.

Wagner felt that later eras lost the Greeks' ideal integration of arts and the connection between art and society. The different arts became fragmented; they developed on their own and lost their strong basis in the folk. Only two later creative figures, Wagner said, manifested the universality and connection to the community characteristic of Greek tragedy—Shakespeare and Beethoven. But each operated within his own art, drama and instrumental music, respectively. It was now time for the arts to come together again in what Wagner called the total artwork, or *Gesamtkunstwerk*. The total artwork would not only unite the arts but help regenerate society in ways that Wagner realized were unlikely to happen through the political sphere, where his hopes for liberal reform had been dashed by the events of 1848.

According to Wagner, opera would be the ideal medium for the total artwork in the modern era, but up to now it had failed to bring the arts together in a convincing manner, largely because the musical dimension had overwhelmed the dramatic one. Even Mozart, whom Wagner admired for his "purely musical-artistic content," was in the later composer's view hobbled by inadequate poets or librettists. This problem persisted well into the nineteenth century, when the greatest music, that of Beethoven, was purely instrumental.

As we saw in Chapter 6, Wagner used the term *absolute music*, often pejoratively, to describe music that had no dramatic or literary purpose, but was created for its own sake—music detached from its roots in dance, gesture, and speech. Instrumental music was mostly "absolute" in this sense, but so were vocal melodies that simply floated over the words, disconnected from any linguistic or poetic basis. For Wagner, Rossini was guilty of writing absolute music and marked the end of "the real *life history of opera*," because "all pretense of drama had been scrupulously swept away" and singers "had been allotted the showiest virtuosity of song as their only task." Wagner described Meyerbeer's operas as "effects without causes," as spectacles with stirring tunes and large crowd scenes but little musical or dramatic coherence.

For Wagner the path forward in opera had been forged by Beethoven in his Ninth Symphony, which (according to Wagner) had reached the limits of absolute music. In the final movement of the Ninth, Beethoven had broken the rules of a traditional symphony by adding soloists and a chorus singing Schiller's *Ode to Joy*; music was, in Wagner's terms, "fertilized" by the word. And from this point there could be no turning back to absolute music: "The last symphony of Beethoven is the redemption of Music from out of her own peculiar element into the realm of *universal art*. . . . Beyond it no forward step is possible; for upon it the perfect artwork of the future alone can follow, the *universal drama* to which Beethoven has forged for us the key."

Wagner was clearly concerned with how music can and should "speak," the very issue we examined in Chapter 6. For him Beethoven's Ninth Symphony marked the limits of instrumental music in this regard. Wagner initially had little esteem for program music. But in 1857, a few years after the aesthetic debate sparked by Hanslick's *The Beautiful in Music* and Liszt's essay on Berlioz and program music, Wagner expressed admiration for the symphonic poems of Liszt (who would later become his father-in-law), especially for "the great, the speaking plainness with which the subject proclaimed itself to me." For Wagner, as for the commentators discussed in Chapter 6, this "subject"—Wagner's German word is *Gegenstand*, really connoting "thing" or "object"—is not fundamentally descriptive, narrative, or perceived cognitively; it is transmitted directly from the music to our emotions.

THE WAGNERIAN ARTWORK OF THE FUTURE

Program music was not to be Wagner's artwork of the future. But its expressive goals, like those of Beethoven's instrumental works, could inform opera, where stories based in myth or legend would place a greater emphasis on emotion than on active comprehension. Wagner refers frequently in his writings to the need for a composer to capture the "unconscious" as the source of feelings, a source beyond the realm of "understanding." In this way he anticipated the psychology of Freud and other later figures.

Emotional expression would propel or motivate the new libretto, whose rhythm and flow must arise from natural speech. Rather than using traditional rhyme schemes, Wagner sought, based on his study of early Germanic literatures, to structure his librettos on what he called "root" rhyme, or *Stabreim*. This is a form of alliteration in which a verse or group of verses is made to cohere by means of similar consonant sounds. Wagner explains that the listener's ear and emotions will be coordinated in that this cluster of sounds will correspond to a particular feeling or set of images.

Here is a characteristic passage from Act 1, scene 3 of *Tristan und Isolde*, where Isolde is describing how she first encountered Tristan:

Von einem Kahn,	*About a boat,*
der klein und arm	*which, small and frail,*
an Irlands Küste schwamm,	*drifted along the Irish coast.*
darinnen krank	*In it a sick*
ein siecher Mann	*and ailing man*
elend im Sterben lag.	*lay miserably dying.*

In these six lines there is a pattern of two short lines followed by a longer one, but no regular rhyme scheme. What provides sonic coherence is the use of words beginning with "k": "Kahn," "klein," "Küste," and "krank," all appearing within four lines. The density with which the "k" words accumulate indicates the intensity of emotion with which Isolde is narrating. There is also a secondary *Stabreim* of "s" words—"schwamm," "siecher," and "Sterben." Such simultaneous use of different root rhymes is typical of Wagner's librettos.

Example 8.1: *Wagner,* Tristan und Isolde, *Act 1, scene 3, Isolde's Narrative*

About a boat, which, small and frail, drifted along the Irish coast. In it a sick and ailing man lay miserably dying.

Wagner's ideal musical setting for such poetry is a "verse melody," which abandons the artificial distinction between recitative and aria but still retains a clear structure. We see an example in his setting of the text passage from *Tristan* cited above (Ex. 8.1; see Anthology 14). Though fluid, the vocal part is far from unstructured. Each three-line unit becomes a phrase of four measures, arranged somewhat like a traditional antecedent and consequent. Moreover, the harmonic frame is also readily graspable in that the first phrase moves to a deceptive cadence on C major, and the second cadences in the passage's real tonic, E minor.

This passage lies within a larger continuous structure that bears only an occasional resemblance to traditional operatic numbers, such as the arias, duets, or ensembles we examined in Chapter 4. Wagner shapes the scenes or acts in his mature operas by means of a basic unit he called the "poetic-musical period" (*dichterisch-musikalische Periode*). Such a period is based on a "principal feeling" (*Hauptempfindung*), which may then be supplemented by or give way to a "secondary" emotion (*Nebenempfindung*). The music reflects this structure: a poetic-musical period is tonally anchored by a main key area and has a main motive, enriched by modulations to other areas and the introduction of other themes.

Wagner never specified the dimensions of poetic-musical periods in his operas, and scholars have long disagreed about this topic, some claiming that a period extends over an entire act (and thus an hour or more). The most reasonable view is that a poetic-musical period lasts between 20 and 40 measures, or several minutes, before giving way to another. A period is often embedded in a larger form that bears traces of more standard structures like rondo, strophic, or ternary form. But in the interest of dramatic and musical continuity, the music remains fluid and almost seamless, evolving by what Wagner called "the art of transition."

The orchestra plays a larger role in Wagner's theories and his mature works than in earlier opera. It furnishes a symphonic web of thematic development that is far more than "accompaniment." Wagner likened the orchestra to a surging sea upon which the poet navigates his ship. He also suggested that the orchestra can communicate "the unspeakable," that which cannot be expressed in words. In this sense the orchestra represents the unconscious for the characters in the opera.

Individual themes, almost always played by the orchestra but not appearing in the vocal parts, are associated with certain feelings, characters, ideas, or objects. The term that has come to characterize such motives in Wagner is "leitmotif," or leading motive. Wagner neither coined nor approved of this word; he tended to use the term "melodic element" or simply "motive." But whatever name it was given, the concept was fundamental to Wagner's compositional principles. Although opera composers from Mozart through Verdi often associated motives with certain characters or ideas, it is in Wagner's music that such motives become both plentiful and fundamentally structural. They undergo the same kind of symphonic processes as in Beethoven, who was Wagner's model in the realm of absolute music. Wagner himself explained the principle as follows:

> The new form of dramatic music will have the unity of the symphonic movement; and this it will attain by spreading itself over the whole drama, in the most intimate cohesion therewith, not merely over single smaller, arbitrarily selected parts. So that this unity consists in a tissue of root themes pervading all the drama, themes which contrast, complete, reshape, divorce, and intertwine with one another as in the symphonic movement; only that here the needs of the dramatic action dictate the laws of parting and combining.

In Wagner's own time critics began to use the term *Musikdrama*, "music drama," to characterize his later works and to differentiate them from "opera." That designation has stuck right down to the present day. Yet Wagner himself dismissed the term, feeling that it put too much emphasis on the libretto and not enough on musical structures. Wagner advised his contemporaries to keep the name "opera" for their works destined for the musical stage. As for his own works, he commented (in 1872) that if "opera" is not deemed adequate, he would gladly call them "deeds of music made visible," an admittedly unwieldy term that nonetheless places appropriate emphasis on the role of music.

In fact Wagner used a variety of terms for his later works. *Tristan und Isolde* was called simply an "action" (*Handlung*). *Die Meistersinger von Nürnberg* was designated an "opera." Those works that were created for the opera house he built at Bayreuth carried the special designation "festival play" (*Festspiel*). Wagner called the four-part *Ring des Nibelungen* (Ring of the Nibelung) a "stage festival play [*Bühnenfestspiel*] for three days and a preliminary evening." *Parsifal* was "a stage-consecrating festival play" (*Bühnenweihfestspiel*).

WAGNER'S MATURE OPERAS

Whatever designations he used, there is no question that Wagner's later operas are pathbreaking works of musical theater. Their titles and dates of composition are as follows:

Das Rheingold (The Rhine Gold) (*Ring, Part 1*): 1853–54

Die Walküre (The Valkyrie) (*Ring, Part 2*): 1854–56

Siegfried (*Ring, Part 3*), Acts 1 and 2: 1856–57

Tristan und Isolde: 1857–59

Die Meistersinger von Nürnberg (The Mastersingers of Nuremberg): 1862–67

Siegfried (*Ring, Part 3*), Act 3: 1869

Götterdämmerung (Twilight of the Gods) (*Ring, Part 4*): 1869–74

Parsifal: 1877–81

In what follows, we will examine some of the main features of these works and their relationship to Wagner's theories of opera.

THE RING OF THE NIBELUNG

The creation of Wagner's four-opera cycle *The Ring of the Nibelung* extended over 25 years. Wagner began to draft the story and librettos in 1848, at the same time he embarked on the prose writings about operatic reform we examined above.

Indeed, the *Ring* operas, especially the first, *Das Rheingold*, became to some extent demonstration works for his new theories. In the late 1850s, seeing that a production of his massive cycle was unlikely, Wagner stopped active work on it. He resumed only in 1869 when a performance seemed a greater possibility, thanks in part to the patronage of King Ludwig II of Bavaria. The last note of the *Ring* was composed in 1874, and the entire cycle had its premiere in 1876.

For the *Ring*, Wagner drew on a number of medieval sources of Norse mythology, including the Eddas and the Volsunga Saga, collections of poems and prose written in Icelandic; and the *Nibelungenlied*, an epic poem written in Middle High German. As with all his later works, he reaches inside the tales for a few basic concepts or plot elements. In the *Ring*, the essential themes include love, lust, greed, power, loyalty, and betrayal. The characters are gods, dwarves, giants, mermaids, and humans. The story, which evolves over several generations, involves the consequences of the theft of a lump of gold from the Rhine River by a dwarf from the race of the Nibelungs, Alberich, who has it fashioned into a ring that gives its wearer ultimate power but also bears a curse. Everyone who comes into possession of the ring after Alberich—the chief god Wotan, the giant Fafner, the hero Siegfried, and finally the Valkyrie warrior maiden Brünnhilde—will perish. At the end of the four-opera cycle, the ring is returned to the waters of the Rhine.

The *Ring* operas call for many special effects that clearly owe something to the legacy of spectacle in French grand opera (see Chapter 4): swimming Rhine Maidens; a singing dragon; and the Valkyries, helmet-clad, horse-riding lady warriors. These characters sometimes elicit a chuckle from modern audiences. But Wagner draws us into his operas primarily by capturing in music psychological situations that seem timeless and very human, such as the relationship between Wotan and his daughter Brünnhilde. In *Die Walküre*, Brünnhilde protects Siegmund (the father of Siegfried) in a battle where Wotan has ordained his death. But in disobeying her father, she fulfills his true wishes. Wagner explores the complex dynamics of parent-child relationships, as does Verdi, whom we examine in the next chapter. (See the excerpts from *Die Walküre* in the Opera Sampler.)

For the *Ring*, Wagner conceived and had built a special opera house in the town of Bayreuth in southern Germany, to be used only for the presentation of his own stage works. The cornerstone was laid in 1872 (with Wagner conducting a performance of Beethoven's Ninth Symphony), and the building was completed in 1876, when the entire *Ring* cycle was performed for the first time. Here Wagner's ideal of a German opera house, first put forward many years earlier, was realized. Singers, directors, and designers worked under the composer's supervision for many months before the cycle was performed.

Among the design innovations specified by Wagner for Bayreuth were a double proscenium arch, intended to create a special illusion of depth, and an orchestra kept largely invisible by being placed underneath the stage in a deep well (Fig. 8.2). Wagner wrote: "We called this the 'mystic chasm,' because its task was

Figure 8.2: *Performance of Wagner's* Das Rheingold *at the first Bayreuth Festival in 1876. The orchestra pit is largely hidden underneath the stage.*

to separate the real from the ideal. . . . The spectator has the feeling of being at a far distance from the events on stage, yet perceives them with the clarity of near proximity; in consequence, the stage figures give the illusion of being enlarged and superhuman." For Wagner, the goal was to create an atmosphere much like that of the art-religion discussed in Chapter 2, where a spectator is completely absorbed in the music and the stage drama, with no other visual distractions.

The Bayreuth house also had an egalitarian seating plan, devised according to Wagner's beliefs about opera as a communal artwork; the auditorium was sloped and fan-shaped, allowing for good sight lines from all seats, which were sold at the same price. Unlike most opera houses, Bayreuth had few boxes for wealthy patrons, and these were arranged along the rear wall (as can be seen in Fig. 8.2). The English writer, Wagnerian, and ardent socialist George Bernard Shaw, who visited Bayreuth in 1889, praised the reversal of social and architectural hierarchy implied by the design: "It is republican to begin with; the 1,500 seats are separated by no barrier, no difference in price, no advantages except those of greater or less proximity to the stage. The few state cabins at the back, for kings and millionaires, are the worst places in the house." The Bayreuth opera house, today still under the management of the Wagner family, remains the site of annual summer performances of Wagner's operas, which are the only works allowed to be staged there.

TRISTAN UND ISOLDE

The work of Wagner that had the greatest musical influence in his time and into the later nineteenth century was *Tristan und Isolde*. Here, as in the *Ring*, Wagner condensed a vast literary source, a medieval poem by Gottfried von Strassburg based on an ancient Celtic legend, into a drama with only a handful of principal characters. Tristan, a knight from Cornwall, is bringing Isolde, an Irish princess, by ship to marry his lord, King Mark (Fig. 8.3.). The marriage is intended to make peace between the warring nations of Cornwall and Ireland. Isolde is resentful at the marriage and feels especially humiliated by the role of Tristan as intermediary: earlier, Tristan had killed her fiancé Morold in battle, and she, not initially knowing his identity, healed Tristan's wound. In Act 1 Isolde's rage and Tristan's indifference turn to love as the two drink what she believes is a death potion, but is really a love potion. Although she marries King Mark, Isolde remains bound in desire with Tristan. In Act 2 the lovers meet in secret and are discovered by Mark and his retinue. In the fight that ensues, Tristan allows himself to be mortally wounded. In Act 3, Tristan lies dying in his castle, awaiting the arrival of Isolde. As soon as she enters, he dies; she too dies, singing the "Transfiguration" monologue over his body. Mark, who has learned the story of the potion, arrives, prepared to forgive the lovers, but he is too late.

Tristan und Isolde has a slower pace and far less action than the *Ring*. It is the close relationship between the psychological drama and the music that makes the work so effective. In Isolde's monologue of Act 1, scene 3 (see discussion of Ex. 8.1 above; analyzed in detail in Anthology 14; Opera Sampler), Wagner traces a whole range of emotional states. At first Isolde is sullen and silent; her servant Brangäne cannot understand why Isolde would not be pleased to marry the

Figure 8.3: *Costume design for Isolde by Franz Seitz for the premiere of Wagner's* Tristan und Isolde, *Munich, 1865*

Cornish king. During the scene we learn from Isolde that she had healed Tristan after his small boat had washed ashore in Ireland. Here as in so many operas, Wagner relies on a character's narration to fill in past events not shown onstage but critical to the drama. Isolde relates that Tristan had revealed himself to her only as "Tantris," a disguised version of his real name. But Isolde recognized him because a fragment missing from his sword matched a piece she had found lodged in the wound in Morold's head. She was about to kill Tristan with his sword, but as he gazed up at her, she let the sword drop and spared his life. At this point, Tristan and Isolde fell in love, though neither is at present conscious of having done so. And now, Isolde tells Brangäne in Act 1, breaking off the narrative, she must suffer the indignity of being led to an arranged marriage by the man who killed her fiancé.

This scene is organized musically around two kinds of themes: leitmotifs that recur and accrue meaning throughout the opera, and themes that are local and serve a more immediate structural role. The orchestra, functioning in part as Isolde's unconscious, reveals to us more about her feelings for Tristan than she herself can. As she describes Tristan on his sickbed, the orchestra plays a rising chromatic figure, first heard in the opera's Prelude, which is often called the "desire" (Sehnsucht) motive (Ex. 8.2; also discussed in Chapter 1, Ex. 1.1). As soon as we hear the desire motive, which Isolde also sings, we understand that the descending main theme specific to scene 3 is a free inversion of it (see the top line in the accompaniment in Ex. 8.1). By creating this relationship between the two themes, Wagner the music dramatist reveals to us, well before the potion is drunk later in the act, the inevitability and all-consuming nature of the love between Tristan and Isolde.

Example 8.2: *Wagner,* Tristan und Isolde, *Act 1, scene 3, Isolde's Narrative*

Hand. . . . He looked into my eyes.

The composition of *Tristan* was inspired in part by Wagner's infatuation with a married woman, Mathilde Wesendonck, whose husband was one of Wagner's patrons and had offered the composer the use of a cottage on his estate near Zurich. Mathilde, an accomplished poet and writer, was a genuine intellectual soul mate for Wagner, who set five of her poems to music in songs known as the *Wesendonck Lieder*. Although they seem not to have had a physical relationship—Mathilde would not transgress the bounds of middle-class propriety—the situation had clear similarities to the Isolde–Tristan–Mark triangle of the story Wagner set to music.

The other great obsession that fed into Wagner's creation of *Tristan* was a more purely intellectual one—with the philosopher Arthur Schopenhauer, whom we have discussed in Chapters 2 and 7. Wagner claimed that his encounter with Schopenhauer's thought moved him from Greek-inspired optimism toward modern pessimism. For Schopenhauer, life is constant unfulfilled striving; it is experienced as suffering that can be escaped only through renunciation. Wagner wrote that in conceiving *Tristan* he thought of a "genuine ardent longing for death, for absolute unconsciousness, total non-existence." The deaths of Tristan and Isolde at the end of the opera are above all acts of renunciation, of ceasing to strive.

DIE MEISTERSINGER AND PARSIFAL

If *Tristan und Isolde* is about love and death, *Die Meistersinger von Nürnberg* and *Parsifal* take up, respectively, themes of Germanness and Christianity. As such, they have become the most controversial operas in his oeuvre. *Die Meistersinger*, Wagner's only comic opera, is set in sixteenth-century Nuremberg, geographically and symbolically in the middle of Germany. Hans Sachs and his fellow burghers are "mastersingers," seeking to preserve the ancient traditions of song composition. They feel threatened by an outsider, a nobleman named Walther von Stolzing, who enters a song contest in order to win the hand of Eva, daughter of one of the masters. In the end, Walther triumphs with a song that represents a reconciliation of rules and poetic inspiration. Sachs and the other masters extol the virtues and uniqueness of German art.

In *Parsifal*, a different tradition is closely guarded by another group of initiates. At a castle called Monsalvat, an order of knights watches over and celebrates the Holy Grail, the cup from which Christ supposedly drank at the Last Supper. Their community is threatened by the evil magician Klingsor, who had once been a Grail knight, and by a mysterious woman who does his bidding, Kundry. Parsifal, a young boy who wanders into the realm of the Grail, defeats Klingsor, resists Kundry's seduction, and at the end becomes the leader of the order of knights. Parsifal is unmistakably a Christ-like figure in Wagner's opera, and the work is filled with Christian symbolism and language. The basic theme of the opera is redemption (*Erlösung*, a word frequently encountered in the libretto).

WAGNER'S NATIONALISM AND ANTI-SEMITISM

Die Meistersinger and *Parsifal* remain immensely popular; they are cornerstones of today's operatic repertory. But understood in their historical and cultural context, they also point up a darker side of Wagner as man and artist. For all his radical theories of drama and of politics, Wagner became in later years an outspoken cultural conservative, strongly opposed to modern commerce, industry, and urbanism. (He also became a vegetarian.) Wagner's frequent public and private expressions of anti-Semitism, including his essay *Judaism in Music* of 1850, were by no means unique in a German culture where anti-Semitism was widespread. But Wagner took the communication of such prejudices to another level.

In *Judaism in Music* Wagner argues that Jews are outsiders; however much they seek to assimilate, they will never be able to speak the cultural, musical, and artistic language of Germany. Jews are depicted by Wagner as interested in money and as dominating commercial life and—more disturbing for him—the world of the arts. The Jew's voice type is described by Wagner as a "creaking, squeaking, buzzing snuffle," a mode of expression that characterizes not only Jewish religious singing, but also their attempts at art music. Even in instrumental music, "the Jew musician hurls together the diverse forms and styles of every age and every master." Meyerbeer, a Jew, also comes in for criticism as an uninspired composer who manipulates his audiences and the operatic system.

It is now generally recognized that some characters in Wagner's operas manifest Jewish stereotypes, even though none is identified as Jewish. In the *Ring*, Mime the dwarf shuffles around and sings in a high-pitched, whining style; his gestures and voice seem a direct evocation of the Jewish traits identified by Wagner and other anti-Semitic writers of the nineteenth century. In *Die Meistersinger*, Beckmesser, Walther's main competitor for Eva, also sings in a high range, and some aspects of his vocal line resemble melismatic Jewish chant. Mime and Beckmesser are both "bad" characters—self-serving, manipulative, and dishonest—and thus reinforce the traits Wagner associated with Jews.

In Wagner's later writings, published between 1877 and 1881, anti-Semitism becomes viewed less in cultural and more in racial, biological terms. Wagner was attracted by the notion of an "Aryan" Christianity developed by contemporary writers like Arthur de Gobineau and Paul de Lagarde, whose theories were to have strong influence on Nazi ideology in the twentieth century. According to this line of thought, Jesus as savior and redeemer of mankind could not have been Jewish or Semitic. Rather, he was descended from a purer Indo-Iranian Aryan race. ("Aryan" originally meant "noble" in Sanskrit, and does not signify Nordic and blond, as in some later connotations.) Thus Wagner sought to disassociate Christianity from any connection with Judaism and the Jews. Wagner calls for the "regeneration" of the German race by a purification of German blood, in part through the elimination of the Semitic element. Historians disagree about whether Wagner advocated actual genocide. He did, from 1850 on, sometimes call for the "destruction" and "annihilation" of Judaism, but it is not clear whether these were metaphorical or literal statements.

Some modern commentators see in *Parsifal* an operatic counterpart to Wagner's later writings on race. In this reading, the brotherhood of the Grail is racially pure, devoutly Christian, and exclusively male. The sorcerer Klingsor and the seductress Kundry who is his slave are impure outsiders and thus marked as Jews. Wagner himself noted Kundry's resemblance to the Wandering Jew, a figure from a medieval legend about a Jew who mocked Christ at the crucifixion and was then cursed to roam the earth until the Second Coming.

Parsifal is perhaps Wagner's subtlest score; its harmonic language and orchestration had an enormous impact on later composers, including Claude Debussy (see Chapter 12). The sound world of *Parsifal* is shaped by an opposition between diatonicism and chromaticism. The main diatonic theme of the opera is the "Dresden Amen," a traditional religious melody from the eighteenth century that here represents the Holy Grail and, more generally, purity or goodness (Ex. 8.3a). Set against this diatonicism is the often turbulent chromatic music associated with Klingsor and Kundry. Kundry's main motive (Ex. 8.3b) is based on a progression from the "Tristan" chord, or half-diminished seventh, to a diminished seventh chord, which is different by only one note (D♮ moves down to C♯).

Example 8.3: *Wagner,* Parsifal, *themes*

(a) "Dresden Amen" or Grail Theme

(b) Kundry's theme

Can we understand Wagner's musical techniques in *Parsifal* as related to his racial ideology—diatonicism as pure and Aryan, chromaticism as sullied and Jewish? Such an association would be too simplistic; tonal music is often based on an opposition of diatonicism and chromaticism. But to ignore the context of these musical techniques would be to go against Wagner's own beliefs. As we saw earlier, Wagner disdained absolute music: music had to be about more than the notes on the page or sounding in the air. Especially in opera, Wagner's chosen medium, music reflects the community that gives rise to it through the agency of the composer who, in the spirit of Greek tragedy, serves as a kind of mouthpiece of the "folk." Thus, we are not misguided when we examine Wagner's operas as manifestations of their culture, even if and when some aspects are unattractive.

WAGNERISM

In its narrowest sense Wagnerism refers to the enormous impact Wagner's works had on other musicians. In Austria, Germany, France, Russia, England, and Italy, countless composers were captivated by the chromatic style of *Tristan und Isolde*, reveling in sonorities like the "Tristan" chord (see Chapter 1) and in broad harmonic-melodic sequences that could travel through remote key areas. The idiom of *Tristan* and the medieval Christian aura of *Parsifal* spawned a host of imitations. Two examples of Wagnerism in this sense are the opera *Der arme Heinrich* (Poor Heinrich, 1893) by the German composer Hans Pfitzner (1869–1949), about a medieval knight cured of leprosy by the offer of self-sacrifice from the wife of one of his vassals; and *Fervaal* (1895) by the Frenchman Vincent d'Indy (1851–1931), in which a Celtic pagan warrior leads his people into a new era of Christianity. In both operas, as in *Tristan* and *Parsifal*, the themes of redemption and sacrifice are paramount; both also are built around recurring leitmotifs.

In a broader cultural and intellectual sense, Wagnerism became an international phenomenon during the last two decades of the nineteenth century. Wagner's operas were produced frequently across Europe and the United States; more books were written about Wagner and his music than about any other composer; and Wagner societies were formed by the dozens. *Lohengrin* became the most popular work in the entire operatic repertory. In Austria and Germany, it was heard 263 times in seventy cities during the 1890–91 season. At the Opéra in Paris, it was given 61 times in 1891–92. Even in Italy, the home of Wagner's great contemporary Giuseppe Verdi, Wagner's operas had many performances (70 in 1890–91). Verdi himself was among the admirers.

In France, Wagnerism spread rapidly across the different arts. Not only musicians, but painters, poets, and novelists also became caught up in the Wagnerian frenzy. Among the first was the poet Charles Baudelaire (1821–1867), who was overwhelmed by a concert of Wagner's music in Paris in 1860 and became one of the composer's strongest defenders after a performance of *Tannhäuser* in 1861 that offended much of the French public. Later in the decade, a group of poets called the Parnassians declared Wagner "a genius such as appears on earth once every thousand years."

Wagner's shadow grew still longer in France after his death in 1883. A chromatic Wagnerian style, strongly redolent of *Tristan* and especially *Parsifal*, was cultivated by the composer César Franck (1822–1890) and his pupils, who included Ernest Chausson (1855–1899) and d'Indy. (We return to Franck in Chapter 10.) Chausson, d'Indy, and other French composers, including the young Claude Debussy (1862–1918), made the pilgrimage to Bayreuth to hear Wagner's operas and were swept up in the fervor. In literature, the Symbolist movement that arose in the 1880s and 1890s took Wagner's work as a direct model. Symbolist writers

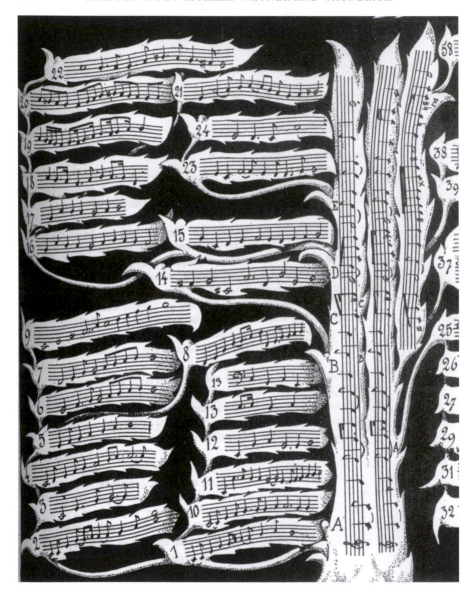

Figure 8.4: *Part of an illustration from the* Revue wagnérienne, *showing the "orientation of the 66 principal motivic-organic elements" of* Parsifal, *1887*

believed that poetry and prose should not depict events, feelings, or objects in a literal way; they should be indirect, suggestive, and allusive. As Jean Moréas, who gave Symbolism its name, wrote in 1886:

The essential trait of Symbolist art consists in never conceptually fixing or directly expressing an idea. And this is why the images of nature, the acts of men, all concrete appearances in this art, must not themselves be made visible, but instead should be symbolized through sensitively perceptible traces, through secret affinities with the original ideas.

Wagner's music inspired the Symbolists not only through its fluidity and frequent avoidance of distinct melody and fixed harmony, but also in its use of actual musical symbols, the leitmotifs. In their poetry and prose, Symbolists sought to create a "music of words" (*musique des mots*), often devoid of any definite meaning, analogous to what Wagner had achieved in his music.

The Symbolists founded a journal called the *Revue wagnérienne* to disseminate Wagner's poetic and philosophical ideas in France. During its three years of existence, from 1885 to 1888, the *Revue* published listings of Wagner performances, detailed discussions of the operas, translations of his writings, reviews of books, and commentary on current cultural issues. Figure 8.4, from the *Revue*, shows an elaborate, eccentric treelike presentation of relationships among the motives in *Parsifal*.

In its most extreme form, French Wagnerism was associated with decadence, a movement in which artists advocated—and sometimes practiced—a retreat from the real world into what Baudelaire had called "artificial paradises" of self-indulgence, including alcohol and promiscuous sex. (Decadence was discussed briefly in Chapter 7 in connection with Nietzsche's ideas.) The most famous work of decadence in France was the novel *Against the Grain* (*A rebours*, which really means "at the limits"), written in 1884 by J.-K. Huysmans, an ardent French Wagnerite and contributor to the *Revue wagnérienne*. In this book, a wealthy aristocrat secludes himself at his country estate in a bizarre world of artificially created sounds, sights, smells, and tastes.

The force of Wagner's work, personality, and ideas reached deep into Western culture of the later nineteenth century in ways that Wagner himself might never have imagined or appreciated. The effete protagonist and the subject matter of Huysmans's *Against the Grain* seem very distant from the mythic heroes and philosophical concepts of Wagner's operas. Yet Wagner was very much a man of his time, incorporating aspects of Romanticism but going "beyond" them in ways that resonated with his culture. Wagnerism itself was a relatively short-lived phenomenon. It barely outlasted the nineteenth century, and even Wagner's own voluminous writings had a limited impact beyond his day. Wagner's most important legacy lies in his operas, whose musical and dramatic power continues to speak to audiences far removed from his own time, well into the twenty-first century.

FOR FURTHER READING

Bayreuth: The Early Years, ed. Robert Hartford (Cambridge and New York: Cambridge University Press, 1980)

Chafe, Eric, *The Tragic and the Ecstatic: The Musical Revolution of Wagner's "Tristan und Isolde"* (Oxford and New York: Oxford University Press, 2005)

Grey, Thomas S., *Wagner's Musical Prose: Texts and Contexts* (Cambridge and New York: Cambridge University Press, 1995)

Millington, Barry, *Wagner*, rev. ed. (Princeton: Princeton University Press, 1992)

Selected Letters of Richard Wagner, ed. Stewart Spencer and Barry Millington (New York: Norton, 1988)

Wagner on Music and Drama, trans. William Ashton Ellis, ed. Albert Goldman and Evert Sprinchorn (New York: Da Capo Press, 1988)

Wagner, Richard, *Judaism in Music and Other Essays,* trans. William Ashton Ellis (Lincoln and London: University of Nebraska Press, 1995)

Wagnerism in European Culture and Politics, ed. David C. Large and William Weber (Ithaca and London: Cornell University Press, 1984)

Ⓢ Additional resources available at wwnorton.com/studyspace

CHAPTER NINE

Verdi, Operetta, and Popular Appeal

Wagner's vision of an opera that would arise from and appeal directly to the "folk" was naive in many respects. His works are complex, sophisticated, and long, taxing the attention span even of devoted followers. The opera house Wagner built at Bayreuth to share his art with the people is today attended by a select few who often wait years to be eligible for tickets that are very expensive.

For all his self-professed uniqueness, Wagner was not alone in seeking a direct connection to society through musical theater. During the period when he was writing down his theories and composing his mature operas, from about 1850 to the mid-1880s, other composers undertook similar quests with different means. These included figures we will examine in this chapter, composers as diverse as Giuseppe Verdi in Italy, Arthur Sullivan (and his partner W. S. Gilbert) in England, and Jacques Offenbach and Georges Bizet in France. The appeal of their works came in part from features Wagner mostly eschewed, like hummable melodies, social critique and satire, and the use of exotic locales or characters.

GIUSEPPE VERDI

Even at its most musically complex, the Italian operatic tradition we examined in Chapter 4 retained a populist strain. Italian composers wrote for a public that was passionate about opera and wanted flesh-and-blood characters and great tunes they could leave the theater singing. The figure who best balanced sophistication and broad appeal across the latter half of the nineteenth century in Italy was Giuseppe Verdi (1813–1901). Born in the same year as Wagner, Verdi was in a sense his counterpart, attempting analogous reforms on the other side of the Alps.

These two titans of opera are often depicted as polar opposites, but the differences between Wagner and Verdi owe less to temperament or artistic vision—both were determined, focused artists—than to their respective national operatic traditions. In his early years Wagner served as kapellmeister or music director in small local German opera houses. Composition formed a relatively small part of his professional activity. Verdi had no such official position—the post of music director did not exist in Italy—but produced operas on demand, often one or two each year, for different Italian houses. This period, which Verdi later referred to as his *anni di galera*, or galley years, lasted from 1839 to 1850, and included 15 operas. Several of these, including *Nabucco* (1842), *Ernani* (1844), and *Macbeth* (1847), point the way to Verdi's mature works.

As discussed in Chapter 4, by the mid-1840s Verdi was able to improve his situation by choosing his own librettists, setting his own deadlines, selecting his own singers, and exerting influence over all aspects of staging. In the 1850s he effectively had a personal agent and watchdog in his publisher, Giulio Ricordi. From about 1856 to 1893 Ricordi issued a set of detailed production guides (*disposizioni sceniche*) for nine of Verdi's operas. These books, prepared mostly from Verdi's own notes and statements, sometimes extend to 100 pages or more, and include diagrams, illustrations, and instructions for staging, scenery, and lighting. All these elements are closely coordinated with what is being sung onstage and played by the orchestra. Thus Verdi sought and achieved a kind of total control over his operas considerably earlier than Wagner, who had to wait for his own theater at Bayreuth in the 1870s.

Like Wagner, Verdi was involved in the political scene of his native land. Italy was, like Germany, in a period of transition to unification. Until after midcentury it was not a nation, but a collection of separate states, some belonging to foreign countries, including France, Spain, and Austria. Beginning in the 1820s, the status quo was challenged by a series of popular uprisings that grew into a movement to unify and democratize Italy, called the Risorgimento ("resurgence"). The Risorgimento took on special urgency with the arrival on the scene of the patriot and politician Giuseppe Mazzini and the revolutionary military leader Giuseppe Garibaldi. Poets and writers also played a role, especially Alessandro Manzoni, whose historical novel *I promessi sposi* (The Betrothed), first published in 1827 and reissued in a definitive form in 1842, was a thinly disguised attack on Austrian and Spanish occupiers of Italian regions.

As happened elsewhere in Europe, the revolutions of 1848 yielded little in terms of liberalization in Italy and in fact led to redoubled repression, except in the kingdom of Sardinia, where a constitution was established under Victor Emanuel II. His prime minister Camillo Cavour led the next, smoother phase of the Risorgimento. In 1861, Victor Emanuel was declared king of Italy, and over the next decade other parts of the peninsula, including the Papal States around Rome, joined to form the nation that is today recognized as Italy.

As the most prominent composer in Italy, Verdi took an active part in the culture of the Risorgimento and its aftermath. Supporters of a unified Italy coined the popular slogan "Viva VERDI," in which the letters of the composer's name became an acronym for "Vittorio Emanuele Re d'Italia" (Victor Emanuel, King of Italy). Cavour was eager to have prominent figures in the new government, and in 1861 he urged Verdi to stand for election as a deputy to the new Italian parliament Verdi won easily and attended sessions in Turin. After Cavour's unexpected death in June 1861, Verdi's participation dropped off, and he did not stand for reelection. But he always retained his loyalty to the constitutional monarchy.

Verdi was clearly attracted, especially in his early operas, to themes of political oppression or injustice. *Nabucco* is based on the Old Testament story of the captivity of the Israelites under the Babylonian king Nebuchadnezzar. The opera's most famous number, *Va, pensiero* (Go, thought), is a slow chorus sung by the Israelites longing for their homeland. It has been suggested by generations of writers that *Va, pensiero* carries a covert patriotic message and that Italians were meant to recognize their own plight in that of the captives on stage. Similar claims are made for the chorus for Scottish exiles, *O patria oppressa* (O, oppressed fatherland), which Verdi wrote for his operatic version of Shakespeare's *Macbeth*.

In fact, there is little evidence to suggest that contemporary audiences interpreted these numbers as distinctively patriotic—even in 1848, the year of the biggest uprisings, when censorship by Austrian authorities in northern Italy was very strong. Indeed, at the premiere of *Nabucco* in Milan in 1842 the military band of the occupying Austrian army played onstage and was apparently welcomed by the Italian locals. Only much later, well after Italy's unification, did *Va, pensiero* become a musical emblem of Italian nationalism, especially when it was sung by hundreds of mourners at a state memorial service after Verdi's death in 1901.

Yet there is no question that through such choruses Verdi helped to create a patriotic-popular musical idiom. He was also drawn to topics relevant to the culture of Risorgimento Italy. A frequent theme in Verdi operas is how the exercise of power and authority affects individuals. Personal relationships are set against the backdrop of a larger national-political drama; lovers or friends are torn apart by conflicting loyalties. In *Don Carlos* (1867, rev. 1884), Elisabeth, the queen of Spain, is in love with Carlos, who fights for the enemy, the kingdom of Flanders. They are betrayed by a jealous Princess Eboli, who is also in love with Carlos. *Aida* (1871) involves a similar struggle between Egypt and Ethiopia, into which are entwined the fates of Radames, an Egyptian prince and warrior; Aida, an Ethiopian princess now enslaved in Egypt and in love with Radames; and Amneris, who exposes their illicit relationship because she also loves Radames. Both *Don Carlos* and *Aida* are strongly influenced by the tradition of French grand opera, where, as we saw in Chapter 4, politics and personal drama are also juxtaposed. (*Don Carlos* was written for the Paris Opéra.)

A passionate and sophisticated reader, Verdi was drawn to high-quality literature as a source for his operas. He sought, above all, distinctive, gripping characters and what he called "strong" situations in which they could interact. Verdi often adapted works written outside his native land, including plays or novels from France, England, Spain, and Germany. Verdi wrote three Shakespeare operas (*Macbeth*, *Otello*, and *Falstaff*) and planned a fourth (*King Lear*). Two operas were adapted from Lord Byron, and five were based on works by the German playwright Friedrich Schiller. Where Wagner looked to the remote past or to myth and legend for his sources, Verdi was sometimes drawn to the works of his own contemporaries, like the French writers Victor Hugo and Alexandre Dumas.

Like nearly all composers of opera (Wagner being the exception), Verdi never wrote his own librettos, preferring to work with excellent literary craftsmen who could help him shape his musico-dramatic vision. Verdi rode hard on his librettists, demanding (and often himself providing) many rewrites. His patient collaborators included Francesco Maria Piave (1810–1876), who worked with Verdi on ten operas, and Arrigo Boito (1842–1918), a poet-playwright and a composer in his own right, who was willing to subordinate his musical ambitions to adapt the texts for *Otello* and *Falstaff*.

RIGOLETTO

After the "galley years," Verdi wrote in relatively close succession the three operas that were to become his most popular and beloved: *Rigoletto* (1851), *Il trovatore* (The Troubadour, 1853), and *La traviata* (The Fallen Woman, 1853). *Rigoletto* was adapted by Piave from Victor Hugo's 1832 play *Le roi s'amuse* (The King Enjoys Himself). In the opera, a court jester named Rigoletto seeks revenge on the man he serves, the Duke of Mantua, for seducing his daughter Gilda. Rigoletto hires an assassin who, in the final tragic moments, kills Gilda instead.

Several aspects of *Rigoletto* epitomize the special qualities of Verdi's mature operas. First, although he remains within the Italian tradition of the "number" opera, with clearly defined arias, recitatives, and ensembles, Verdi strives for greater musical and dramatic continuity, as well as greater compression. Act 3 of *Rigoletto*, lasting just over half an hour, moves seamlessly and breathlessly across a variety of number types toward its tragic denouement.

Second, each mature opera of Verdi has a special coloration, called by Verdi a *tinta*, which is imparted by the orchestration and certain kinds of melodic and harmonic gestures. In *Rigoletto*, the *tinta* includes a prevalent E-minor harmony, snarling brass, and sobbing melodic gestures. Verdi also uses lighter music in very dark situations, as with the Duke's aria in Act 3 (to be discussed below). In Act 3, Verdi enriches the *tinta* with an untexted humming chorus moving in parallel thirds, meant to suggest an impending storm, and flute arpeggios to convey flashes of lightning. Like Wagner, Verdi greatly expanded the role of the orchestra in opera.

A third important Verdian feature is what the composer called the *parola scenica*, literally the scenic or stage word. These are short phrases in the libretto, set to music in a memorable way that captures or focuses a dramatic situation. In Verdi's own words, the *parola scenica* "sculpts and makes the situation precise and evident." Verdi would often push his librettists to include or expand such elements. In *Rigoletto*, the most noticeable *parola scenica* involves the word *maledizione* (curse) and Rigoletto's phrase "Quel vecchio maledivami" (The old man cursed me). In Act 1, Count Monterone confronts the womanising Duke for having seduced his daughter. Rigoletto publicly mocks Monterone, who then pronounces a curse that unsettles, even terrifies the jester. Rigoletto's memorable musical phrase embodies both his fear and his tragic fate (Ex. 9.1): it is his own daughter Gilda who is pursued by the Duke (something Rigoletto will learn only later) and who will die violently. Sung in declamatory style on a high single note, over a memorable harmonic progression featuring an altered sixth chord, the phrase recurs twice in its original form, and is alluded to on other occasions. Rigoletto's last utterance in the opera, as he weeps over the body of his daughter, recalls the *parola scenica*: "la maledizione!"

Example 9.1: *Verdi,* Rigoletto, *Act 1, scene 1, the curse motive*

(Quel vec - chio ma - le - di - va - mi!)

morendo

(That old man cursed me!)

A fourth significant aspect of Verdian musical dramaturgy the strategic deployment of melodies, as with the most famous aria in *Rigoletto*, *La donna è mobile* (Woman is fickle) (Ex. 9.2). The catchy main tune of this number serves a structural role far beyond its mere characterization of the caddish Duke who sings it. It is not woven into the orchestral fabric like a Wagner leitmotif. But its three appearances are as dramatically effective as anything in Wagner. The Duke first sings the full two strophes of *La donna è mobile* at an inn where he flirts with Maddalena, the sister of the assassin Sparafucile. Then, as he is about to retire for the night, the Duke reprises a portion of one strophe in a fragmented version that indicates he is dropping off to sleep. Near the end of the act, he reprises in full the first strophe of the song. Here it is punctuated by short outbursts from Rigoletto, who is standing outside the inn. As he recognizes his master's voice, Rigoletto realizes that the Duke, whom he hired Sparafucile to murder, is still alive. By this point the irony of Verdi's simple ditty has become devastating, because we know more than Rigoletto: that it is Gilda, the Duke's former "donna," who has been killed instead of the jester's intended victim.

Example 9.2: *Verdi*, Rigoletto, *Act 3*, La donna è mobile

Woman is fickle like a feather in the wind

A fifth characteristic of Verdi's style is the simultaneous presentation by different characters of multiple viewpoints on a single dramatic situation. Mozart and Rossini had developed this technique, especially in their act finales (as we saw in Chapter 4 with Act 1 of Rossini's *Il barbiere di Siviglia*). But in the quartet from Act 3 of *Rigoletto* (see Anthology 15 and Opera Sampler), Verdi might be said to transcend his models. The pairs of characters are physically separated here: Gilda and Rigoletto are outside the inn, Maddalena and the Duke are inside. The Duke is trying to seduce Maddalena; she is amused and skeptical but finds him attractive. Gilda, looking in through the window, is distraught at the Duke's betrayal of her. Rigoletto encourages her revenge upon the Duke. These divergent emotions are all brought together musically by Verdi in an ensemble of stunning power, in which each voice has its individual profile. Nowhere are Verdi's powers more apparent than in this great ensemble, where we are at once beguiled by musical beauty and stirred by the dramatic situation.

We recall from Chapter 2 that Victor Hugo, author of the play on which *Rigoletto* is based and one of the chief figures of French Romanticism, advocated that artists

mingle strongly contrasting elements, including "darkness and light, the grotesque and the sublime." Verdi's opera and its source embody just such extremes
in the characters of Rigoletto and Gilda—he the sour and vengeful hunchback,
muttering about the curse; she the innocent girl spinning long, ethereal melodies.
And as we have seen, the juxtaposition of lighter and darker music is part of the
opera's *tinta*. All these aspects help make *Rigoletto* a Romantic work. But especially
in the scenes of naturalistic dialogue, the opera also goes beyond Romanticism
in ways that, as suggested in Chapter 7, are characteristic of the second half of the
nineteenth century.

LATER VERDI

In his later years Verdi wrote fewer operas. Famous and well off, he became still
more selective about topics and librettists. But it was hard to refuse a generous
commission from the khedive of Egypt to write a new work, *Aida* (1871), for the
recently opened opera house in Cairo. The basic plot, which was part of the commission, appealed to Verdi in that it embeds a personal drama within a broader
political context, here involving a conflict between the ancient Egyptians and
Ethiopians.

Aida is Verdi's best-known opera to depict characters and cultures foreign to
western Europe. Such works are often described as exoticist or Orientalist. In
the nineteenth century, the latter term was relatively neutral or benign, indicating the artistic use (or the scholarly study) of subject matter from the "Orient"
or East, in contrast to the Occident or West. Orientalism has a long history in
opera, where plots are sometimes set in locales distant from the Western world,
like the Middle East or Asia. Mozart produced one of the most famous such operas with *Die Entführung aus dem Serail* (The Abduction from the Seraglio, 1782).
A later example is Giacomo Puccini's *Madama Butterfly* (1904–7), to be discussed
in Chapter 12. Verdi's *Aida* occupies a special place in this tradition in that a
prominent Western composer received the commission not from a European
opera house, but from the Orient itself—Egypt, where the premiere also took
place. The Egyptian aspects of *Aida* were strongly played up by all concerned
with the opera, including the publisher of the score, Ricordi (Fig. 9.1).

In 1978 the literary scholar Edward Said identified *Aida* as Orientalist in a
more pejorative sense. Said redefined Orientalism as a complex relationship of
power and domination that arises when a Western culture views a non-Western one from a position of superiority—a position shaped by European imperialist activities of the eighteenth and nineteenth centuries. But is *Aida* really
Orientalist in Said's meaning? To be sure, the scenario came from a French
Egyptologist, Auguste Mariette, who may have been inspired by images made
earlier in the century during the Napoleonic invasions of North Africa that depict an Egypt idealized and subjugated for European consumption. There are

Figure 9.1: *Illustrated cover for score of Verdi's* Aida, *featuring Egyptian motifs, 1873*

certainly musical aspects of *Aida* that depict Egypt as exotic, including flutes and harps, a modal scale with lowered second degree, and Middle Eastern–inspired dances. But we need not conclude that Verdi viewed such music as inferior to the traditional Italian operatic style that prevails in *Aida*. Within the opera's plot, Egypt is not a victim of European domination, but rather the imperialist aggressor toward Ethiopia. Thus it might be more accurate to understand *Aida* in the context of some of Verdi's earlier works, like *Nabucco* and *Don Carlos*, where a minority struggles against a brutal invader.

In the 1880s and early 1890s, after working on revisions of earlier operas, Verdi was coaxed out of retirement to create two final masterpieces, *Otello* (1887) and *Falstaff* (1893). Both operas were adapted from Shakespeare by Arrigo Boito (1842–1918), a member of a group of younger artists seeking to revitalize Italian culture by opening it up to more foreign influences. Among those influences was Wagner's music, which (as discussed in Chapter 8) began to be performed in Italy, and which the elderly Verdi came to know and admire. Yet there are few traces of Wagner in Verdi's later works. Traditional Italian forms or "numbers" still lie at the core of these operas—as in the cabaletta-like vengeance duet between Otello and Iago at the end of Act 2 of *Otello*. They are embedded in continuous scenes whose flow is governed less by Wagnerian principles than by Verdi's unique and ever more subtle control over all aspects of musical and dramatic expression. To capture the fast-paced action and zany situations in *Falstaff*, his only mature comic opera (based on *The Merry Wives of Windsor* and scenes from *Henry IV*), Verdi developed an especially fluid and brilliant musical language of quicksilver, able to adapt from moment to moment.

OPERETTA

In the world of musical theater, the popular had always coexisted alongside, or sometimes even within, the serious. The eighteenth century had seen the rise in Italy of the comic intermezzo, where servants mingled with (and often outwitted) nobility, and the birth of *opéra comique* (comic opera) in France. Popular tunes from other composers' operas, as well as his own, appear in Mozart's *Don Giovanni*. Don Giovanni's serenade in Act 2, accompanied by mandolin, is an attempt to imitate a popular genre. As we have seen, the presence of *La donna è mobile* within Verdi's *Rigoletto* is a powerful dramatic use of the popular style within a tragic framework.

In the latter half of the nineteenth century, popular types of musical theater—today usually grouped under the name "operetta"—thrived in a number of countries, including France, Austria, Spain, and England. Operettas grew out of theatrical forms that were initially little more than collections of songs strung along a thin comic plot line, interspersed with spoken dialogue. Operettas are the precursors to American musical comedy of the twentieth century.

JACQUES OFFENBACH

The father of the modern operetta was a German-born Jew, Jacques Offenbach (1819–1880), who came to Paris as a young man to study cello and established a career as soloist and conductor. In the 1850s Offenbach began to compose works he called *opéras bouffes*, with spoken dialogue and lively musical numbers. The comic plots usually poked fun at the Paris of Napoleon III. Offenbach's first big success came in 1858 with *Orphée aux enfers* (Orpheus in the Underworld), a parody of the Greek Orpheus myth, whose score contained the composer's most famous dance number, the can-can (actually a "gallop") in a brisk duple meter.

A few years later Offenbach joined forces with the librettist team of Ludovic Halévy and Henri Meilhac. Their long collaboration was to produce a series of comic hits, including *La belle Hélène* (Beautiful Helen, 1864), *La vie parisienne* (Parisian Life, 1866), *La Grande-Duchesse de Gérolstein* (The Grand Dutchess of Gerolstein, 1867), and *La Périchole* (1868). Offenbach was a major star of the Parisian musical scene (Fig. 9.2).

La belle Hélène was, like *Orphée*, based on classical mythology, here the story of Queen Helen of Sparta, whose abduction by the Trojan prince Paris set off the Trojan War. Offenbach's sparkling score is filled with waltzes, hymns, marches, patriotic choruses, and other popular forms, as well as numbers that parody more elevated operatic styles, such as the mock-serious ensemble in the finale of Act 1, *L'homme à la pomme* ("the guy with the apple," referring to Paris, who presented an apple to Venus). The operetta, a thinly disguised parody of life in the Second Empire in France, pokes fun at royalty, politics, war, marriage, and religion. In *Hélène*, the kings of Greece (Agamemnon, Achilles, and Ajax) organize

Figure 9.2: *Caricature of Jacques Offenbach conducting "a frenetic round of his works," whose titles and main characters are displayed*

a competition they call the "day of intelligence" at which they are outsmarted by Paris, disguised as a shepherd. The High Priest Calchas, whose character is a send-up of the Catholic clergy, enables the tryst between Paris and Helen and cheats when playing a board game with the kings. Calchas's role so alarmed the French censors that they demanded its alteration. Perhaps the baldest religious parody comes in Act 3, when Paris impersonates a Grand Priest of Venus in order to abduct Helen. Instead of singing a solemn invocation, he yodels his way through a "tyrolienne," a dance number imitative of Alpine folk music (Ex. 9.3).

Example 9.3: *Offenbach,* La belle Hélène, *Act 3,* Tyrolienne

Offenbach proved that he could be an equal master in a more serious vein with his most beloved and enduring work, *Les contes d'Hoffmann* (The Tales of Hoffmann, first produced 1881), an *opéra fantastique* (as he called it) based on stories by the German Romantic writer E.T.A. Hoffmann, whom we discussed in Chapter 2. Offenbach died while the opera was in rehearsal and not quite complete; it was finished by the composer Ernest Guiraud. Since its premiere, many alternate versions of *Hoffmann* have appeared, some far removed from the composer's intentions, which more recent editors, producers, and conductors have sought to respect by reconstructing the opera from the fragmentary original materials that survive.

JOHANN STRAUSS, JR.

In Vienna, the enormous success of Offenbach's operettas spawned a local industry initially dominated by the Austrian composer Franz von Suppé (1819–1895). Then, in the 1870s, Johann Strauss, Jr. (1825–1899), member of a famous family of composers and already renowned for orchestral waltz suites to which the city had been dancing for years, put his distinctive stamp on Viennese operetta in works that capture much of the political, cultural, and social climate of his time. Strauss's most popular work—indeed, today the best-known operetta in any language—was *Die Fledermaus* (The Bat, 1874), with a libretto adapted by Carl Haffner and Richard Genée from a French play by Offenbach's librettists Meilhac and Halévy. Strauss would write a total of 15 operettas over the last quarter of the nineteenth century; among his best known are *Eine Nacht in Venedig* (A Night in Venice, 1883) and *Der Zigeunerbaron* (The Gypsy Baron, 1885).

Unlike *La belle Hélène*, where the satire is displaced to ancient Greece, *Fledermaus* takes place in contemporary Austro-Hungary, at "a spa town, near a big city" that is obviously intended to be Vienna. The characters are all recognizable urban types that run the gamut of social classes—nonhereditary nobility (Gabriel von Eisenstein), émigré royalty (the Russian Prince Orlovsky), bourgeoisie (Dr. Falke, a notary), and servants (the maid Adele). The plot revolves around disguises, mistaken identities, marital intrigues, and flirtations. It also pokes fun at the Austrian legal system: the main story involves an excessively harsh prison sentence given to Eisenstein for assaulting Falke. The operetta takes its name from a masquerade costume worn by Falke. But the title is also a symbol for the dissimulation or illusion that lies at the core of the plot and, by implication, of Austro-Hungarian society.

Die Fledermaus had its premiere just after a serious stock market crash and economic crisis in Vienna in 1873. Especially in its second act, which takes place at a ball at Orlovsky's villa, the operetta celebrates a life style that was now seriously in jeopardy, but also looks forward optimistically to its resumption. Champagne, which flows freely at the party, is celebrated at the end of the operetta as the "king" of wines, whose "majesty is acknowledged throughout the land."

Die Fledermaus is often characterized as a "waltz operetta," and indeed some of its most famous numbers are radiant waltzes, the musical emblem of nineteenth-century Vienna and of Strauss himself (as in his famous *Blue Danube Waltz*). But Strauss and his collaborators also make *Fledermaus* a subtle musical portrait of the different national identities that were part of the Austro-Hungarian Empire, created in 1867 under an agreement by which the Habsburgs would share power with a separate Hungarian government, dividing the territory of the former Austrian Empire between them.

A ballet sequence in Act 2 includes a series of Scottish, Russian, Spanish, Bohemian, and Hungarian dances, which then culminate in a waltz—a sequence that has been seen as reflecting the cultural and national superiority that German-speaking Vienna felt over "Others" (Fig. 9.3). Individual musical numbers capture distinct ethnic difference, especially the aria *Klänge der Heimat* (Sounds of the Homeland), sung by Eisenstein's wife Rosalinde, who is disguised as a Hungarian countess. The aria is specifically labeled by Strauss as a *csárdás*, a form associated with Gypsy or Roma music, with a slow first part in a highly ornamental style (called *lassú*, though not so indicated by Strauss; Ex. 9.4a) and a fast second part in lively duple meter (called *friska* or, in German, *frischka*; Ex. 9.4b).

Figure 9.3: *Waltz in Act 2 ballroom scene from* Die Fledermaus *by Johann Strauss, Jr. Set and costume design by Ludwig Kainer (Berlin, 1930).*

Example 9.4: *Strauss,* Die Fledermaus, *Act 2, Rosalinde's aria*

(a)

Sounds of my homeland, you awaken my longing.

(b)

Fire and zest for living swell the true Hungarian breast.

Prince Orlovsky in *Fledermaus* is a trouser role—a man sung by a woman. Although such cross-dressing was common in opera and operetta of the eighteenth and nineteenth centuries, the character was normally a young, prepubescent boy, like Cherubino in Mozart's *Marriage of Figaro*. Strauss and his collaborators were doing something unusual, perhaps even transgressive, in having a mature man played by a woman. This casting reinforces the foreignness, the "otherness" of Orlovsky, as does the music of his Act 2 aria *Chacun à son gout* (To each his own), which is a slow march representing a vaguely exotic or "Eastern" style different from the prevailing Viennese musical idiom.

Eisenstein's pedantic and bumbling lawyer is named Dr. Blind, a clear jab at his profession. He also embodies a Jewish stereotype of the kind discussed in Chapter 8 in connection with Wagner's ideas. Instead of melodies, Blind sings repeated notes in declamatory rhythms; he paces, complains, and argues with his client. Even though Jews were in many respects assimilated in Viennese society—by 1870 they had full rights of citizenship and were prominent in commerce, law, medicine, and the arts—anti-Semitism was widespread. It worsened toward the end of the nineteenth century, especially when the right-wing Christian Social party took power in Vienna 1897. In creating the caricature of Blind in *Fledermaus*, Strauss and his collaborators were no different than many contemporaries, for whom (unlike Wagner) anti-Semitism was more an unfortunate habit than an ideology. But we should recognize this dark underside of Austrian culture, in which Jews, as much as Gypsies and Russians, were sometimes viewed as "Others."

GILBERT AND SULLIVAN

The influence and popularity of Offenbach extended not only across the Rhine to Germany and Austria, but also across the English Channel to Great Britain, where W. S. Gilbert (1836–1911) and Arthur Sullivan (1842–1900) joined forces to become one of the greatest librettist-composer teams in the history of music. They first collaborated on an operetta in 1871; over the next quarter-century they were to create 13 more classics of the genre. These works were the so-called Savoy Operas, named for the theater that the impresario Richard D'Oyly Carte built to house them. Among the most beloved and famous are *HMS Pinafore* (1878), *The Pirates of Penzance* (1879), and *The Mikado* (1885).

HMS Pinafore, subtitled *The Lass That Loved a Sailor*, explored several themes that were ripe for parody in British society. First was the relationship between the classes. Ralph, a sailor, and Josephine, the daughter of Captain Corcoran, are in love. The difference in their class presents an apparently insuperable obstacle to the union, as does the fact that the First Lord of the Admiralty, Sir Joseph Porter, also loves Josephine. A lower-class woman who sells goods to the sailors, Little Buttercup, reveals that as foster mother she mistakenly exchanged Ralph and Captain Corcoran as babies. At the end of the operetta the two switch ranks, and Sir Joseph gives Ralph and Josephine permission to marry. The former captain weds Buttercup, and Sir Joseph agrees to marry his cousin Hebe.

Pinafore was also an affectionate parody of one of the British Empire's greatest symbols of power, the Royal Navy. At the time of *Pinafore*, British imperial expansion was nearing its peak; the empire "on which the sun never sets," as a saying went, would soon comprise 400 million people, spread over more than 14 million square miles. It was the Royal Navy that enabled this worldwide domination. ("Britannia rules the waves," according to an eighteenth-century popular song.)

Pinafore presents an idealized image of the sailor's life aboard a Victorian Navy ship. In fact, seamen were frequent victims of illnesses like scurvy and alcoholism. Captains had almost absolute authority, and mutinies (most famously depicted in the novel and films *Mutiny on the Bounty*) were not uncommon. As punishment, sailors would be given 40 lashes with a cat-o'-nine-tails. But *Pinafore* also reflects reforms that were underway by the later nineteenth century, when the common sailor was given more rights and status and was treated more humanely. Sir Joseph encourages the sailors to dance the hornpipe, and composes a lighthearted part-song for them so as, in his words, "to encourage independent thought and action in the lower branches of the service, and to teach the principle that a British sailor is any man's equal, excepting mine." Ralph's confession of love for Josephine is met not with flogging, but with a more gentle confinement in the ship's "dungeon cell."

Another aspect of Navy life that may be alluded to indirectly in *Pinafore* is that of homosexuality, which had long been recognized but not openly acknowledged. Sir Joseph arrives and compliments the Captain on his "remarkably fine crew" and "splendid seamen"—and offers to teach the hornpipe personally to a sailor after dinner. There is of course no overt homosexual behavior here, but many recent productions of *Pinafore* play up the campy subtext of this scene, and Sir Joseph is often presented as somewhat effeminate.

The basic structure of an act of *Pinafore*, as of the other Savoy Operas (and, indeed, of nineteenth-century operetta in general), is a series of numbers arranged as recitative, aria, ensembles, and choruses, interspersed with spoken dialogue. Like many operas, each act has a finale yoking together different segments into a more continuous, complex whole, culminating in a big chorus. In *Pinafore*, Gilbert and Sullivan draw on a wide range of musical styles from both popular and classical music. These include glees and hornpipes (*We sail the ocean blue*, *A British tar*); waltzes (*I'm called Little Buttercup*); melodrama, or spoken dialogue over orchestral accompaniment (*The hours creep on apace*); and full-fledged Italian-style aria (*A simple sailor lowly born*).

When I was a lad, sung by Sir Joseph, is a strophic number with choral interjections that pokes fun at the Royal Navy's tradition of putting men with little practical training or experience into positions of authority. Sir Joseph relates good-naturedly how he worked his way up from office boy to a seat in Parliament, but had never in fact been on a ship. He thus advises the sailors: "Stick close to your desks and never go to sea, / And you all may be rulers of the Queen's Navee" (Fig. 9.4). As contemporaries readily recognized, Gilbert modeled the character of Sir Joseph on William Henry Smith, a businessman and politician who served as First Lord of the

Figure 9.4: *Henry A. Litton as Sir Joseph Porter in* HMS Pinafore *by Gilbert and Sullivan, 1878*

Figure 9.5: *Lobby of the Opéra in Paris, designed by Charles Garnier*

Admiralty between 1877 and 1880—thus at the time of the premiere of *Pinafore*—and who, like Sir Joseph, had no naval experience when appointed to his post. After the premiere of the operetta, he became known as "Pinafore Smith."

FRENCH OPERA

Perhaps no operatic work of the later nineteenth century better embodies popular appeal, a strategic mixture of styles, and an engagement with issues of social and ethnic identity than Georges Bizet's *Carmen* (1875). To place it in context, we need first to return to the operatic world of late-nineteenth-century Paris, where each theater was associated with a distinct type of work. Offenbach's operettas or *opéras bouffes* were primarily written for the Théâtre des Bouffes-Parisiens and the Théâtre des Variétés. The other most important venues were the Paris Opéra, the Opéra-Comique, and the Théâtre Lyrique.

From the 1870s the Opéra was housed at a spectacular and ornate building designed by Charles Garnier. Both the architecture and technology of the Palais Garnier, as it was known, were advanced for the time. Especially striking was the Grand Staircase, a massive double stairway created from marble of different colors (Fig. 9.5). In such a setting the patrons themselves became part of the show, as Garnier intended: "The spectators leaning on the balconies garnish the walls, rendering them alive, as it were, while those going up and down the stairs themselves added to this impression. In adding materials and hanging draperies, chandeliers and candelabra, and with the marble adorned with flowers, a sumptuous and brilliant composition will result." For its productions the Opéra used the most up-to-date gas lighting system, equipped with an "organ" of distribution pipes that could simulate night or day at the pull of a lever. In 1881, electric lighting was installed. Operas performed at the Palais Garnier included works by Meyerbeer, Verdi, Gounod, and (in the 1890s) Wagner and Camille Saint-Saëns.

The Opéra-Comique, which had been established in 1783, was the main rival to the Opéra. Its name reflected the genre that it was created to produce. *Opéra comique* refers not to "comedy" in a narrow sense, but to plots or situations on a more human scale that steer clear of the epic, historical, and often tragic themes that dominated at the Opéra. Until 1864, all operas staged at the Opéra-Comique were required by law to have spoken dialogue rather than recitative in between the musical numbers, another feature that distinguished them from grand opera. As the nineteenth century wore on, many of these differences began to erode, and after 1870 any firm link between genre and theater was broken. Operas produced at the Opéra-Comique often dealt with serious topics and sometimes involved strong, independent heroines. Examples included Bizet's *Carmen*, about a rebellious, defiant Gypsy woman; Jules Massenet's *Manon* (1884), tracing the decline of a young girl into deceit and promiscuity; and Gustave Charpentier's *Louise* (1900), about a poor dressmaker in working-class Paris. The Opéra-Comique also presented the premiere of Debussy's *Pelléas et Mélisande* (1902), the Impressionist masterpiece about doomed lovers.

During its 18 years of existence, from 1852 to 1870, the Théâtre Lyrique was the most important rival to the Opéra and Opéra-Comique. During the directorship of Léon Carvalho the house was especially known for introducing major works by contemporary French composers that fell between grand and comic opera, including Charles Gounod's *Faust* (1859) and *Roméo et Juliette* (1867). The Théâtre Lyrique also familiarized Parisian audiences with foreign works in translation, among them Italian operas by Bellini, Donizetti, and Verdi, and German works by Weber and Wagner.

BIZET'S *CARMEN*

From its somewhat modest beginnings at the Opéra-Comique, Bizet's *Carmen* has become perhaps the most popular of all operas. The authors of its libretto, based on a novella by Prosper Mérimée, were also Offenbach's collaborators, Meilhac and Halévy. Halévy would later recall how the codirector of the Opéra-Comique, Adolphe de Leuven, was dubious about Bizet's idea for this opera. "Carmen! The Carmen of Mérimée?" de Leuven exclaimed. "Wasn't she murdered by her lover? And the underworld of thieves, Gypsies, cigarette girls—at the Opéra-Comique, the theater of family, of wedding parties? You would put the public to flight. No, no, impossible!" Halévy tried to reassure de Leuven:

> I persisted, explaining that ours would be a softer, tamer Carmen. In addition, we would introduce a character in the tradition of the Opéra-Comique—a young innocent girl, very pure [Micaëla]. True, we would have Gypsies, but Gypsy comedians. And the death of Carmen would be glossed over at the very end, in a holiday atmosphere, with a parade. . . . After a long, difficult struggle, M. de Leuven acceded. "But I pray you," he said, "try not to have her die. Death—at the Opéra-Comique! This has never been seen!"

Carmen's death at the end of the opera can hardly be said to be "glossed over" by a holiday atmosphere at the bullfight, but Halévy did make good on many of his promises.

In *Carmen*, a Spanish soldier (Don José) on duty in Seville is seduced by Carmen, a rebellious cigarette factory worker who has been arrested and is under his watch. The love-struck Don José abandons his responsibilities to join Carmen and her Gypsy friends in smuggling activities. Even a visit from his hometown girlfriend, Micaëla, does nothing to dissuade Don José. Eventually Carmen abandons him for the handsome matador Escamillo and is murdered by her jealous former lover.

One can understand de Leuven's concern: the character of Carmen in Bizet's opera is an Other embodying several stereotypes that would have seemed threatening—but at the same time alluring—to the French bourgeoisie. Carmen is a foreigner, an ethnic outsider; she comes from the lower class; she flouts the law; she is sexually available and promiscuous, even if not specifically a prostitute. The character of Micaëla (invented for the opera, as we have seen) is her polar opposite—a sweet, somewhat sexless white middle-class woman who espouses family values. Don José is caught directly between these women, and it is his inability to resolve the conflict that leads ultimately to his demise.

Bizet conveys these character types and relationships with extraordinary musico-dramatic skill. He sets off the musical numbers with spoken dialogue, as was still the norm at the Opéra-Comique. The Gypsy world is captured by instruments like castanets and tambourines, and the use of Spanish-style dances, rhythms, and melodies. Carmen's two best-known solo numbers, the *Habanera* and the *Seguidilla*, evoke Hispanic dance prototypes. (See Anthology 16 and the Opera Sampler.) The *Habanera*, although suitably exotic in this context, would have sounded familiar to many in the audience, as Bizet based it on a song in Afro-Cuban style by a Spanish composer whose work was popular in Parisian cabarets. In *Carmen*, the respectable bourgeois world of Micaëla is conveyed by a tuneful musical style more characteristic of the Opéra-Comique.

The two musical idioms, exotic and conventional, clash most directly in the duet between Don José and Carmen in Act 2, a long, complex number that shows the great range of Bizet's musico-dramatic ability. Carmen dances

Example 9.5: *Bizet,* Carmen, *Act 2, Carmen–Don José duet*

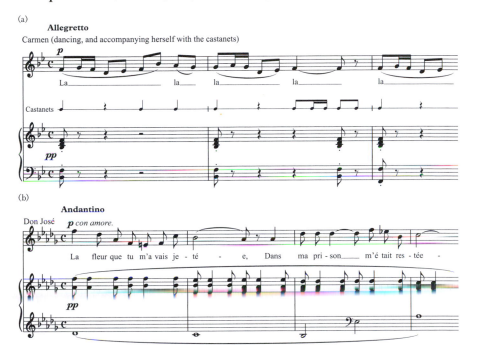

The flower you tossed me, I kept in my prison.

seductively and plays castanets while singing a wordless Spanish-style vocalise. The melody, simple and repetitive, is really only one part of her "multimedia" act, an accompaniment to her dance (Ex. 9.5a). The sounds of an offstage bugle remind Don José of his military duties, which Carmen defies him to obey. Don José responds with a passionate aria, *La fleur que tu m'avais jetée* (The flower that you tossed to me), with pulsating rhythms, a broad lyrical melody, and chromatic harmonies (Ex. 9.5b). It ends with the phrase "Carmen, je t'aime" (Carmen, I love you), expressing feelings that she will never reciprocate. In this duet, each character has reverted to type, and we sense that their relationship is doomed.

As might have been predicted, at the opera's premiere in 1875 the role of Carmen offended many of the French bourgeoisie. One critic described Carmen as "a savage; a half Gypsy, half Andalusian; sensual, mocking, shameless; believing neither in God nor in the Devil . . . she is the veritable prostitute of the gutter and the crossroads." Such reactions fit Carmen and her music neatly into an Orientalist frame, as discussed above, in the sense that Bizet and his librettists present her as a stereotype to whom the audience can feel superior. But there is more to Carmen. Recent feminist readings of the opera, and stagings influenced by them, have interpreted the main character not as a shameless savage, but as a heroic woman with the courage to resist sexual and societal exploitation, and as a tragic victim of violence in personal relationships. Both interpretations—Orientalist femme fatale and defiant heroine—are part of the rich legacy of this opera.

Soon after its premiere, *Carmen* won a place in the international operatic repertory, a development Bizet did not live to see. Praise came from distinguished figures outside France as different as Tchaikovsky, Brahms, Wagner, and Nietzsche. But there is a twist: *Carmen* became famous (and is often still heard today) not in its original form, but in a version from later in 1875 for which the composer Ernest Guiraud (mentioned above in connection with the completion of Offenbach's *Contes d'Hoffmann*) replaced the original spoken dialogue with recitatives. This significantly alters *Carmen* by giving it the more continuous style and feel of grand opera. At the same time, the change—which Bizet himself was apparently considering before he died—allowed it to be played more easily on stages across the world. The opera "industry" discussed earlier in this book can be both harmful and benevolent: even as it distorted the original form of *Carmen*, it helped to perpetuate and canonize the work.

As we have seen in this chapter, music theater of the later nineteenth century, designed mainly as entertainment and contained within four walls and a proscenium, was often a reflection of what happened outside the theater. Political tensions, the struggle for nationhood, differences between social classes, the role of women, and the status of "Others"—these issues and more were explored by the best composers and librettists of the day, including Verdi, Offenbach, Sullivan, and Bizet; and Piave, Boito, Meilhac, Halévy, and Gilbert. Whether the work was comic, tragic, or somewhere in between—whether the intention was to evoke laughter, tears, or just attentive engagement with the musical drama onstage—audiences in this era beyond Romanticism were always made to appreciate the tensions between art and the real world.

FOR FURTHER READING

Ainger, Michael, *Gilbert and Sullivan: A Dual Biography* (Oxford and New York: Oxford University Press, 2002)

Budden, Julian, *The Operas of Verdi*, 3 vols. (Oxford and New York: Oxford University Press, 1992)

The Cambridge Companion to Verdi, ed. Scott L. Balthazar (Cambridge and New York: Cambridge University Press, 2004)

Crittenden, Camille, *Johann Strauss and Vienna: Operetta and the Politics of Popular Culture* (Cambridge and New York: Cambridge University Press, 2006)

Kracauer, Siegfried, *Jacques Offenbach and the Paris of His Time*, trans. Gwenda David and Eric Mosbacher (New York: Zone, 2002)

McClary, Susan, *Georges Bizet: Carmen* (Cambridge and New York: Cambridge University Press, 1992)

Williams, Carolyn, *Gilbert and Sullivan: Gender, Genre, Parody* (New York: Columbia University Press, 2011)

Ⓢ Additional resources available at wwnorton.com/studyspace

CHAPTER TEN

Concert Culture and the "Great" Symphony

In the last half of the nineteenth century, instrumental genres thrived alongside the musical theater of Wagner, Verdi, and their contemporaries. The symphony, serenade, suite, concerto, chamber music, and piano sonata had their origin in the eighteenth century in some kind of private venue—courts or castles—but by the mid-nineteenth century all were essentially public genres. Their main locus of performance was the concert hall. We can speak of a "concert culture" for which this music was composed and in which it was heard. In this chapter, after examining the broader phenomenon of concert culture, we will focus on its most prestigious product, the "great" or large-scale symphony. We will see how the symphonic inheritance of Beethoven was transformed, according to the pressures and demands of concert culture in different regions, by several major composers of the period, including Johannes Brahms, Anton Bruckner, Camille Saint-Saëns, César Franck, and Pyotr Il'yich Tchaikovsky.

CONCERT CULTURE

Concert culture was a creation of the educated middle classes, who, as we have seen earlier in this book, replaced the aristocracy as the primary consumers of music.

In large urban centers across the middle and later part of the century, new concert halls were built, or preexisting ones expanded. St. James's Hall, with an audience capacity of 2,000, opened in London in 1858 (Fig. 10.1); the Grosser Musikvereinsaal in Vienna, in 1870; and an enlarged Gewandhaus in Leipzig, in 1884. Concerts were no longer meant primarily as social occasions interrupted by occasional listening, but as educational, and even quasi-religious, experiences, as exemplified by the concept of art-religion discussed in Chapter 2.

To understand how these attitudes helped change concert programming between the late eighteenth and late nineteenth centuries, we can compare the circumstances of the Vienna premiere of Mozart's Symphony No. 35 (*Haffner*, K. 385) in 1783 with that of Brahms's Third Symphony in the same city 100 years later, in 1883. Mozart's work was performed during Lent at a private concert or "academy," as it was called at the time. This was a one-time event, not part of any regular series, and it had to be organized by Mozart himself. Unlike in a modern performance, Mozart's *Haffner* was broken up and spread across the program. The first three movements opened the concert; the last one appeared at the end.

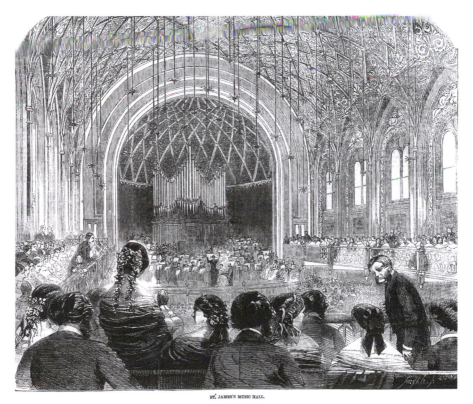

ST. JAMES'S MUSIC HALL.

Figure 10.1: *St. James's Hall in London, which opened in 1858 and had an audience capacity of 2,000*

after Schumann's Third Symphony of 1850 (chronologically the last of his four works in the genre) the symphony fell into something of a decline. Fewer were written, and those that did emerge often had a hard time getting space on concert programs. Critics were often savage, comparing new symphonies unfavorably with the masterworks by Haydn, Mozart, and Beethoven. Schumann himself had made such a comparison in 1838, noting that "we find many too close imitations [of Beethoven], but very, very seldom, with few exceptions, any true maintenance or mastery of this sublime form." These words, echoed by critics for many decades thereafter, had a chilling effect on even the best younger composers. Brahms, Bruckner, and Dvořák each began to work on a symphony in the 1860s. But they delayed completing and unveiling their works until the 1870s, intimidated by Beethoven's long shadow and by attitudes like Schumann's. "I will never compose a symphony!" Brahms reportedly said in 1871. "You have no idea how it feels to one of us when he continually hears behind him such a giant [Beethoven]."

JOHANNES BRAHMS AND ANTON BRUCKNER IN VIENNA

From the 1870s to near the end of the century, the two dominant figures in Viennese symphonic life were Johannes Brahms (1833–1897) and Anton Bruckner (1824–1896). Both were bachelors living modestly in the large cosmopolitan city to which they had emigrated, but they were very different in background, outlook, and musical style. Each had ardent supporters who came from different ideological and social spheres, a situation that sheds light on the special relationship between cultural forces and musical works in Vienna of this period.

Brahms had been born and raised in the north German city of Hamburg, Bruckner in the Upper Austrian town of Ansfelden, near Linz. Brahms was a lifelong Lutheran Protestant, with a profound knowledge of the Bible, but he had a secular education and did not attend church regularly. By contrast, Bruckner was a devout Catholic who was educated as a choirboy at the monastery of St. Florian and later worked there for many years as a teacher.

Sacred vocal works were an important part of the compositional output of both Brahms and Bruckner. Brahms wrote in the Lutheran tradition of works with German texts. Among his sacred choral compositions were motets modeled on those of Heinrich Schütz and J. S. Bach; his largest choral work, and the one that made him a famous composer around Europe, was the *German Requiem* (1868), which, as discussed in Chapter 7, combined these historical influences in a work of great originality. Brahms's choral works are nonliturgical, that is, not intended to be a part of any religious service. They are part of the broader concert culture of the nineteenth century, meant to be performed in secular venues like the concert hall. Bruckner presents a very different picture.

His sacred vocal music, created with Latin texts and within Catholic traditions, includes three Masses, a Te Deum, and a Magnificat, as well as motets. While these have become concert works today, many were liturgical in origin, written specifically for churches where Bruckner worked, or intended for similar ones.

Bruckner and Brahms settled permanently in Vienna in the same year, 1868. Bruckner took a post teaching harmony, counterpoint, and organ at the Vienna Conservatory. Brahms, who rarely sought regular positions of that kind, was able to make a good living as a free-lance composer, conductor, and pianist. Vienna had an active concert life centered on several halls, large and small, including the sumptuous 1,600-seat Grosser Musikvereinsaal, which was home to the Vienna Philharmonic. It was in these venues that ambitious young composers sought to make a place for themselves in concert culture, especially with the great symphony, a genre to which both Brahms and Bruckner contributed significantly. In addition, Brahms enriched concert culture with more than 25 chamber works, including string quartets, quintets, and sextets; piano trios, quartets, and a quintet; and compositions featuring solo clarinet and horn.

Brahms and Bruckner occupied such different places in Vienna's concert culture that music historians often refer to a Brahms–Bruckner "conflict" or "controversy." The conflict stemmed in part from the tensions in Viennese politics and society. During the decades Brahms and Bruckner lived in Vienna, Austria was a constitutional monarchy strongly shaped by the politics of Liberalism. Liberalism, which had arisen in the aftermath of the revolutions of 1848 discussed in Chapter 7, espoused a belief in individual and religious freedom, human and scientific progress, and a flexible economic system. The members of the Liberal party tended to be drawn from the intellectual and social elite, German speakers and assimilated German-Jewish citizens from the middle and upper-middle classes. Liberals were strongly secular and anticlerical. In the 1880s Liberalism began to be challenged by other groups or parties, including those coming from the lower or working classes, nationalists from the Slavic areas of the empire, extreme pan-Germanists who believed Austria should be part of a larger nation that was culturally and linguistically German, and Catholics who saw themselves as excluded from government. These groups fomented anti-Semitic rhetoric (as discussed briefly in Chapter 9), harshly attacking many of Vienna's Jews.

These political issues played out in concert culture, especially among the respective supporters of Brahms and Bruckner. Many patrons of the arts in Vienna tended to come from the Liberal elite who admired and helped Brahms. These were bankers, businessmen, physicians, and university professors. Brahms moved comfortably in their social circles and shared their values. Among those values was the idea of listening to music and striving to understand complex forms and processes as a means to improve or develop oneself. For Liberals, music was an integral part of what was called in German *Bildung,* meaning formation or education in the broadest sense (see Chapter 3).

Bruckner drew his support from Catholics, from the ranks of pan-Germans, and from an anti-Liberal group called the Academic Wagner Society, which promoted not only Wagner's operas but some of his cultural-social ideas that we explored in Chapter 8, including racial purity and folk-based populism. For these groups, Bruckner was a simple, authentic man of the countryside, not a cosmopolitan elitist; his music was seen as capable of direct emotional contact with an audience through sensuous melody and massive orchestral effects. These same people claimed the opposite of Brahms: that his symphonies were too esoteric and intellectual. "Brahms's symphonies do not inspire and delight the human heart," wrote the Bruckner enthusiast and music critic Hans Paumgartner in 1890, "and will therefore never become popular." Attacks like these were countered by one of Vienna's most powerful music critics, Eduard Hanslick, whose ideas on music we examined in Chapters 6 and 7. Hanslick, already known as one of Wagner's main opponents, found Bruckner's symphonic work "strange," "repugnant," and "interminable." He upheld Brahms as the only true heir to Beethoven, writing in 1886, "Brahms is unique in his resources of genuine symphonic invention; in his sovereign mastery of all the secrets of counterpoint, harmony, and instrumentation; in the logic of development combined with the most beautiful freedom of fantasy."

BRAHMS'S SYMPHONIES

Brahms's four symphonies, completed between 1876 and 1885, form an important part of his contribution to concert culture. Given his connections to the Viennese musical and cultural elite, it is no surprise that his Second (1877) and Third (1883) Symphonies were premiered on subscription concerts by the Vienna Philharmonic, and that his First (1876) and Fourth (1885) were played by the orchestra not long after their first performances elsewhere. All became a regular part of the orchestra's repertory, displaying what the Liberal elite most valued in music. These features, as articulated above by Hanslick, include technical mastery and logic, to which we might add another component of proper *Bildung*—a knowledge of the past.

As we saw in Chapter 7, Brahms was one of the great musical historicists of his age. His symphonies were created for a sophisticated concert public that was assumed to be familiar with the music of Haydn, Mozart, Beethoven, Schubert, Mendelssohn, and Schumann, and it is easy to discern the presence of these composers in the symphonies. The main Allegro theme of the finale of Brahms's First bears a strong resemblance to the *Ode to Joy* theme of Beethoven's Ninth Symphony. When the similarity of themes was pointed out to Brahms, he is reported to have said that "any jackass" could notice it. His sarcasm reveals that he was not seeking to hide or deny the allusion to Beethoven, but rather to celebrate his dialogue with the music of the past.

Another characteristic of Brahms's symphonies is the intensity of their motivic processes, also a hallmark of Haydn, Mozart, and especially Beethoven, where large-scale forms were often shaped by the continuous development of small thematic units. The first movement of Brahms's First updates this tradition for a late-nineteenth-century, musically educated audience. The movement is in a standard sonata form—with a slow introduction, exposition, development, recapitulation, and coda—but the different parts of the form are woven tightly together (see Anthology 17). The harmonic and thematic language surges continuously; rarely does it settle down into longer melodic phrases or stable tonal areas. Brahms's main allegro theme is a complex of three ideas (labeled *x, y,* and *z* in Ex. 10.1), which are unfolded successively, then simultaneously— that is, played in counterpoint with each other. To follow this motivic complex throughout the movement demands a high level of listening. Even Hanslick, Brahms's biggest supporter, found the work tough going. In a review, he wrote, "Brahms seems to favour too one-sidedly the great and the serious, the difficult and the complex, and at the expense of sensuous beauty."

Example 10.1: *Brahms, Symphony No. 1, Op. 68, movement 1, mm. 38–46, main Allegro theme*

The finale of Brahms's Fourth Symphony fully embodies the musical and cultural principles for which the composer stood: compositional integrity and logic, and historical consciousness. For the movement's structural framework Brahms reached back past the Classical forms to the Baroque chaconne, in which a set of variations is constructed upon a short repeated bass line. The Canon by Johann Pachelbel (1653–1706) and Bach's Chaconne in D Minor for solo violin (the last movement of his Second Partita, BWV 1004) are among the examples best known today. The eight-measure chaconne theme of the finale of Brahms's Fourth Symphony is modeled on the last movement of Bach's Cantata No. 150. Brahms had played Bach's theme to a friend in 1882, commenting,

"What would you think about a symphony written on this theme some time? But it is too clumsy, straightforward. One must alter it chromatically in some way." Indeed, Brahms did modify his model by adding a chromatically raised fourth degree, A♯, by enriching the harmony, and by placing the theme initially in the top voice, not the bass (Ex. 10.2).

Example 10.2: *Brahms, Symphony No. 4, Op. 90, movement 4, mm. 1–8, chaconne theme*

From here Brahms goes on to construct a powerful set of 30 variations and a coda. In the course of the finale, the chaconne theme moves into different parts of the texture; sometimes it is a bass, sometimes a melody, sometimes an inner voice. Although the variations remain anchored in E minor, Brahms manages— while keeping the chaconne theme almost unchanged—to modulate to the keys of E major, A minor, and C major. He also superimposes elements of a sonata-form design on the variation form, such that the theme and variations 1–15 act as a kind of exposition, variations 16–24 as a development, and variations 24–30 as a free recapitulation. The whole movement is richly scored. There are powerful climaxes for full orchestra, a delicate flute solo (variation 12), and an elegiac chorale for trombones (variation 14). The finale of Brahms's Fourth, to which one cannot deny the "sensuous beauty" Hanslick sometimes found lacking, fuses historical and contemporary practices in a way unique in the symphonic literature.

BRUCKNER'S SYMPHONIES

If Brahms's symphonies are tightly constructed and characterized by complex motivic development, Bruckner's go in the opposite direction. They are massive in all senses of the term. Some last almost 80 minutes in performance, twice as long as a Brahms symphony, and are scored for an orchestra closer in size to that used by Wagner than by Beethoven or Schumann. Their musical processes are also on a broad scale, with long arching melodies, extended harmonic sequences, and frequent repetition of thematic and rhythmic figures, rather than development or transformation.

Between 1863 and his death in 1896, Bruckner worked on 12 symphonies, of which 11 reached a performable state. Two of these—symphonies in F minor and D minor (now sometimes numbered "00" and "0")—were not considered by Bruckner to be part of his official symphonic output, which comprises nine numbered works. Because, as discussed above, Bruckner was not embraced by the Viennese elite that dominated concert culture, his symphonies entered the repertory more slowly than Brahms's. The early success of Bruckner's Second Symphony (1872), which he conducted with the Vienna Philharmonic in 1873, was not followed by any regular hearings of his works until the 1890s, when Liberal culture was beginning to wane. The first performance of the Third in 1877 was a disaster with the public. One critic reported that "even before Herr Bruckner raised the baton, part of the audience began to stream out of the hall and this exodus assumed ever greater proportions after each movement, so that the Finale ... was only experienced to the last extreme by a little host of hardy adventurers."

Bruckner's symphonic vision and its distinctive place in concert culture come from several sources. First there is Bruckner's Catholicism. His incomplete Ninth Symphony was dedicated to "Beloved God." Although they contain no explicitly sacred content, Bruckner's symphonies have sometimes been dubbed "cathedrals in sound." They feature broad chorale-like themes that are not actual church melodies but are often played by groups of brass and woodwind instruments that give the effect of a choir, or perhaps of an organ. Indeed, Bruckner's approach to orchestration shows his experience as a church organist. The different blocks of sound—strings, woodwinds, brass tend not to be blended, but set off against each other in a fashion characteristic of the organ.

Second, like Brahms, Bruckner was powerfully influenced by the musical past. But Bruckner's historicist approach is very different, as can be seen by comparing the finale of Bruckner's Fifth Symphony (1878) with that of Brahms's Fourth, discussed above. Bruckner, like Brahms, seeks to synthesize older and contemporary practice, in this case Baroque fugue and Classical sonata form. But where Brahms compressed his 30 variations on the chaconne theme into about 10 minutes, Bruckner writes an expansive 25-minute movement brimming with counterpoint. The first theme of the sonata exposition is a full imitative presentation of a fugue subject, characterized by bold octave leaps and dotted rhythms (Ex. 10.3a).

At the end of the exposition Bruckner introduces as a closing theme a new chorale-like tune, which is played fortissimo by the entire brass section—four horns, three trumpets, three trombones, and a tuba (Ex. 10.3b). The development section consists of a double fugue based on a simultaneous presentation of the first theme and the chorale (Ex. 10.3c). The recapitulation returns to the initial fugue subject, which in the coda is then rejoined by the chorale played triple *forte* in blazing glory by the brasses. The chorale appears in augmentation, that is, with its original note values doubled, a technique that derives directly from Baroque contrapuntal practice and drives home the historicizing dimension of Bruckner's symphony. If the historicism of Brahms's Fourth is restrained—perhaps only the most sophisticated listeners could recognize the chaconne form—that of Bruckner's finale is hard to miss, even by an audience not schooled in contrapuntal subtleties.

The third main influence on Bruckner's symphonic style comes from the more recent composers he revered, Beethoven, Schubert, and Wagner. In the Vienna of Bruckner's day, as we saw above, Wagnerism had become associated

Example 10.3: *Bruckner, Symphony No. 5, movement 4*

with anti-Liberal, populist movements, from which much of Bruckner's support came. He was personally devoted to Wagner, to whom he dedicated his Third Symphony (1873). In its original form—it later went through several revisions—the symphony is replete with quotations from Wagner's operas.

The most effective Wagnerian moment in Bruckner's symphonies comes in the Adagio of the Seventh Symphony, a movement written to commemorate Wagner's death in February 1883. Bruckner calls for four "Wagner tubas," instruments combining aspects of a tuba and French horn that Wagner commissioned for his *Ring* operas. In the coda of the Adagio, the tubas play a chorale-like theme that recalls a famous Wagner passage, Siegfried's Funeral March from the last act of *Götterdämmerung* (Ex. 10.4). In Bruckner's passage, Wagnerism, historicism, and spirituality combine to create an affecting symphonic utterance that represents the heart of Bruckner's contributions to concert culture.

Example 10.4: *Bruckner, Symphony No. 7, movement 2, mm. 185–188*

CONCERT CULTURE IN FRANCE

Far more than in Austro-German areas, concert culture in France in the later nineteenth century was centralized around a single locale, the capital city of Paris. Paris had an enormous concentration of cultural institutions, most of them heavily subsidized by the state, which in France always played a more prominent role in the arts than in Austria and Germany. During the Third Republic, which began after France's defeat in the Franco-Prussian War in 1870 and lasted until World War II, music was seen as an agent of cultural regeneration. Political leaders believed that music should serve the public good, and an active concert life was an important way of achieving that goal. By contrast, in Vienna, as we have seen, the Liberals (for all their belief in individual rights) maintained an elitist view of musical culture.

The development of French concert culture had begun well before the Third Republic. In 1828, François-Antoine Habeneck (1781–1849) founded a concert series at the Paris Conservatoire that introduced the Beethoven symphonies to France, alongside works by contemporary French and Italian composers. The concerts were revelatory for young composers like Berlioz, who had powerful formative experiences with symphonic masterpieces that they would then seek to emulate.

The Conservatoire concerts had a relatively restricted audience, since the general public was not admitted. In 1861 the conductor Jules Pasdeloup (1819–1887) tried to remedy this situation with a series of large-scale and very successful events, the Concerts populaires, which took place at the Cirque Napoléon, a hall that seated 5,000. Pasdeloup's orchestra of 110 players offered a broad repertory. The Austro-German masters, including Beethoven, Haydn, Mozart, and Mendelssohn, appeared alongside contemporary French composers like Berlioz, Edouard Lalo (1823–1892), and Jules Massenet (1842–1912). In the inclusion of living composers, such concerts showed a more progressive side than those in Austria and Germany.

These trends toward cultivating a broad audience among the general public continued in the Third Republic. In 1873, Edouard Colonne (1838–1910) founded the Concerts nationals (later renamed Concerts Colonne). The first program (Fig. 10.3) shows clearly the mixture of Austro-German and contemporary French composers that Colonne achieved: Schubert, Mendelssohn, and Schumann are balanced by Saint-Saëns, Bizet, and Ernest Guiraud. Still another conductor who helped shape the concert life of Paris in the Third Republic was Charles Lamoureux (1834–1899), whose Concerts Lamoureux, begun in 1881, promoted younger French composers alongside the music of Wagner, a figure who, as we saw in Chapter 8, played an enormous role in French culture of this period.

Perhaps the organization that best symbolized concert culture in France in the latter half of the nineteenth century was the Société Nationale de Musique

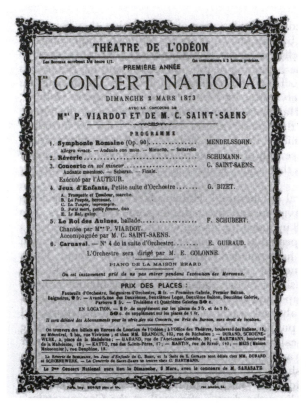

Figure 10.3: *Program for first Concert national at the Théâtre de l'Odéon, Paris, 1873*

(National Society of Music), founded in 1871 in the aftermath of the Franco-Prussian War by a group of musicians led by Saint-Saëns. The French were no less prone to nationalist sentiment in this era than the Germans, Italians, Russians, and Czechs we discussed in Chapter 7. The Latin motto of the society, "Ars Gallica" (Gallic art), reflected an explicit desire to promote French music at a time when national pride needed a strong boost. This goal did not mean the exclusion of German music, despite the fact that France had suffered defeat at German hands. Indeed, the society viewed the weightiness of Austro-German instrumental music as an important model for French composers and audiences.

The Société Nationale gave its first concert on November 17, 1871. Saint-Saëns would later recall, "It is permissible to say that on that date the aim of the Société was achieved and from then onwards French names appeared on concert programmes to which no one had hitherto dared admit them." The society continued its activities until 1939. During its early years, it gave premieres of new works by figures who were to become major composers, including Emmanuel Chabrier, Ernest Chausson, Gabriel Fauré, César Franck, Edouard Lalo, Maurice

Ravel, Claude Debussy, and Paul Dukas. Several of these composers were ardent Wagnerians (as suggested in Chapter 8). Neither their passion for the German-born Wagner nor his influence on their musical style prevented them from being an integral part of the newly conceived Ars Gallica.

French concert culture of the later nineteenth century also had a distinctive historicist dimension. Concerts in Paris often featured the performance of early music (la musique ancienne), especially from the Baroque era. The choral works of Bach and Handel were extremely popular. Especially in the aftermath of the Franco-Prussian War—and (to reiterate) despite the fact that the composers were German—their works were seen as beneficial for morale, embodying values of strength and courage. Old and new compositions were often juxtaposed on the same concerts. Lamoureux performed oratorios by Charles Gounod and Jules Massenet alongside one by Handel. In other concerts, French music from the era of Louis XIV and XV (the seventeenth and eighteenth centuries) was played with works by Gounod and Bizet. Such concerts served another goal of the Third Republic: listeners were encouraged to hear relationships between the music of past and present, and thus to appreciate the continuity of French history. Indeed, Colonne planned his 1885–86 season specifically (in his words) to "form a complete summary of the history of music." These concerts were furnished with program notes distinctive for being written by a musical scholar and archivist at the Paris Opéra, Charles Malherbe.

France had long showed an appetite for the genre of the symphony. Both Haydn and Mozart had composed symphonies for the Parisian public, as had Classical-era French composers like François-Joseph Gossec (1734–1829) and Étienne-Nicholas Méhul (1763–1817). As we saw in Chapter 6, Berlioz viewed his *Symphonie fantastique* (1830) as a descendant of the Beethovenian symphony. In the 1850s, Gounod and Bizet each produced symphonies that would become much admired. But the genre was not to establish a real presence among French composers until the next generation, with Saint-Saëns, Franck, and their followers. In keeping with the goals of the Ars Gallica, their symphonies sought to blend musical values from a variety of national traditions.

CAMILLE SAINT-SAËNS AND CÉSAR FRANCK

Camille Saint-Saëns (1835–1921) wrote prolifically in all genres, including symphony, concerto, chamber music, choral music, and opera. His most famous opera was *Samson et Dalila* (Samson and Delilah, 1876). Somewhat like Mendelssohn in Germany decades earlier (see Chapter 5), Saint-Saëns took an active role in the public musical life and concert culture of France. In addition to working as codirector of the Société Nationale, he composed large-scale works like the cantata *Le feu céleste* (Heavenly Fire), written to celebrate the invention of electricity; he performed frequently as a pianist and conductor; he wrote music criticism; and he helped prepare editions of earlier French music. Saint-Saëns was definitely seeking to make music matter.

César Franck (1822–1890), born in Belgium, was a more reclusive figure who spent much of his professional career in relative obscurity as an organist at Paris churches, most notably at Ste. Clothilde from 1858 until his death. Unlike Saint-Saëns, Franck did not have a large compositional output, and most of it was produced in the last 20 years of his life. Franck's musical language, strongly influenced by Wagner and Liszt, is far more chromatic than Saint-Saëns's. Its rich harmonies, dense voice-leading, and extended sequences held enormous appeal for a younger generation of French composers. Franck's group of dedicated pupil-disciples included Vincent d'Indy, Henri Duparc, and Ernest Chausson. In 1886 Franck was elected president of the Société Nationale, an event that set off a conflict between his followers and those of the more musically conservative Saint-Saëns.

Saint-Saëns's Third Symphony in C Minor (1886) and Franck's contemporaneous Symphony in D Minor (1888) are two of the finest French works in the tradition of the "great" symphony in the later nineteenth century. In keeping with the ecumenical spirit of the Ars Gallica, to which both composers adhered despite differing outlooks, the symphonies are deeply indebted to the compositional principles of Franz Liszt. Liszt's music, as we saw in Chapter 6, featured both the emphasis on color and sensuous effect and the values of structure and coherent form, principles he had adapted in part from Berlioz. Saint-Saëns dedicated his Third Symphony to the memory of Liszt, who died in 1886 and had been an important patron and friend to both composers.

Saint-Saëns and Franck adopted the techniques of thematic transformation and of cyclic return. As we saw in Chapter 6, thematic transformation was pioneered by Berlioz in the *Symphonie fantastique*, where the recurring *idée fixe* keeps its basic shape and contour, but at each appearance changes mood, instrumentation, meter, and tempo. Liszt took up this principle in many of his works, including the symphonic poems. He also used the related technique of cyclical return: as discussed in Chapters 3 and 6, cyclic form enabled composers to provide coherence or unity in a large-scale work by having themes recur at important structural moments, especially at the end.

Saint-Saëns's Third Symphony had its premiere at London's massive St. James's Hall (see above, Fig. 10.1). With substantial parts for piano and organ—it is nicknamed the *Organ* Symphony—it hearkens back to the eighteenth-century French tradition of the *symphonie concertante*, which featured solo instruments. Saint-Saëns's Third has the four standard movements of the great symphony, but they are arranged into two large units, such that the first movement Allegro moderato and the Poco adagio are linked without pause, as are the scherzo and finale. The organ makes its appearance only in the slow movement and finale, the piano in the scherzo and finale.

The Third Symphony is unified by the recurrence of a main motive that is first presented by the strings in agitated sixteenth notes (Ex. 10.5a) and then re-appears in each of the movements in a stunning display of transformation and cyclic form. In the slow movement, it becomes a mysterious pizzicato in the low strings; in the scherzo, a fleeting figure in the woodwinds. The finale is dominated by the motive in many transformations, which unfurl one after the other. It becomes a stately organ chorale in a broad meter (Ex. 10.5b), then an energetic fugue subject. At one point near the end of the finale, the motive is adapted in such a way as to recall the famous *Dies irae* melody, in what might be a historical reference to Berlioz's *Symphonie fantastique*. In the final pages, the motive returns briefly to the form it had at the opening of the symphony before concluding the work with a final spacious transformation.

Example 10.5: *Saint-Saëns, Symphony No. 3, thematic transformation*

(a) First movement, mm. 12–14

(b) Second movement, mm. 392–395

Like Saint-Saëns, Franck finds an ingenious way of incorporating the traditional four movement types in an unusual design. The D-Minor Symphony has three movements, of which the middle one, an Allegretto in B♭ minor, combines the functions of a slow movement and scherzo. The main theme is a plaintive melody for English horn, accompanied by the steady plucking of harp and pizzicato strings. Embedded in the middle of the movement is a contrasting scherzo-like section in G minor, with skittish triplet rhythms in the violins. A bit later, the original English horn theme is superimposed over the violins' scherzo such that we have a "double" return, or one that serves two functions simultaneously (Ex. 10.6). Many of the symphony's themes are related by transformation. The cyclic aspects of the symphony are emphasized when first the Allegretto theme, and then the slow introduction and the closing exposition theme of the first movement, all return at the end of the finale.

With their imaginative reinventions of the great symphony, Saint-Saëns, Franck, and some of their contemporaries showed what a vital role the genre could play in French concert culture of the later nineteenth century. Their

Example 10.6: *Franck, Symphony in D Minor, movement 2, mm. 200–203*

symphonies demand close, intelligent listening, in order to follow the formal innovations, but are also attractive in the richness of melodic style and the use of organ, piano, harp, English horn, and other special instrumental colors. In these ways, the French symphony projected the values of the Third Republic, where concert music was meant both to educate and to appeal.

RUSSIAN CONCERT CULTURE AND TCHAIKOVSKY'S SIXTH (*PATHÉTIQUE*) SYMPHONY

In imperial Russia, concert culture centered on two cities, St. Petersburg and Moscow. St. Petersburg, the national capital until 1918, stood at the forefront of Russian musical life. Geographically and culturally closer to western Europe, it had long been the more cosmopolitan of the two cities. Concerts and musical "academies" were held frequently in the noble palaces, private houses, and public spaces of St. Petersburg. The St. Petersburg Philharmonic, founded in 1802, gave 205 symphony concerts during the century of its existence. The St. Petersburg Conservatory was opened in 1862.

In Moscow, musical life prospered after midcentury. The Russian Musical Society was founded in 1859 by Nikolay Rubinstein (1835–1881); its concerts were organized and conducted by his younger brother Anton Rubinstein (1829–1894), who also became the first director of the new Moscow Conservatory they co-founded in 1866. The Moscow Philharmonic was created in 1883.

As its contact with the West developed in the course of the century, Russia developed strong native traditions of chamber and orchestral music. Anton Rubinstein, who completed six symphonies between 1850 and 1886, was eventually eclipsed by the Russian symphonists who began to emerge in the 1860s and 1870s: Mily Balakirev, Aleksandr Borodin, Nikolay Rimsky-Korsakov, and Pyotr Il'yich Tchaikovsky (1840–1893). Of these figures—the first three were discussed briefly in Chapter 7 as members of the "Mighty Handful" based in St. Petersburg—Tchaikovsky alone was professionally trained; he studied with Rubinstein at the St. Petersburg Conservatory.

Among the Russian composers, Tchaikovsky also produced the most sustained, high-quality work in the genre of the great symphony, earning him an international standing in concert culture that his compatriots did not achieve. Tchaikovsky received an honorary degree from the University of Cambridge in England (Fig. 10.4) and also conducted his works at Carnegie Hall in New York City. In his six symphonies he developed a unique fusion of technique and expression. His Sixth (*Pathétique*) Symphony (1893) is one of the last works in the concert culture of the nineteenth century that both respects and transforms conventions in ways that were immediately appreciated by audiences. (As we will see in Chapter 12, Gustav Mahler's symphonies did not often enjoy that kind of reception.)

The composer's title of *Pathétique* and the dark outer movements of the Sixth Symphony have often been associated with his death, which occurred only nine days after the premiere on October 28 (in the Western calendar), 1893. It was rumored at the time—and this echoed down through much of the twentieth century—that Tchaikovsky committed suicide because of shame over revelations about his homosexuality. This story has been discredited in recent years; it is now generally accepted that Tchaikovsky died, as was announced at the time, of cholera probably contracted from drinking a glass of unboiled water in the midst of an epidemic.

It has also been suggested that Tchaikovsky viewed the Sixth Symphony as his own requiem. In fact, Tchaikovsky's title for the symphony, *Pateticheskaia simfonia* in Russian (but usually rendered in French), does not indicate "pathos"

Figure 10.4: *Tchaikovsky in academic robes for his honorary degree from the University of Cambridge, England, 1893*

in the sense of suffering, but rather a more general emotion like "impassioned" or "passionate." And although the work ends with one of the most wrenching symphonic movements ever created, there is no evidence to connect its mood directly with a personal premonition of death. Indeed, moments after conducting the triumphant premiere, Tchaikovsky was reported as being "utterly happy and content" at the work's success and as having "joked and laughed" with a friend.

Tchaikovsky's *Pathétique* Symphony boldly reimagines the conventions of the great symphony. As we have seen in this chapter and earlier in the book, it is usual for the exposition of a sonata form to be built from two large thematic areas of roughly equal weight; the second is normally preceded by a transition characterized by harmonic and rhythmic momentum. Tchaikovsky's first movement modifies this process to place emphasis on a single powerful melody, the second theme. After a slow introduction, the first theme (a transformation of the introduction, as in Franck) is unstable and scherzo-like. It lasts barely a minute, then dies away—no momentum here—to be succeeded after a short transition and a fermata by a lyrical and expansive second theme in D major (Ex. 10.7). Tchaikovsky unabashedly tips the balance of his exposition toward this passionate theme, whose iterations and extensions stretch to almost five minutes.

Example 10.7: *Tchaikovsky, Symphony No. 6* (Pathétique), *movement 1, mm. 90–97*

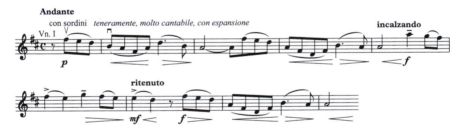

The lyric intensity of the first movement is balanced by that of the finale, the Adagio lamentoso, one of the most psychologically devastating movements in the entire Western concert repertory (see Anthology 18). The movement has an ABA'B' form in which both main themes feature stepwise descents that recall the four-note descending lament figure of the Baroque (as heard, for example, in Claudio Monteverdi's madrigal *Lamento della ninfa* [Lament of the Nymph]). The radiant B theme, which appears first in D major, reflects in key and in spirit the broad second theme of the first movement, and thus helps to bring the symphony to a close (Ex. 10.8).

The spacious outer movements of the *Pathétique* frame two faster inner movements. The second is a dance, marked Allegro con grazia, in D major, and especially famous for its irregular $\frac{5}{4}$ meter, which has been called a "limping waltz" because the

Example 10.8: *Tchaikovsky, Symphony No. 6* (Pathétique*), movement 4, mm. 39–46*

measures are subdivided into units of 3 + 2 beats. This dance occupies the traditional position of a slow movement, which—as we come to realize—is displaced to the final position in this symphony. The third movement begins like a scherzo (in duple meter), but gradually builds into a colossal march. As it develops, this robust movement develops the feel of a triumphant symphonic finale. Yet the sense of an ending is premature, since the march is followed by the Adagio lamentoso. Tchaikovsky's radical reweighting of the great symphony in the *Pathétique* is one of the boldest creative acts of nineteenth-century concert culture.

Each in his own way, the composers discussed in this chapter engaged with the paradigms and pressures of the "great" symphony in the second half of the nineteenth century. In Austria, Germany, France, and Russia, concert culture created certain expectations for new works. Symphonies needed to bear some clear relationship to the classics—the symphonies of Haydn, Mozart, and Beethoven—so that they could be programmed alongside them. At the same time, they had to present some kind of "twist" or angle that distinguished them from conventional symphonies. Balancing these demands, Brahms, Bruckner, Franck, Saint-Saëns, and Tchaikovsky all managed to secure a place in concert culture that they retain today. In Chapter 12 we will examine how beginning in the late 1880s (and thus contemporaneously with some of these composers) Gustav Mahler began a further transformation of the great symphony in ways that would bring it well beyond Romanticism, into the sphere of Modernism.

FOR FURTHER READING

Brown, A. Peter, *The European Symphony from ca. 1800 to ca. 1930: Great Britain, Russia, and France* (Bloomington and Indianapolis: Indiana University Press, 2008)

Brown, A. Peter, *The Second Golden Age of the Viennese Symphony: Brahms, Bruckner, Dvořák, Mahler, and Selected Contemporaries* (Bloomington and Indianapolis: Indiana University Press, 2003)

The Cambridge Companion to Bruckner, ed. John Williamson (Cambridge and New York: Cambridge University Press, 2004)

Frisch, Walter, *Brahms: The Four Symphonies* (New Haven and London: Yale University Press, 2003)

Hanslick, Eduard, *Hanslick's Music Criticisms*, trans. and ed. Henry Pleasants (New York: Dover, 1988)

Notley, Margaret, *Lateness and Brahms: Music and Culture in the Twilight of Viennese Liberalism* (Oxford and New York: Oxford University Press, 2007)

Pasler, Jann, *Composing the Citizen: Music as Public Utility in Third Republic France* (Berkeley and Los Angeles: University of California Press, 2009)

Wiley, Roland John, *Tchaikovsky* (Oxford and New York: Oxford University Press, 2009)

Ⓢ **Additional resources available at wwnorton.com/studyspace**

CHAPTER ELEVEN

Musical Life and Identity in the United States

At the dawn of the nineteenth century, the United States was still young and its culture very much in transition. The nation, consisting of 16 states strung mainly along the Eastern seaboard, was overwhelmingly rural and agrarian; only 5 percent of the population lived in big cities. A century later the United States was well on its way to being a major world and economic power. It had undergone a wrenching civil war, had expanded across the continent to the Pacific Ocean, had taken part in the Industrial Revolution, and was enjoying what has been called a Gilded Age of prosperity and culture. By 1900, cities claimed 40 percent of the American population. The three largest were New York, with almost 3.5 million people, and Chicago and Philadelphia, each with about 1.5 million. Across the latter part of the nineteenth century, with successive waves of immigrants arriving from Ireland, Germany, and then other countries, the cities saw ever greater ethnic diversity and—inevitably—growing economic inequality among residents. Life in the densely populated urban areas was "gilded" for relatively few.

Well before the arrival of settlers and colonizers in the early seventeenth century, there had of course been "American" music—that of the Native Americans. Our principal record of this music is from non-natives who heard and described it, and sometimes wrote it down in Western notation. The Europeans also brought with them music and musical practices, some of which were imposed upon the native peoples. During the post-Revolutionary period and the nineteenth century, an extraordinary diversity developed in American music. Music created and performed by white, African, Hispanic, Asian, and Native Americans would play a crucial role in defining the identity not only of individual racial, ethnic, and social groups, but of the nation as a whole.

Throughout this book we have focused on the so-called classical music traditions of Western Europe, especially within the broader cultural contexts of performers, consumers, and institutions, and the arts in general. Given the history and richness of these traditions (also referred to as "genteel," "cultivated," or "high-brow") and the structure of most music history curricula, it is perhaps understandable that little attention is given to European "popular" and folk musics. The United States presents a different picture, however, and different challenges to the music historian, because the classical traditions arguably form a smaller part of what has always made American musical life distinctive. The other part is popular music in the broadest sense, whether newly composed and notated, or passed down orally as folk music. A single chapter cannot possibly do justice to the complexity of American musical life in the nineteenth century, which includes traditions like Native American chants and black spirituals, as well as genres associated with people of European descent. In keeping with the cultural and contextual focus of this book, we will consider selectively the ways in which both the classical and popular impulses manifested themselves in American places, people, institutions, and musical works.

We begin with snapshots of musical life from three different areas of North America in the first decades of the nineteenth century—the sophisticated context of urban Boston, the frontier world of the Spanish colonial missions in California, and the vibrantly multicultural city of New Orleans. Each local scene was dominated by a key figure who, much like European counterparts examined in Chapter 5, sought to make music matter in the New World.

FEDERAL BOSTON

In the first decades of the new American republic, often called the Federal period (1780–1820), Eastern cities cultivated a concert life based on European models. The most prestigious musical group was the Handel and Haydn Society of Boston, which was founded in 1815 and continues to this day. The creators of the society wanted music to become an integral part of the civic, social, and political fabric of the nation. They wrote in their charter:

> While in our country almost every institution, political, civil, and moral, has advanced with rapid steps, while every other science and art is

cultivated with success flattering to its advocates, the admirers of music find their beloved science far from exciting feelings or exercising the powers to which it is accustomed in the Old World. Too long have those to whom heaven has given a voice to perform and an ear that can enjoy music neglected a science which has done much towards subduing the ferocious passions of men and giving innocent pleasure to society.

The clear intention here is to give classical music in the United States the status it had in the "Old World," in Europe. Initially the Handel and Haydn Society focused its efforts on the sacred music of Handel and Haydn and other "eminent" composers. The first concert was held on Christmas Eve 1815, and included numbers from Handel's *Messiah* and Haydn's *Creation.* The reaction was enthusiastic. One Boston newspaper acknowledged the performance's "superiority to any ever before given in this town." The society sought to commission a new work from Beethoven, who declined but said he felt honored by the offer. Societies were formed in other American cities in emulation of the Handel and Haydn Society.

In 1822 the society issued the *Boston Handel and Haydn Society Collection of Church Music*, compiled by Lowell Mason (1792–1872), who would go on to have an enormous influence on musical life in the United States. Mason, a native of Massachusetts, had put the volume together by drawing on English collections, arranging instrumental and vocal works of Classical composers, and composing some numbers anew. The *Collection* would eventually go through 22 editions, sell more than 50,000 copies, and bring considerable wealth to both the society and Mason.

Mason's ambitions extended far beyond assembling hymn tunes. He sought nothing less than to transform the relationship between the American people and their music. As music director of several churches in the Boston area, Mason understood the community-building role that music played in congregations. In the 1830s he actively desired—and this was his key insight—to transfer to the secular sphere the principles of societal cohesion he saw in the churches. Mason became head of the Handel and Haydn Society. He set up the Boston Academy of Music, to train teachers in new methods for encouraging a more active, participatory style of learning. In 1838 Mason also became superintendent of music in the Boston public school system. By the time he died in 1872, many other educational and musical reformers had taken up Mason's ideas, and musical life in the largely urban northeastern United States had changed forever.

SPANISH COLONIAL AMERICA

Around 1815, an entirely different picture was presented by the western side of the North American continent, thousands of miles from New England. California, populated by Native Americans and Spanish colonists, would not become a part of the United States for many decades. There were no large cities and no organizations for the promotion of European musical works. Outside the music of the indigenous peoples, musical life centered exclusively on the Catholic missions, the first of which had been founded in 1697. In a manner that was different from Boston's Handel and Haydn Society but had something of a similar purpose, the Catholic priests used music as a tool for conversion and for what they understood as civilization. Music was deployed to accomplish what the Boston society had called "subduing the ferocious passions of men"—in this case not European settlers but Indians. Today we interpret such practices as a form of subjugation, but the motives of the Franciscan priests were not necessarily exploitative.

A key figure in the mission movement was Father Narciso Durán (1776–1846), who was born in Catalonia, Spain, and arrived as a missionary in California in 1806. In some ways his goals and his vision were similar to those of Lowell Mason. Like Mason, Durán had a passion for teaching young people; he believed that music could improve the soul and the body. At the Mission of San José (Fig. 11.1), which he headed for over 25 years, Durán developed a high level of musical skills among the Native Americans, who were taught to sing and read music and to play instruments. Durán also devised theories of simplified notation that would allow others to teach with his method.

In 1813, again not unlike Mason, Durán compiled a choir book of polyphonic masses with a pedagogical goal, which he set out in an extraordinary prologue. At first, he reported, the Native Americans had trouble memorizing the Christian

Figure 11.1: *A photograph of San José Mission in California as it appeared in the 1860s*

chant. Their performance "had neither feet nor head, and seemed a howl rather than a song." "Therefore," he continued, "what is most necessary at a Mission is to teach the boys the Sacred Chant according to rules or principles so that they will not have to trust everything to memory, but will be able to read notes and sing by themselves whatever is plainly written." Durán went on to explain the system of clefs, scales, and accidentals he devised for teaching the boys to read music.

The music in the choir book includes the *Misa de Cataluña* (Catalonian Mass), which Durán may have composed himself or adapted from another source. In it we see an example of the simple but elegant four-part polyphonic writing he taught to the Native Americans (Ex. 11.1). European visitors to the Mission of San José often reported hearing in this music a haunting or melancholy quality which they also recognized in the Native Americans' own music. This similarity suggests that even though he was seeking to teach them music based on the European Catholic tradition, Durán was sensitive to the nature of their indigenous chant.

Example 11.1: Misa de Cataluña, *Kyrie, mm. 1–3*

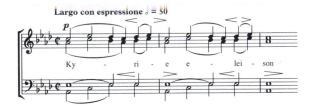

Lord have mercy

The most evocative account of what Indians singing the Mass may have sounded like comes from later in the century, well after the Mission period. In 1879, the writer Robert Louis Stevenson reported how moved he was by a visit to a church in Carmel, California. His description gives us a hint of the special sounds that Durán likely elicited from his singers:

> The Indians troop together, their bright dresses contrasting with their dark and melancholy faces; and there among a crowd of somewhat unsympathetic holiday makers, you may hear God served with perhaps more touching circumstances than in any other temple under heaven. An Indian, stone blind and about eighty years of age, conducts the singing; other Indians compose the choir; yet they have the Gregorian music at their finger ends, and pronounce the Latin so correctly that I could follow the meaning as they sang. The pronunciation was odd and nasal, the singing hurried and staccato. "In saecula saeculo-ho-horum," they went, with a vigorous aspirate to every syllable. I have never seen faces more vividly lit up with joy than the faces of these Indian singers.

NEW ORLEANS AND LOUIS MOREAU GOTTSCHALK

New Orleans, lying on the coast of the Gulf of Mexico over a thousand miles from both Boston and California, was home to a vibrant and diverse culture that included French, Spanish, and African elements. Already in the nineteenth century New Orleans was a site of a kind of musical fusion that would eventually lead to the creation of jazz, one of the greatest art forms produced in the United States. The city had many street musicians and several theaters, each with its own orchestra. Music was made in numerous dance halls, churches, and saloons, and played by army bands.

Into this milieu was born Louis Moreau Gottschalk (1829–1869), whose lineage reflected the city's ethnic and racial diversity. His father was an English Jew of German descent, his mother a Haitian of French and African descent. Gottschalk started playing the piano at age three and at thirteen was sent off to Paris, where he soon became part of the cult of pianism and virtuosity that included such figures as Liszt and Chopin. Chopin was in the audience for Gottschalk's public debut. In the early 1850s Gottschalk returned to the United States and began extensive concert tours on the East Coast. Later he would focus his travels on the Caribbean and Latin America, especially Cuba and Brazil.

Gottschalk wrote almost 300 compositions, mainly for solo piano, and played them extensively around the world. Most are based on musical themes and idioms from the places he lived and traveled. The piano piece *La gallina* (The Hen), subtitled *danse cubaine,* was probably written during one of Gottschalk's trips to Cuba in the late 1850s. It features several popular Latin or Caribbean rhythmic patterns (Ex. 11.2; see Anthology 19). In measure 3 the right hand plays a form of the *amphibrach* with a characteristic syncopated first beat; the left hand plays the *habanera*, the same pattern that Bizet would use in *Carmen* (see Anthology 16). Gottschalk's works transport us back to a hybrid musical world, where a gifted

Example 11.2: *Gottschalk,* La gallina, *mm. 1–5*

composer-performer could blend European and New World traditions in a style that had virtuosity, panache, and popular appeal.

Gottschalk's final tour of North America before his early death at age 40 shows the grueling schedule he maintained. In his diary of December 1862 he reported from New York:

> I have just finished . . . my last tour of concerts for this season. I have given eighty-five concerts in four months and a half. I have travelled fifteen thousand miles by train. At St. Louis I have seven concerts in six days; at Chicago, five in four days. A few weeks more in this way and I should have become an idiot! Eighteen hours a day on the railroad! Arrive at seven o'clock in the evening, eat with all speed, appear at eight o'clock before the public. The last note finished, rush quickly for my luggage, and en route until next day, always to the same thing!

This passage gives a vivid impression of the frenzied life of a touring musician, especially one working in the United States, with its vast distances between cities. Gottschalk's star status came at a price.

Gottschalk had a huge impact on American musical life that continued even after his death. Biographies began to appear, and sheet music of his compositions was published in North and South America and in Europe. *Notes of a Pianist,* the 1881 publication of Gottschalk's diaries, makes for one of the nineteenth century's most colorful and informative books about music. Gottschalk presents not only many details of his extensive tours, but also a view of music as a potential force for physical and social good—attitudes that make him a kindred spirit of Lowell Mason and Narciso Durán, as well as other European figures who, as we saw in Chapter 5, sought to make music matter. In one passage from 1865, Gottschalk argues that music "is one of the most powerful means of ameliorating and ennobling the human mind, of elevating the morals, and, above all, of refining the manners of the people."

Among other stories, Gottschalk tells one of how a deeply psychotic Parisian priest was transformed by singing regularly in a church choir. In the spirit of Mason, Gottschalk also praises the communal musical societies in Europe, which bring together people from different walks of life. Participation in such choral groups, Gottschalk argues, may keep down violent crime and drunken behavior: "In fact, you are better, your heart is in some way purified, when it is strongly impregnated with the noble harmonies of a fine chorus, and it becomes difficult not to trust as a brother him whose voice is blended with your own and whose heart is united with yours in a community of pure and joyful emotions." If such groups are established in America, Gottschalk writes, "be assured that the barrooms—the scourge of the country—and revolvers will cease to be national institutions." Gottschalk may have been naive in imagining how choral singing might curb the abuse of alcohol and firearms. But he also may not have been aware how far the civilizing mission of Mason and others in Boston had developed.

Gottschalk represented a unique amalgam of what made American music special in the nineteenth century. He had popular appeal, and his music was rooted in both American and European traditions. He was also a truly American entrepreneur and self-promoter, making a considerable profit off his tours and his music. Gottschalk bridged a number of worlds that up until his time had been very separate: Europe, North America, and Africa; popular and classical music; and the consumer and the artist. Gottschalk's passionate belief in the powers of music helps explain the punishing schedule of tours and concerts to which he subjected himself. A man with a mission to spread the gospel of music, he did so across a far greater geographical area than was possible for Mason or Durán—from Canada to Brazil, and from San Francisco to Boston.

STEPHEN FOSTER AND AMERICAN POPULAR SONG

Gottschalk based one of his most popular compositions, *The Banjo* (1855), on a tune by an American composer who would surpass him in fame without ever leaving the Northeast, Stephen Foster (1826–1864). Gottschalk used Foster's *Camptown Races*, a song which for him and many other Americans was so much a part of the national psyche that it became a sort of folk song—widely known and not specifically associated with the composer's name. In 1852, a writer in the *Albany State Register* noted the extraordinary popularity of another Foster song, *Old Folks at Home*, composed the preceding year:

> Pianos and guitars groan with it, night and day; sentimental young ladies sing it; sentimental young gentlemen warble it in midnight serenades; volatile young "bucks" hum it in the midst of their business and their pleasures; boatmen roar it out stentorially at all times; all the bands play it; amateur flute players agonize over it at every spare moment; the street organs grind it out at every hour; the "singing stars" carol it on the theatrical boards, and at concerts; the chamber maid sweeps and dusts to its measured cadence.

A native of Pittsburgh who later settled in New York, Foster published about 200 songs in his short life. Their range in many ways maps out American culture in the middle years of the nineteenth century. Foster wrote parlor songs based on English, Irish, and Scottish models; songs that drew on Italian operatic styles; and minstrel and other song types drawing on African-American models.

Foster's first big successes came in this last category, also the most problematic part of his oeuvre for us today. American minstrelsy emerged in the 1830s and 1840s as a form of musical-theatrical entertainment in which white performers, their faces blackened with burnt cork, would sing, dance, and act in ways that poked fun—often maliciously—at African-American life. Minstrels and their songs were also sometimes called "Ethiopian." Certain stereotypes were common among minstrel characters, including Jim Crow, the naive plantation slave, and Zip Coon, the slick urban sophisticate. Groups like Christy's Minstrels, formed in 1843, increased the demand for minstrel songs, and the repertory became more substantial and of higher quality. Foster fed the craze with some of his earliest songs, including *Oh! Susanna* (1848).

In 1850 Foster married, and the following year a daughter was born. But he soon separated from his family, left Pennsylvania, and moved to New York. From then on Foster's songs take on more overtones of loss, pain, and regret. His "plantation songs," as he called them to distance them from his earlier minstrel or "Ethiopian" ones, are calmer and more reflective. In each, a solo verse alternates with a chorus written in harmony. *Old Folks at Home* (1851), Foster's most famous plantation song, uses black dialect to convey nostalgia (Ex. 11.3; Fig. 11.2).

Example 11.3: *Foster,* Old Folks at Home

Such lyrics might seem to reinforce stereotypes of black Americans. As in Verdi's *Aida* and Bizet's *Carmen* (see Chapter 9), we have a case of a white man of European descent creating music in the voice of an Other. With a song about a slave's fond memories of life on the plantation, Foster is domesticating, even falsifying, for white consumption what was certainly a degrading, dehumanizing existence. But Foster, who would side with the North in the Civil War and was generally sympathetic to black Americans, saw things differently. He wrote to Christy in 1852:

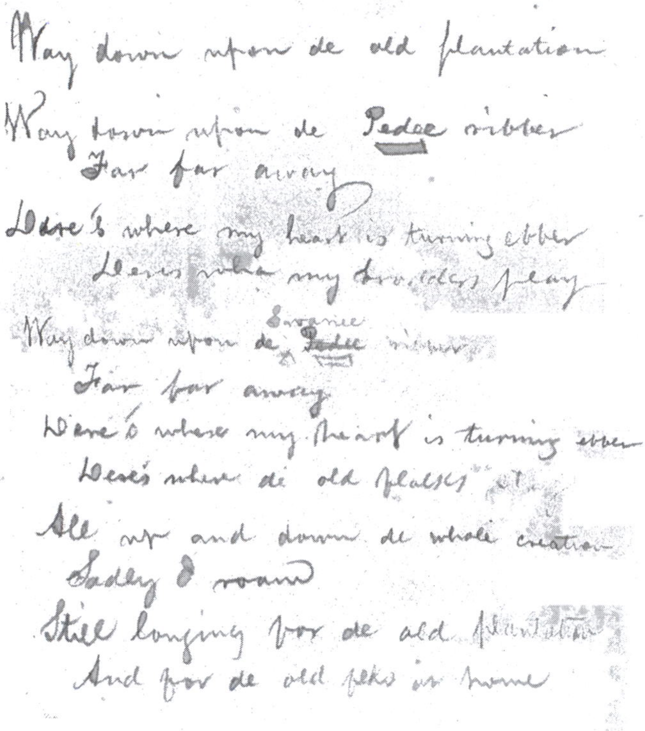

Way down upon de old plantation
Way down upon de Pedee ribber
Far far away
Dere's where my heart is turning ebber
Dere is wha my brodders play
Way down upon de Swanee ribber
Far far away
Dere's where my heart is turning eber
Dere's where de old plafys—
All up and down de whole creation
Sadly I roam
Still longing for de old plantation
And for de old feks at home

Figure 11.2:
*Stephen Foster,
early draft of lyrics
for* Old Folks at
Home, *1851*

I find that by my efforts I have done a great deal to build up taste for the Ethiopian song among refined people by making the words suitable to their taste, instead of the trashy and really offensive words which belong to some songs of that order. Therefore I have concluded to pursue the Ethiopian business without fear or shame.

In the wake of Foster's achievements, popular song became a powerful vehicle of American cultural values and experiences. Nowhere was this clearer than during the Civil War, fought from 1861 to 1865 on American soil by armies made up of Americans. The country felt passionately about the issues surrounding the war, which included not only slavery, but states' rights, taxation, and strong socio-cultural differences between a rural, agrarian South and an increasingly industrialized, urban North.

Rallying songs began appearing early in the Civil War, and as the conflict raged on, important battles and heroes were celebrated in music. Sentiments included stirring ones like those reflected in the marching song *Battle Hymn of the Republic*, whose words were written by Julia Ward Howe in 1861 to the tune of a camp-meeting hymn from the 1850s:

Mine eyes have seen the glory of the coming of the Lord:
He is trampling out the vintage where the grapes of wrath are stored;

He hath loosed the fateful lightning of His terrible swift sword:
    His truth is marching on.
    Glory! Glory! Hallelujah! (*3 times*)
    His truth is marching on.

The hardships and ravages of war also inspired more sober songs that expressed nostalgic longing for better, calmer times. The chorus of *Tenting on the Old Camp Ground*, written late in 1862 by Walter Kittredge, is a plaintive call for peace:

    Many are the hearts that are weary tonight,
    Wishing for the war to cease,
    Many are the hearts looking for the right
    To see the dawn of peace.

During the later nineteenth century, popular song in America continued to reflect the nation's experiences and aspirations. Many songs captured the westward expansion, none more famously than the song that came to be known as *Home on the Range*, whose lyrics were written in the early 1870s by Brewster M. Higley and set to music by Daniel E. Kelly. Higley's title for the song was *My Western Home*, and in fact the word "range" does not appear in his original version, where the chorus goes:

    A home! A home!
    Where the Deer and the Antelope play,
    Where seldom is heard a discouraging word,
    And the sky is not clouded all day.

The West depicted in this song, like the South in so many "plantation" songs, is an idealized world, showing little struggle or deprivation. Such lyrics romanticize the West or the South as places to escape from the ever more crowded, industrialized cities of the North. It is remarkable that the song manages to turn the wide-open spaces of the prairie into the idea of "home," normally something much smaller-scale and intimate. The fact that the song is a lilting waltz domesticates it still further, and associates it with the Anglo-European traditions from which it sprang.

AMERICA AT THE OPERA

Like most classical music in the United States, opera was mainly an import. In the first half of the nineteenth century, English operas, and the occasional French and Italian one, prevailed in New York, Boston, and Philadelphia.

One advocate for Italian opera was none other than Mozart's former librettist, Lorenzo Da Ponte (1749–1838), who came to the United States in 1805. In 1829, Da Ponte, already 80 years old, brought an Italian opera company on tour to New York and Philadelphia. He then worked to help raise funds for the first building in the nation designed exclusively for opera, the Italian Opera House in New York, which opened in 1833 and presented two seasons before debt forced it to close.

It took time for opera to catch on in America in part because the social and institutional structure was different from Europe. Opera in the United States was not supported by the state or by aristocracy; all funds had to be raised from private donors or ticket sales. At least in its early phase, before about 1850, opera was relatively egalitarian, and ticket prices were modest. American audiences were less clearly separated by class than in Europe, in part because material wealth was spread more widely (if not evenly) throughout the society. Audiences in the theater and at opera in America were thus, in the words of one contemporary observer, "a strange medley of manners and deportment," displaying no "conformity of dress, behavior, or appearance." Opera also pointed up important gender distinctions in American society. Although it was men who wrote, produced, and staged operas, women were the principal consumers; they made up most of the audiences. Many middle-class American males—unlike their noble or wealthy bourgeois counterparts in Europe—felt that art, especially an emotional, extroverted art like opera, was the domain of women. Men were supposed to take care of business and politics.

But women were also, of course, stars on the operatic stage. For much of the century, "opera" in the United States meant the tours of famous singers. The cult of the virtuoso performer, which Gottschalk exploited so successfully (and which we examined in Chapter 3), also embraced divas—goddesses of the operatic stage—including Jenny Lind (1820–1887). Dubbed the "Swedish Nightingale," Lind launched a successful operatic career in Europe in the late 1840s. She arrived in New York on September 1, 1850, on a tour masterminded by the impresario P. T. Barnum, better known today for his circuses. Over nine months and 95 concerts, Lind's journey became one of the most famous cultural events in nineteenth-century American history (Fig. 11.3). The clever Barnum stirred up excitement by having a public auction for the first ticket for each concert. In Philadelphia and Boston, these went for $625, a sum which, adjusted for inflation, would be over $16,000 today!

Lind never performed in an actual opera in the United States, but her tour, and those of several divas who followed her, helped spark a new passion for staged operas, including the desire for theaters dedicated specifically to opera. At midcentury wealthy citizens of the major cities on the East Coast planned opera houses of enormous size and splendor. In New York, the 1,800-seat Astor Place Opera House opened in 1847. By now opera was a much less egalitarian

Figure 11.3: *Jenny Lind giving a concert at Castle Garden in New York City, 1851*

effort than earlier in the century. Astor Place was run by a group of 50 wealthy shareholders, who also claimed the prime seats. The elitism of the house offended many New Yorkers, as did the apparent domination by non-American-born singers and actors. A kind of xenophobia is apparent in the comment of a New York reporter from 1844: "The opera—the ballet—the acted drama—are all abominations maintained by foreigners, and imported into this country by 'foreigners.'" Only a year and a half after its opening, Astor Place was the site of a deadly riot stirred up by such isolationist sentiments; 22 people were killed.

Despite the financial and cultural challenges, opera continued to thrive in New York. In 1854, the New York Academy of Music opened as the largest opera house in the world, with 4,500 seats. As at Astor Place, newer Italian and French operas were featured, in particular the recent works of Verdi, *La traviata* and *Rigoletto*, and a work that became the most popular opera in America for the last part of the century, Gounod's *Faust*. The next big step for opera in New York came in 1883 with the creation of the Metropolitan Opera, which is still the most prestigious opera company in the nation.

One of the biggest opera fans in midcentury New York was the poet Walt Whitman (1819–1892), who wrote about opera for the *Brooklyn Daily Eagle*. His passion for the genre is evident in his most famous work, *Leaves of Grass* (1855), where some poems powerfully evoke scenes and characters from the works he saw on the stage, including Bellini's *Norma*, Donizetti's *Lucia di Lammermoor*, and Verdi's *Ernani*:

> Across the stage with pallor on her face, yet lurid passion,
> Stalks Norma brandishing the dagger in her hand.
> I see poor crazed Lucia's eyes' unnatural gleam,
> Her hair down her back falls loose and dishevel'd.
> I see where Ernani walking the bridal garden,
> Amid the scent of night-roses, radiant, holding his bride by the hand,
> Hears the infernal call, the death-pledge of the horn.
> To crossing swords and gray hairs bared to heaven,
> The clear electric base and baritone of the world,
> The trombone duo, Libertad forever!

It has been suggested that the structure of some of Whitman's poems and their use of a kind of "melodic" repetition was based on the arias of Italian opera.

CLASSICAL MUSIC IN THE CITIES

Classical instrumental music grew alongside opera in the United States, supported by wealthy citizens with more leisure time and disposable income than earlier in the century. Some Americans were more favorably disposed to instrumental and choral music than to opera. Nowhere was this more apparent than in Boston, a city founded by Puritans. Many New Englanders had at least a suspicion of, if not a distaste for, opera, which they deemed too sensuous and superficial. As we saw earlier, for much of the Federal period sacred choral singing was considered the most appropriate communal activity in New England.

In the 1830s and 1840s, Boston's leading music writer, John Sullivan Dwight (1813–1893), became a champion of classical instrumental music, especially the symphonies of Beethoven. Dwight, a graduate of the Harvard Divinity School and an ordained minister, admired Beethoven's music less for its ability to entertain than for its uplifting and inspiring qualities (much like the goal of German *Bildung* that we discussed in Chapter 3). Dwight was also an important figure in the early American Transcendentalist movement that included Ralph Waldo Emerson and Henry David Thoreau. In line with that mode of thought, Dwight saw Beethoven's symphonies as signaling the dawn of a new age of progress toward universal harmony as the resolution of human conflict. The Ninth Symphony was for Dwight "the music of the high hour of Human Brotherhood; the triumph of the grand unitary sentiment, into which all the passions and interests of all human hearts are destined finally to blend."

Dwight's views helped elevate instrumental music to a new status, which in turn spawned the creation of institutions to support it. The Boston Academy of Music, originally founded in 1833 to promote singing, soon began to give orchestra concerts, including the local premiere of Beethoven's First Symphony in 1841. The repertory of these concerts was almost exclusively German. For Dwight and like-minded thinkers, German music was authentic, natural, and organic; Italian music was less imaginative, more formulaic. "In Germany, songs grow," Dwight wrote. "Italian opera airs are full of melody and sweetness, but one is too much like another."

In 1842 the first permanent, fully professional orchestra in the United States was founded. The New York Philharmonic Society, whose aim was announced as "the advancement of instrumental music," is still in existence today. The first concert, given on December 7, 1842, began with Beethoven's Fifth Symphony. An anonymous reviewer recognized the significance of this event: "We must undoubtedly reckon Wednesday evening last, as the commencement of a New Musical era, in this western world. The concert which was then given . . . was the first of an attempt to form an approved school of instrumental music in this country."

The sense of mission and of the raising of standards and tastes that comes from all these activities in Boston and New York—as well as the sense of New World entrepreneurship needed to make it all happen—was nowhere better embodied than in the man who would become the nation's leading conductor in the later nineteenth century, Theodore Thomas (1835–1905). Thomas's family had come to New York from Germany in 1845, as part of the wave of immigration we discussed in Chapter 7. In 1854 he joined the first violin section of the New York Philharmonic Society. He soon began conducting, as well as organizing concerts from both musical and business sides. In 1865 he founded the Theodore Thomas Orchestra, which toured throughout the United States and Canada on what came to be called the "Thomas Highway," stretching from Montreal and Maine, to Georgia, New Orleans, and San Francisco. These profitable tours sustained the orchestra and allowed Thomas to spread the gospel of classical instrumental music throughout North America, to people in all walks of life. One audience member at a Thomas concert in Mississippi in 1877 recalled that "life was never the same afterward." The experience had shown him that "there really existed as a fact, and not as something heard of and unattainable, this world of beauty, wholly apart from everyday experiences."

In 1877 Thomas became music director of the New York Philharmonic Society, a position he held, together with that as conductor of his own Thomas Orchestra, until 1891. In that year he was invited to Chicago to become the inaugural music director of the Chicago Symphony Orchestra, which was to be the first American orchestra to offer its musicians full-time employment for a season that included 28 weeks in residence and 8 on tour. Thomas had almost complete authority over all aspects of the organization. His contract read: "The Musical Director is to determine the character and standard of all performances . . . make all programmes, select all soloists." Such an arrangement was Thomas's dream, and he left New York for Chicago, where he remained until the end of his life.

In the meantime, Boston's musical life continued to thrive and develop. The Boston Symphony Orchestra, one of the nation's most prestigious ensembles, was founded in 1881. Its first conductor was the German-born George Henschel (1850–1934). Boston also became at this time the locus of the first real "school" of American musical composition—a cluster of like-minded composers writing mainly instrumental music for the concert hall. Sometimes referred to as the Boston Classicists or Second New England School, this group included John Knowles Paine (1839–1906), Horatio Parker (1863–1919), Arthur Foote (1853–1937), George Chadwick (1854–1931), and the sole woman, Amy Marcy Cheney Beach (1867–1944; Fig. 11.4). Several held or assumed academic positions. Paine was the first professor of music at Harvard, Parker at Yale, and Chadwick taught at the New England Conservatory. They tended to come from and move in the same social circles of upper-crust Boston.

Though they were mostly trained in the Germanic instrumental tradition of symphonic and chamber music—and many had studied in Europe—these composers were concerned with creating an American music with an identity different from European models. One figure who entered this discussion vigorously

Figure 11.4: *Amy Marcy Cheney Beach, prominent American composer and pianist in Boston and New York*

was the Bohemian Antonín Dvořák, whom we discussed in Chapter 7. Regarded as the leading composer of the Czech nationalist movement, Dvořák lived in New York from 1892 to 1895 as head of the National Conservatory of Music. He urged his American colleagues to base a genuinely national music on the music of Native Americans and African Americans, especially the latter. "I am now satisfied that the future music of this country must be founded on what are called negro melodies," Dvořák declared in a newspaper interview of May 1893. "There is nothing in the whole range of composition that cannot be supplied with themes from this source." As a demonstration of what he had in mind, Dvořák composed his Ninth Symphony, entitled *From the New World*, whose melodies evoke the musical language of African Americans. The second theme from the first movement, based on a pentatonic scale, is similar to the famous spiritual *Swing Low, Sweet Chariot* (Ex. 11.4). Both move down to the sixth and fifth degrees of the scale (E, D), then rise through a tonic arpeggio to the high D.

Example 11.4: *Comparison of Dvořák, Symphony No. 9* (From the New World*), theme from movement 1, mm. 157–164, and* Swing Low, Sweet Chariot

Dvořák's suggestions met with mixed reactions. The prominent Boston critic Philip Hale observed, "The great majority of Americans are neither negro nor Indian, nor are they descendents of negroes or Indians. How then can folk songs attributed to the negro or Indians be distinctively, peculiarly American?" Hale was being obtusely literal, but others defended a similar position more fully. Beach agreed with Dvořák that vernacular music could reinvigorate art music. But, along the lines of Hale, she argued that American composers should rather base their music on their own heritage: "We of the North should be far more likely to be influenced by the old English, Scotch, or Irish songs, inherited with our literature from our ancestors." In 1894–96, as a counterexample to Dvořák's *New World* Symphony, Beach composed her *Gaelic* Symphony, which through the use of Irish folk melodies was to depict the sufferings and struggles of the Irish people, "their laments . . . their romance, and their dreams."

Beach is worth further consideration here because she emerged as the first major female composer of large-scale concert music in the United States, and she did so despite the obstacles faced by musicians of her gender. Born into a prominent New England family, she was trained as a pianist and composer in

Boston and began a promising concert career. In 1885 she married Dr. Henry Beach, a physician 24 years her senior. Henry Beach was typical of middle-class men who felt women should not be actively involved in the "business" of music, sentiments similar to those expressed by Felix Mendelssohn and his father about Fanny Mendelssohn Hensel, as discussed in Chapter 5. He urged his wife to limit her public performances to one a year, with the proceeds donated to charity. In some ways this proved a fortunate arrangement, because it allowed her to concentrate on composition. Yet even in this area her path to acceptance was not smooth. In the patronizing rhetoric endured by so many female professionals of the era, Amy Beach was welcomed by Chadwick in the New England School as "one of the boys." After her husband's death in 1910, she resumed an active international career as pianist and composer.

Beach's music shows a complete command of traditional forms and contemporary harmonic idioms. Her A-Minor Violin Sonata from 1896 can more than hold its own among the great works of nineteenth-century chamber music, including those of Brahms, which it evokes without ever being imitative. The scherzo of Beach's sonata brings together contrapuntal intricacy, rhythmic energy, and harmonic sophistication in ways that are compelling and original (Ex. 11.5; see Anthology 20). Nowhere does American music of the late nineteenth century better reimagine the Germanic tradition.

Example 11.5: *Beach, Violin Sonata in A Minor, Op. 34, movement 2, mm. 1–6*

In conclusion we return to the question of American musical identity at the close of the nineteenth century. Relevant in this context are the thoughts and experiences of one prominent American composer, Edward MacDowell (1860–1908), a remote member of the New England School who was born and worked mainly in New York. Already in 1891—before Dvořák set foot on American soil and issued his dictum to composers—MacDowell had become interested in Native American themes that had been transcribed in a publication of 1882. On these he based his *Indian Suite* for orchestra, which had its premiere in 1896.

Yet MacDowell was ambivalent about whether such a work was distinctly or meaningfully American. "I do not believe in 'lifting' a Navajo theme and furbishing it into some kind of musical composition," he wrote to a friend. "That is not American music." MacDowell frequently said he did not want to be considered an "American" composer. He claimed that "there is no such thing as American music" and refused to have his works performed on all-American programs. MacDowell's ambivalence is clear. He was trained in Germany and by no means sought to reject that musical heritage. At the same time he felt that achieving national identity required more than simply adapting indigenous musical materials.

Perhaps the aspirations, challenges, and contradictions of creating an American music at the dawn of the twentieth century are best articulated by Arthur Farwell (1872–1952), a key figure in the "Indianist" movement that sought to combine Native American and Western European elements in music. In 1903 Farwell wrote:

> The promise of our national musical art lies in that work of our composers which is sufficiently un-german; that is, in which the German idiom is not the dominant factor. It will cost American culture many pangs to learn this simple fact. The German masterpieces are unapproachable, especially from another land and race. All that we do toward imitating them must necessarily be weak and apologetic, bringing honor neither to the German tradition nor to American music. It is only by exalting the common inspirations of American life that we can become great musically.

Farwell defines the task of the American composer as resisting the Germanic musical hegemony of Bach and Beethoven. As we have seen in this chapter, not everyone shared his view. But as we have also seen, American composers did share Farwell's goal of "exalting the common inspirations of American life," which they pursued in many compelling ways.

FOR FURTHER READING

Block, Adrienne Fried, *Amy Beach, Passionate Victorian: The Life and Work of an American Composer* (Oxford and New York: Oxford University Press, 1998)

Crawford, Richard, *America's Musical Life* (New York: W. W. Norton & Company, 2001)

Dizikes, John, *Opera in America: A Cultural History* (New Haven and London: Yale University Press, 1993)

Dvořák in America, 1892–1895, ed. John C. Tibbets (Portland, OR: Amadeus Press, 1993)

Gottschalk, Louis Moreau, *Notes of a Pianist*, ed. Jeanne Behrend (New York: Knopf, 1964)

Hamm, Charles, *Music in the New World* (New York: W. W. Norton & Company, 1983)

Horowitz, Joseph, *Classical Music in America: A History of Its Rise and Fall* (New York: W. W. Norton & Company, 2005)

Ⓢ Additional resources available at wwnorton.com/studyspace

CHAPTER TWELVE

The Fin de Siècle and the Emergence of Modernism

In Chapter 7 we discussed ways in which the second half of the nineteenth century moved "beyond Romanticism." Some of the "isms" we identified, including materialism and realism, can be interpreted as feeding into a larger "ism" that emerged in the last 15 years of the century: Modernism. Like Romanticism, Modernism was not a single movement but a broad aesthetic and worldview shared by many creative artists, in this case those working in the years around 1900—the period often identified by the French term *fin de siècle*, or end of century.

In 1859 the French poet Charles Baudelaire wrote of "modern" as reflecting "the transient, the fleeting, the contingent," thus a kind of impermanence and fragmentation. He associated these qualities with life and culture in large cities, which grew ever more populous in the later nineteenth century. But, like the idea of Romanticism for the earliest writers on that phenomenon (see Chapter 2), for Baudelaire the concept of the modern was not limited to a specific historical period; it could be present in any time. This view reflects the original meaning of the word: "modern" comes from the Latin *modo*, meaning "just now." Indeed, for many centuries, "modern" had been part of a binary opposition setting the present against the past. This juxtaposition was very much a part of the culture of the later nineteenth century; we recall from Chapter 10 how concert organizations in Paris in the 1870s and 1880s presented programs of old and new music.

Modernism is often described as a quest for the new, or a rejection of the past. But as Joseph Auner points out in his volume in this series, *Music in the Twentieth and Twenty-first Centuries*, Modernism just as often captured "a sense of possibility," a desire on the part of artists to explore different paths of expression and technique that might lead forward, sideways, or even backwards. Auner discusses these dimensions of Modernism in the careers of composers who lived primarily in the twentieth century. In the present chapter, after exploring the broader cultural and intellectual context of the fin de siècle, we will discuss composers born around 1860 who came to maturity in the waning years of the nineteenth century. They include important figures of early Modernism, some already touched on in Chapter 7: Richard Strauss and Gustav Mahler in the Austro-German realm, Giacomo Puccini in Italy, and Claude Debussy in France. Each built upon native musical traditions but also explored a range of "possibilities" that proved critical for twentieth-century music.

CONNECTIONS AND CONTRADICTIONS

The world in which Modernism emerged in the later nineteenth century was one of connections and contradictions. People were brought into more immediate contact than ever before; at the same time, extreme disparities in intellectual, cultural, and economic status led to an increasing sense of depersonalization and alienation. The world was becoming global. The planet had been almost entirely mapped, if not fully visited, and large parts of it were connected by technology. Some connections were of the kind we would today call virtual, thanks to the telegraph and then the telephone, and some were physical, thanks especially to railways and steamships. By the 1880s telegraph cables had been laid across the oceans, from Europe to North America, India, and Australia, allowing rapid communication of information around the globe. The effects on commerce, industry, and politics were incalculable. At the same historical moment, almost three million train cars were rolling across the earth, carrying cargo and some two billion passengers per year. Other inventions of the later nineteenth century, like the phonograph, the light bulb, and the automobile, also served to facilitate connection and communication. The world was rapidly shrinking.

These advances had a great impact on musical culture. As we saw in Chapter 7, the science of acoustics progressed rapidly in the nineteenth century, especially through the work of Hermann von Helmholtz. Musical instruments also became sturdier, more powerful, and able to project into bigger spaces. Sophisticated stage engineering allowed for more complicated theatrical effects. Wealth generated by industry and commerce created more robust patronage of the arts. All these factors led to the construction of larger public performance spaces across the globe in the later nineteenth and early twentieth centuries. The Palais

Example 12.1: *Elgar,* Imperial March, *Op. 32, mm. 1–5*

Garnier, home of the Paris Opéra, opened in 1875, seating 2,200 people. Carnegie Hall, seating 2,800, opened in New York in 1891. The Teatro Colón, which held 2,500 spectators, opened in Buenos Aires in 1908. These and other halls served quite literally as agents of connection, bringing large numbers of people together for common artistic experiences.

But because these kinds of progress were available to relatively few people around the world, they also contributed to enormous inequities. Of the two billion train passengers mentioned above, over 90 percent were within northern Europe and North America. Not only did many people in the underdeveloped areas of Africa, Asia, the Middle East, and South America derive little benefit from technology; that very progress made possible more efficient and even brutal colonization than ever before.

These contradictions were stark within the larger cities of Europe, which continued to increase in size and density. In 1800, only 17 cities in Europe had more than 100,000 people, with a total urban population under 5 million. By 1890 there were 103 such cities, and the urban numbers had swelled to about 30 million. In Paris, Berlin, and New York, the newly wealthy built luxurious residences; they enjoyed music at new or rebuilt opera houses and concert halls. By contrast, factory workers and other laborers lived in squalid tenements, barely eking out a living; they had little time or money to enjoy the arts.

Creative artists were inspired by both sides of the social, political, and economic divide. Some celebrated the power of their nations, as in the *Imperial March,* Op. 32, written in 1896 by Edward Elgar (1857–1934) for the Diamond Jubilee of Queen Victoria. Its grand tunes and majestic rhythms project the prestige of the British Empire (Ex. 12.1). A very different picture is captured in a poem from 1886 by the Berlin writer Arno Holz, who focused in graphic detail on the plight of the urban poor:

Five worm-eaten steps lead up
to the top floor of a workers' tenement;
the north wind likes to linger here,
and the stars of heaven shine through the roofing.

What they catch sight of, oh, it is plenty enough
to make us weep sympathetically at the misery:
a small crust of black bread and a pitcher of water,
a worktable and a stool with three legs.

The window is nailed shut with a board,
and yet the wind whistles through now and again,
and on that bed stuffed with straw
lies a young woman sick with fever.
Three small children are standing around her . . .

Figure 12.1: *Käthe Kollwitz,* Misery, *1895–96, showing living conditions of the urban poor in turn-of-the-century Berlin*

The German artist Käthe Kollwitz, a contemporary of Holz, depicted precisely such scenes in some of her paintings and engravings, such as the powerful *Misery* of 1895–96 (Fig. 12.1), where a distraught mother hovers over a sick child in what appears to be a tenement apartment.

STRAUSS, MAHLER, AND THE MODERN WORLD

Works such as Holz's poem and Kollwitz's *Misery* suggest how artists of the later nineteenth century sought to engage with the harsh realities of the modern world. In the Austro-German sphere, a new generation of composers found relevance in the issues that had been discussed heatedly around 1850 by Hanslick, Wagner, Liszt, and others concerning what music—often deemed remote from the world—was able and even obligated to express. The most prominent were Gustav Mahler and Richard Strauss, whom we examined briefly in Chapter 7 for ways in which they sought to make music more realistic.

Strauss and Mahler were successful at negotiating the gap between an interior artistic world and the increasingly urban and commercial bourgeois world. Both maintained essentially full-time careers as conductors, taking advantage of rapid transportation to travel widely among European cities—and even to the United States and (in Strauss's case) Egypt. Strauss held important positions successively in the opera houses of Munich, Weimar, Berlin, and Vienna. Mahler worked in Kassel, Prague, Budapest, Hamburg, Vienna, and finally New York, at both the Metropolitan Opera and the New York Philharmonic. For Strauss and Mahler, composing was often a summertime activity. Strauss retreated to rural parts of his native Bavaria. Mahler spent his summers working in composing huts situated in bucolic lakeside or mountain areas of Austria (Fig. 12.2).

Both Strauss and Mahler were strongly shaped by German intellectual traditions of the nineteenth century. In their student years—in Munich and

Figure 12.2: *Gustav Mahler's summer composing hut in Steinbach, Austria, where he wrote his Second and Third Symphonies*

Vienna, respectively—each was part of groups that actively discussed the writings of Schopenhauer and Nietzsche. Both composers (Strauss in the early part of his career) focused their attention on orchestral music, which they saw as the prime medium for embodying philosophical or aesthetic concepts like striving and transcendence. They sought to update symphonic genres in the aftermath of Liszt and Wagner.

Yet Strauss and Mahler were different in temperament and outlook. Strauss had a sunnier, more confident disposition, and success came to him more easily. Mahler was a more tortured artist, struggling to create and promote his compositions. A friend of both men during the last decade of the nineteenth century captured the contrast: "Richard Strauss, the productive artist deliberately pursuing his goal and keeping his feet firm on the ground however high he aspired—Gustav Mahler, consumed by his artistic intensity, struggling restlessly towards the loftiest goals." Both composers sought to forge a new musical language that could nonetheless build upon the Wagnerian legacy. Mahler described his relationship to Strauss with an image from Schopenhauer of two miners who dig tunnels from opposite sides of the mountain and eventually meet.

RICHARD STRAUSS AND THE TONE POEM

Strauss is characteristic of his generation in that he began as a composer who moved beyond Romanticism, in ways outlined in Chapter 7, and into Modernism. His early years were dominated by what he called *Brahms-schwärmerei* (literally "Brahms ecstasy"), an overwhelming enthusiasm for the music of Brahms. When serving as assistant to the conductor Hans von Bülow at Meiningen in the mid-1880s, Strauss helped prepare the premiere of Brahms's Fourth Symphony, which he praised as "beyond all question a gigantic work, with a grandeur in its conception and invention, genius in its treatment of forms, periodic structure, of outstanding vigor and strength, new and original."

At the same time Strauss was eager to explore new musical possibilities. From Bülow he learned the importance of curiosity and openness to many styles. Strauss was also exposed to the eccentric Alexander Ritter, a composer and violinist who played in the Meiningen Orchestra. Ritter, married to Wagner's niece, was devoted to the music and ideas of the Bayreuth master and of the New German School, and above all to the concept that music must serve a higher purpose.

Strauss began to write one-movement orchestral works on the model of Liszt's symphonic poems. In 1888–89 Strauss composed three 20-minute pieces he called "tone poems": *Macbeth, Don Juan,* and *Tod und Verklärung* (Death and Transfiguration), based on, respectively, a literary work, a character, and a progression of ideas. They call for an expanded and colorful orchestra, with large brass and percussion sections. During the 1890s and into the first decades of the twentieth century, Strauss went on to compose six more tone poems, of increasing length.

Strauss explained his turn to the genre of the tone poem—and away from the Brahms symphonic tradition—by saying he found the conventional instrumental forms to be exhausted and inadequate to express "musical-poetic" ideas:

> I have found myself in a gradually ever-increasing contradiction between the musical-poetic content that I want to convey and the ternary sonata form that has come down to us from the classical composers. . . . I consider it a legitimate artistic method to create a correspondingly new form for every new subject, to shape which neatly and perfectly is a very difficult task, but for that very reason the more attractive.

Strauss's claim of creating a "new form" is somewhat misleading in that his tone poems make use of standard forms like sonata, rondo, and variation. However, in a way characteristic of early Modernism, these formal principles are often played off against each other in a single work.

Don Juan unfolds in a structural process that involves both sonata and rondo elements. The first portion clearly resembles a sonata-form exposition: a vigorous first theme group in the tonic (E major), representing the main character, is followed by a modulation to a more lyrical second theme in the dominant (B major), depicting one of his female conquests (Ex. 12.2). As in many sonata forms, the second key area is prepared by a long secondary dominant F♯. Especially characteristic of Strauss are the athletic melodies, fluid rhythms, and wide-ranging harmonic progressions. In the space of only seven measures the initial theme (12.2a) rockets up past three octaves, then tumbles back down. The theme also stuns us with its harmonic bravado, beginning on a C-major chord, then lurching to B major, which in turn becomes the dominant of the tonic E major, reached in measure 3. For the broadly lyrical second theme (12.2b), Strauss manages to create the feel of a lilting waltz within the $\frac{4}{4}$ meter by using triplet rhythms. With the return of the main theme and a new lyrical episode in G major (representing another of the Don's female conquests), *Don Juan* seems to shift into a more rondo-like form. The structural perspective shifts again in a more developmental passage, a modified sonata-like recapitulation, and a long, dark coda that ends in E minor.

Strauss's *Don Juan* is based on a version of the famous legend related as a series of dramatic scenes in verse form by the German Romantic writer Nikolaus Lenau (1802–1850). Lenau's Don Juan is a more contemplative and ironic figure than the self-assured protagonist of the Mozart–Da Ponte opera *Don Giovanni*. At the end, admitting "boredom" with his life of sexual excess and with dueling, Lenau's Don allows himself to be run through by his opponent's sword. As a preface to his score of *Don Juan*, Strauss excerpted 32 lines of Lenau's work, concluding with a passage in which the Don admits his flame is literally "burnt out." He has become

Example 12.2: *Strauss,* Don Juan, *Op. 20*

an antihero, a Schopenhauerian, post-Wagnerian Don Juan, who abandons all striving for fulfillment and resigns himself to death. The play of formal processes in Strauss's *Don Juan* reflects these aspects of Lenau's poem. The rondo-like, potentially open-ended pursuit of different women is ultimately unsatisfactory (and, of course, exploitative); at the same time, any sonata-like sense of resolution or confirmation (moving toward the first theme and E major) is implausible. Thus, in the end, both structures are abandoned in the long, somber coda.

Strauss's tone poems of the 1890s show a wide range of expression characteristic of post-Romanticism and early Modernism. *Death and Transfiguration* depicts the death of an artist, who sees his life pass before him and whose soul is finally "transfigured" or released. Such narratives of redemption or transfiguration are common in the music of the later nineteenth and early twentieth centuries, from Wagner's *Tristan und Isolde* (1859, see Chapter 8), which ends with Isolde's transfiguration and death; to Arnold Schoenberg's string sextet *Verklärte Nacht* (Transfigured Night, 1899), a programmatic work about two lovers; to Mahler's colossal Eighth Symphony (1906), which ends with Faust's soul transfigured in heaven.

Also sprach Zarathustra (Thus Spake Zarathustra, 1896), written, in Strauss's words, "freely after Nietzsche," begins in a triumphant, transfigured realm, with the bold theme made famous in Stanley Kubrick's film *2001: A Space Odyssey* (1968). But it ends in a cloud of doubt with one of the most adventurous harmonic effects of the early Modern period: an unresolved juxtaposition of two keys a half step apart, B major and C major. In *Don Quixote* (1898), Strauss ingeniously combines the genres of theme and variations and solo concerto to depict characters and episodes in the life of Cervantes's famous character. Don Quixote is represented by the solo cello, and his sidekick Sancho Panza by the solo viola and tenor tuba. This work reflects Modernist realism (as discussed in Chapter 7) in the use of a wind machine (variation 7) and in representing the bleating of sheep by flutter-tonguing techniques in the brass instruments (variation 2).

Shortly after the turn of the century Strauss turned his attention from tone poems to the musical stage. The year 1905 saw the premiere of his one-act opera *Salome*, adapted from a play by Oscar Wilde about the biblical princess of Judea who demands the head of John the Baptist and then proceeds to make love to it onstage. With *Salome* Strauss deliberately scandalized his audience. The opera, which nonetheless became an enormous artistic and financial success, marks a new phase in Modernist music in which the relationship between the composer and his bourgeois public often became more confrontational. The first two decades of the twentieth century saw several concerts of new music at which riots or disturbances broke out, an occurrence that was far less common in the nineteenth century.

GUSTAV MAHLER: SYMPHONY AND ORCHESTRAL SONG

Although it may have seemed that Mahler and Strauss were tunneling to Modernism from the opposite sides of the mountain, they had a similar starting point: Brahms. Mahler received his musical education closer to the epicenter of the Brahms world, at the Vienna Conservatory, under that composer's close associates, including Robert Fuchs. An early Piano Quartet from 1876–78 demonstrates Mahler's obvious "Brahms ecstasy." Mahler also became interested in the music of Liszt and Wagner, and he attended university lectures by Brahms's rival Anton Bruckner, whose expansive symphonic style (as discussed in Chapter 10) would exert an influence. But Mahler reached back well past the contemporary era. His distinctive compositional voice and worldview were shaped significantly by the symphonic tradition of Beethoven and the imaginative world of early German Romanticism, especially an anthology of folk poetry called *Des Knaben Wunderhorn* (The Youth's Magic Horn, 1805–8).

Where Strauss found the traditional symphony a dead end, Mahler struggled to create within it an entire world of content and expression. In the massive length and complex design of his works, he went well beyond the conventions of the "great" symphony as discussed in Chapter 10. Between 1888 and 1909 Mahler completed nine numbered symphonies, five of which include solo or choral singing. At the same time a genre explored by few earlier composers, the orchestrally accompanied song, became an integral part of his symphonic universe. Mahler's first four symphonies were composed during the last dozen years of the nineteenth century: Symphony No. 1 (1888–89), No. 2 (1888–94), No. 3 (1893–96), and No. 4 (1899–1900). Like Strauss, Mahler strove in these works for an ideal expressive relationship between music and its poetic or programmatic content.

Mahler's struggle with the title and designation of his First Symphony is symptomatic of an evolution in his attitudes. At its premiere in Budapest in 1889, the work was called "a symphonic poem in two parts." Four years later it was performed as *Titan*, "a tone poem in the form of a symphony," and each movement was given a descriptive title. The finale was labeled "From the Inferno," and was said by Mahler to depict "the sudden outburst . . . of despair of a deeply wounded and broken heart." A decade later, in 1899, the full score was published simply as Symphony No. 1 in D Major. The pattern was similar with the next three symphonies, for which Mahler eventually discarded movement titles and explanations.

In 1896 the critic Max Marschalk asked the composer why he had suppressed the programmatic indications in the First Symphony. Mahler's reply is revealing. He said that after the work was complete, he had been persuaded by his friends to create a title and "some sort of program notes" to help them understand it. He was now omitting the notes not only because they were inadequate, but because "I have experienced the way the audiences have been set on the wrong track by them. Believe me, even Beethoven's symphonies have their inner programmes, and close acquaintance with such a work brings understanding of the development of feeling appropriate to the ideas. It will eventually be the same with my works." In other words, when Mahler's symphonies were better known, their "ideas" or "inner programs" would be clear without any verbal explanation.

Like Strauss, Mahler's starting point is often sonata, rondo, or variation forms, which are then expanded or transformed well beyond the traditions of the great symphony. The massive finale of Mahler's First, which lasts about 20 minutes, has segments that resemble a slow introduction, exposition, development, recapitulation, and coda. The exposition has two contrasting themes that stand in an expressive and harmonic relationship well within nineteenth-century norms (energetic, in F minor, versus lyrical, in D♭ major). But in an instance of what has been called progressive or directional tonality, the finale ends in D major, far removed from the F minor where it begins, yet bringing us back to the key of the first movement. D major does not make an appearance until halfway through the finale, with a new chorale-like melody related to the first movement. This chorale and the key of D then disappear, only to return in the final minutes.

This resolution is the result of processes largely independent of the conventions of sonata form. The D-major chorale is reached by what a prominent writer on Mahler, Paul Bekker, called a "breakthrough" (*Durchbruch*); it seems to arrive from some place outside the symphony, as if coming to rescue the work and bring about its conclusion. Beethoven was the first to create such "breakthrough" moments, especially in his Ninth Symphony. Bruckner and Strauss also employ the technique. But nowhere is it as powerful and effective as in Mahler's symphonies.

Mahler's first four symphonies are sometimes called the "Wunderhorn" symphonies because each has movements that include or are based on his own earlier settings of poetry from *Des Knaben Wunderhorn* or similar sources. (We saw in Chapter 3 how Franz Schubert made a similar connection between song and instrumental music.) In addition to about 25 different settings of *Wunderhorn* texts, Mahler also created several orchestral song cycles or groups of songs. These include the *Lieder eines fahrenden Gesellen* (Songs of a Wayfarer), composed for piano and voice in 1883–85 and orchestrated in the following decade, set to poems written by Mahler in the folk style of the *Wunderhorn* texts; and two cycles (1901–4) set to the texts of an early Romantic poet who was a special favorite of Mahler, Friedrich Rückert. Mahler's last cycle of orchestral songs, *Das Lied von der Erde* (The Song of the Earth, 1908–9), was based on translations of Chinese poetry.

The *Wayfarer* songs are closely related to the First Symphony, where themes from two of the songs reappear prominently. The fourth of the songs, *Die zwei blauen Augen* (The two blue eyes), offers an excellent example of Mahler's unique fusion of symphonic and song style (see Anthology 21). Sent out into the world by the painful memory of the beautiful eyes of his beloved, who has married another man, the lonely poet finds rest and solace under a linden tree. The song is a small-scale example of the kind of progressive tonality heard in the finale of the First Symphony: it begins in E minor but moves to F major and concludes in F minor, a process that mirrors how the poet ends up physically and emotionally in a place different from his starting point.

Also characteristic of Mahler is the sense of bitter irony at the end of the song. The music turns first to F major at the mention of the linden tree (Ex. 12.3a), with a lyrical theme that reappears in the third movement of the First Symphony in the same key, where it is marked to be played "like a folk tune." We expect the song to remain in that key and mood. But in the last two measures, Mahler suddenly pulls the music back into the minor with a return of the grim marchlike theme from the opening (Ex. 12.3b). The poet's peace of mind has been fleeting and illusory. The sense of isolation is reinforced by the orchestration. Mahler calls for a large ensemble, of the same dimensions as Strauss's; but instead of rich, blended textures, he favors sparse sonorities that highlight individual instruments or small groups of similar tone color—a technique he was to richly develop throughout his symphonic writing.

Example 12.3: *Mahler,* Lieder eines fahrenden Gesellen, *No. 4,* Die zwei blauen Augen

(a) mm. 41–44

On the road stands a linden tree; there for the first time I found rest in sleep!

(b) mm. 66–67

Irony and a sense of removal from, or conflict with, the world were essential features of the Romantic imagination, as discussed in Chapter 2. The ways in which they are intensified in *Die zwei blauen Augen* shows vividly how Mahler moved beyond Romanticism, toward Modernism.

ITALIAN VERISMO IN OPERA

Italy, too, had a generation of composers who came to maturity in the last dozen years of the century. They transformed opera, that nation's most important musical genre, with the same balance of innovation and tradition that Strauss and Mahler had displayed in symphonic music. As in Austria and Germany, one force driving Italian Modernism was a desire for greater realism, which, as discussed in Chapter 7, offered a way of moving beyond Romanticism.

The term *verismo* (realism) has become closely associated with, and is often restricted to, a few Italian operas of the 1890s, especially *Cavalleria rusticana*

(Rustic Chivalry, 1890) by Pietro Mascagni (1863–1945) and *Pagliacci* (Clowns, 1892) by Ruggiero Leoncavallo (1857–1919). These two operas are both short, high-intensity music dramas about love, jealousy, revenge, and murder in small rural towns. The impulses underlying verismo reach back further into the nineteenth century. Like Zola and Flaubert in France (see Chapter 7), some Italian writers in the 1870s created stories that focused on lower social classes and on themes of crime, prostitution, deformity, and brutality in contemporary society. These *veristi* set themselves against the *idealisti* (idealists), who favored traditional plots often set in an historical or mythological past.

In opera, attempts at realism took a number of different forms well before the actual term verismo came to be used in that context. An important precedent was Bizet's *Carmen* (1875; see Chapter 9), with its earthy, highly sexual heroine and its emphasis on the local color of Spain. Verdi (also discussed in Chapter 9) was an even earlier pioneer of realism. *Rigoletto* (1851) used naturalistic declamation in place of lyrical melody to convey powerful emotional moments or conversations between characters. As we saw in Chapter 7, *La traviata* (1853) was based not on a grand historical plot, but on a play set in contemporary Paris about a high-class prostitute.

In his last two operas, *Otello* (1887) and *Falstaff* (1893), Verdi moves in a veristic direction not by his choice of subject matter—both operas are based on Shakespeare—but by breaking down the traditional number structures that had dominated Italian opera. Arias and duets abandon or greatly attenuate the two-part, slow-fast form we discussed in Chapter 4; the showy cabaletta disappears entirely. The vocal ornamentation characteristic of the bel canto style is all but eliminated.

Instead of long-breathed melodies Verdi often writes intense musical phrases that capture a dramatic idea or moment. Perhaps the most famous example is the "kiss" (*bacio*) theme in *Otello*, which appears in Act 1 at the climax of the love duet between Otello and Desdemona (Ex. 12.4). The theme is carried mainly by the orchestra; Otello and Desdemona sing only short fragments of it in a way that conveys the realism of halting conversation (or lovemaking). The kiss theme

Example 12.4: *Verdi,* Otello, *Act 1, scene 3*

A kiss ... Otello ... A kiss

is heard only once in the love duet, as the culmination rather than the main theme in any conventional sense. Nor is the kiss theme a leitmotif in the Wagnerian manner. It is not continuously repeated and transformed during the opera; it re- appears only in the final moments of the tragic last scene after Otello has killed Desdemona. Once again it is vocalized in a fragmentary manner, now by Otello alone. The kiss theme is a magnificent late example of the Verdian *parola scenica* we discussed in Chapter 9, a verbal-musical phrase that uniquely crystallizes a situation.

PIETRO MASCAGNI AND RUGGIERO LEONCAVALLO

Virtually at the same time as Verdi's last two operas, the much younger Mascag- ni and Leoncavallo, members of what was sometimes called the *Giovane Scuola* (Young School), explored realism less by breaking down traditional forms than by compressing dramatic situations into shorter frameworks. Both are in some ways more conservative musically than the elderly Verdi in that they employ the closed forms of recitative, aria, ensemble, and chorus. But these conventional elements are often fluidly incorporated in continuous scenes.

Cavalleria rusticana and Pagliacci each has a small cluster of five main charac- ters and lasts about 70 minutes. (Though never intended as a pair, they are often performed together in today's opera houses.) The libretto of Cavalleria is adapt- ed from a story by one of the leading *veristi*, the Sicilian writer Giovanni Verga. Verga claimed to be investigating "the science of the human heart"; his goal was to explore in depth the customs and mind-sets of his characters, yet maintain an impersonal authorial distance. *Cavalleria* is set in a Sicilian village on Easter morning. The young peasant Turiddu has abandoned his girlfriend Santuzza for a former lover, Lola, who is now married to a local cart-driver named Alfio. The jealous Santuzza tells Alfio of his wife's infidelity. Alfio challenges Turiddu to a duel; after asking his mother to look after Santuzza, Turiddu is killed in the fight. In the opera, the personal drama is set against the musical background of Mass being sung in the church.

Leoncavallo wrote his own libretto for *Pagliacci*, based on a crime report from a newspaper about a tale of jealousy and murder among a small troupe of actors. The verismo of *Pagliacci* consists in part of the actors stepping in and out of their "stage" roles, that is, their roles in the play-within-the-play. The opera begins with a striking Prologue in which the character Tonio comes in front of the curtain in his costume as Taddeo, telling the audience that "the author has tried to paint a picture of real life" and entreating them, "Above all, do not consider so much our poor flimsy costumes, but consider our hearts, because we are men of flesh and bone." In the final scene of the opera, the troupe is performing their play for an onstage audience. Canio, the male lead and jeal- ous lover, stabs his unfaithful real-life wife Nedda and announces to the audi- ence—both onstage and in the opera house—"La commedia è finita" (The play is over). Here is a late example of the kind of destruction of illusion, of breaking the dramatic or narrative frame, which we saw as characteristic of Romantic irony in Chapter 2.

GIACOMO PUCCINI

During the 1890s another member of the Young School, Giacomo Puccini (1858–1924), emerged as a major figure of the operatic scene in Italy. Among his generation Puccini forged the most effective synthesis of the older Verdian operatic tradition with the newer interest in realism. Puccini's three most influential operas were composed in the years around 1900: *La bohème* (1896), *Tosca* (1900), and *Madama Butterfly* (1904–7).

Like the novelists of naturalism, Puccini did careful research into the historical contexts of his plots. *Tosca* opens in the Roman church of Sant'Andrea della Valle in the year 1800, during the Napoleonic occupation of the Vatican States. Puccini insisted that the costumes match exactly what the choir and clergy wore in that church at that time. The medieval Te Deum chant that the choir sings at the end of Act 1 is the precise version of the melody that would have been in use at Sant'Andrea around 1800. A passage for bells at the beginning of Act 3, set in the Roman fortress Castel Sant'Angelo, re-creates the patterns and pitches of the morning bells of the churches in the neighborhood around the building—including the low E of St. Peter's Basilica. In *Tosca* the sadistic character Scarpia, who heads the secret police in Rome, is a figure worthy of the repressive Metternich era discussed in Chapter 3.

In preparation for writing *Madama Butterfly* (Opera Sampler), set in contemporary Japan, Puccini consulted the wife of the Japanese ambassador to Italy, researched Japanese music in a variety of printed and recorded sources, and attended performances of the Imperial Japanese Theatrical Company. He used at least seven Japanese melodies in the opera. Aspects of the stage design, especially the focus on the house of the title character and the ritual ceremonies that take place within it, also reflect a concern with being authentic. In these ways, Puccini and his collaborators went beyond the practices of most other exoticist or Orientalist composers of the later nineteenth century (as discussed in Chapter 9).

Puccini's *La bohème*, one of the most popular operas in the entire repertory, was adapted by the librettists Luigi Illica and Giuseppe Giacosa from a series of short stories in French, *Scènes de la vie de bohème* (Scenes from Bohemian Life), by Henry Murger. The realist lens is here turned on poor, hungry artists living in a Paris garret. Puccini and his librettists aim for a compactness and fluidity similar to Mascagni and Leoncavallo. The entire opera contains only an hour and 45 minutes of music, divided into four brief acts.

La bohème still relies on some closed numbers in the older Italian tradition, such as the love duet between Mimì and Rodolfo in Act 1. But elsewhere

Puccini responded to his librettists' use of short verses to mimic natural dialogue. Illica and Giacosa write in plain, everyday language to convey the spontaneity of certain moments, as when Marcello says in the first scene, "Ho un freddo cane" ("I'm damned cold"; the Italian slang means, literally, "I have a cold dog"). Puccini sets such passages in a flexible melodic style that is removed from both traditional recitative and aria.

Act 2 of *La bohème* achieves naturalism in a way that would become significant for the twentieth century—by simultaneously juxtaposing very different styles of music in a kind of collage. The act takes place on Christmas Eve at the Café Momus amid the hustle and bustle of a crowded street in the Latin Quarter of Paris. The stage is described by Puccini and his librettists as bringing together a cross-section of urban types: "a vast, diverse crowd: middle-class people, soldiers, maidservants, children, babies, students, dressmakers, gendarmes, etc. Outside their shops vendors are shouting at the top of their voices to attract customers" (Fig. 12.3). The opera's main characters, Rodolfo, Mimì, Colline, Schaunard, and Marcello, are part of the scene, as are Musetta, who is Marcello's former girlfriend, and Alcindoro, her current companion. In an act that is certainly one of the most compact of any opera of the nineteenth century, lasting under 20 minutes, Puccini creates a dizzying array of sights and sounds, including a marching band that comes onstage at the end. Act 2 of *La bohème* comes as close as one could, within the musical language of the nine-

Figure 12.3: *Puccini,* La bohème, *Act 2 street scene near the Café Momus, in Franco Zeffirelli's production at the Metropolitan Opera, New York. Photo by Cory Weaver/ Metropolitan Opera.*

teenth century, to creating a real-life polyphony of an urban street scene. Fifteen years later the Modernist Russian composer Igor Stravinsky (1882–1971) would go further in this direction when depicting a bustling street fair in the first scene of his ballet *Petrushka* (1911).

Example 12.5: *Puccini,* La bohème, *Act 2, Musetta's Waltz*

When I go alone on the street, people stop and stare . . .

Especially effective is Puccini's deployment of one of his most famous tunes, Musetta's Waltz, in which she celebrates her own beauty and tries to make Marcello jealous (Ex. 12.5; Anthology 22; Opera Sampler). Many opera lovers who hum this memorable theme and arrangers who have adapted it do not realize that it is just one component in a complex finale to the act (as with Verdi's *La donna è mobile* in *Rigoletto*, discussed in Chapter 9). Musetta's goal is to win back Marcello and dump Alcindoro. As she sings her number, other voices join in the counterpoint—

not only the other main characters, but people from the crowd. When all the vo-cal parts dissolve into short motives of confused chatter, the full orchestra plays Musetta's melody, as if stepping in to take over from the distracted characters. Finally the waltz and the drama of Musetta and her lovers are overtaken by the approach of the military band, and the act ends in a benign chaos controlled by Puccini's master hand.

COLOR AND SONORITY: CLAUDE DEBUSSY

If some creative artists in the latter part of the nineteenth century sought to practice, in Verga's words, the realistic "science of the human heart," it might be said that Claude Debussy (1862–1918), another member of the generation we have been discussing, explored the science of the human ear. We recall from Chap-ter 7 how Helmholtz and other researchers after midcentury sought to bridge a gap between the properties of sound and their aesthetic effects by investigat-ing the acoustic relationships between noise and musical tone, and consonance and dissonance. Debussy was no materialist or empiricist in that sense. But he became fascinated with the possibilities of liberating musical sonority from the conventions that had dominated Western art music for centuries.

It is no coincidence that Debussy's music was associated with two Modernist movements in the arts, also based in France: Symbolism and Impressionism. Symbolism, as we saw in Chapter 8, sought to dissolve any fixed relation be-tween an idea and the word or image used to represent it. The Impressionist painters, who included Claude Monet and Auguste Renoir, downplayed form and line—the traditional building blocks of painting—in favor of color and light (Fig. 12.4). Inspired by recent developments in optics and visual perception, the Impressionists sought to record the effect that light and color had upon the eye. In Impressionist canvases, objects or people are often refracted into individual spots of color and rendered in prominent brushstrokes, as in the canvas from which the Impressionist movement received its name, Monet's *Impression: Sunrise* of 1872. The viewer's eye must actively put these details to-gether to make a coherent image.

Debussy entered the Paris Conservatoire at age ten and remained there for 11 years. His originality was apparent early on. A fellow student copied down a revealing conversation between Debussy and his composition teacher Ernest Guiraud, who is best known today for having completed or made additions to op-eras by Offenbach and Bizet (as discussed in Chapter 9). Debussy told Guiraud:

> I have no faith in the supremacy of the C-major scale. The tonal scale must
> be enriched by other scales. . . . Rhythms are stifling. Rhythms cannot be
> contained within bars. . . . Music is neither major nor minor. Minor thirds
> and major thirds should be combined, thus becoming more flexible. The

Figure 12.4: *Claude Monet,* London, The Parliament, Sun in the Fog, 1904

mode is that which one happens to choose at the moment. It is inconstant. . . .
Themes suggest their orchestral coloring.

Guiraud is exasperated by such remarks and by Debussy playing a series of free-floating chords on the piano. Guiraud observes, "I am not saying what you do isn't beautiful, but it's theoretically absurd." To which Debussy replies, "There is no theory. You merely have to listen. Pleasure is the law."

Although intended to provoke, these comments genuinely reflect Debussy's compositional practice. We saw in Chapter 1 that in the song *En sourdine* (Muted) from 1891 Debussy uses Wagner's "Tristan" chord as a coloristic sonority that floats without forward motion (Ex. 1.3; Anthology 23). Unlike in Wagner, the chord is not approached or left by stepwise voice leading that would give it a functional harmonic role. The vocal melody hovers around the note D♯. The repetition within the piano accompaniment, where the motives of the languid melody reappear several times, also imparts a static quality to the song. As its title implies, the poem *En sourdine*, by the Symbolist Paul Verlaine, is filled with characteristically subdued images: "calm," "twilight," "profound silence," and "vague languor."

Debussy's musical techniques are the perfect analogue to Symbolism, whose influence he readily acknowledged. Debussy frequented the Parisian

Example 12.6: *Debussy,* Prélude à l'après-midi d'un faune, *mm. 1–5*

salon of one of the most important Symbolists, Stéphane Mallarmé, and in 1894 wrote a ten-minute orchestral piece, *Prélude à l'après-midi d'un faune* (Prelude to the Afternoon of a Faun), inspired by a Mallarmé poem that presents a faun's erotic daydreams of an encounter with two beautiful nymphs. We are never certain whether the meeting actually happened; the faun asks, "Did I love a dream?" There are many musical gestures in Debussy's *Prélude* that capture the poem's Symbolist aesthetic, especially the initial melody for solo flute, which floats free of the barline and any fixed tonality, and then returns in that form throughout the piece (Ex. 12.6). The first chord we hear, played by woodwinds and horn, is none other than the "Tristan" chord (*x* in the example, spelled C♯–E–G♯–A♯). As in *En sourdine*, it hangs in the air, in this case resolving to another dissonant chord, a dominant seventh (*y*), and perpetuating the uncertainty and ambiguity.

Debussy felt an affinity with the Impressionists, as is evident from his remark that music was even better able than painting to bring together "all manner of variations of color and light." According to one contemporary critic, Camille Mauclair, Debussy's music resembled the landscape paintings of Monet in being based on "the relative values of sounds in themselves." Mauclair saw Debussy composing in a manner analogous to Monet, with *"taches sonores"* (sonorous spots). The chords and melodic fragments that hover in Debussy's music, and which the listener's ear must then assemble, are indeed similar to the spots of light and color that make up Impressionist paintings.

The works of Mahler, Strauss, Puccini, and Debussy from the fin de siècle mark a turning point at which musical styles and cultural values linked to the past begin to give way to something new. Other members of this generation whom we have not had space to examine in this chapter, including Jean Sibelius (1865–1957) in Finland and Edward Elgar (1857–1934) in England, also participated in this shift, which affected genres large and small: from opera and symphony or symphonic poem to piano pieces and song.

Some of these composers later became ambivalent about the directions Modernism would take in the hands of a newer generation comprising Arnold Schoenberg, Béla Bartók, and Stravinsky, who are discussed by Joseph Auner in his volume in this series. Debussy was offended by the savage style of Stravinsky's *Le sacre du printemps* (The Rite of Spring, 1913). Sibelius had no sympathy for the radical atonality of Schoenberg's Piano Pieces, Op. 11 (1909). But in the musical and cultural scene of the fin de siècle, well before those tensions surfaced, the early Modernists were not a disgruntled lot. With no sense of contradiction or confusion, they could live in the present, draw securely from the past, and point confidently toward the future.

FOR FURTHER READING

Budden, Julian, *Puccini: His Life and Works* (Oxford and New York: Oxford University Press, 2005)

Fischer, Jens Malte, *Gustav Mahler*, trans. Stewart Spencer (New Haven and London: Yale University Press, 2011)

Frisch, Walter, *German Modernism: Music and the Arts* (Berkeley and Los Angeles: University of California Press, 1995)

Kennedy, Michael, *Richard Strauss: Man, Music, Enigma* (Cambridge: Cambridge University Press, 1999)

Lockspeiser, Edward, *Debussy: His Life and Mind*, 2 vols. (New York: Macmillan, 1962–65)

Mallach, Alan, *The Autumn of Italian Opera: From Verismo to Modernism*, 1890–1915 (Boston: Northeastern University Press, 2007)

Schorske, Carl E., *Fin-de-Siècle Vienna: Politics and Culture* (New York: Knopf, 1980)

Youmans, Charles, *Richard Strauss's Orchestral Music and the German Intellectual Tradition* (Bloomington and Indianapolis: Indiana University Press, 2005)

Ⓢ **Additional resources available at wwnorton.com/studyspace**

CHAPTER THIRTEEN

The Sound of
Nineteenth-Century Music

In the fall of 1889, an assistant to Thomas Edison traveled around Europe to demonstrate recent improvements in phonograph technology, in particular the use of wax rather than tinfoil as a recording medium. In Vienna he stopped by to visit the most famous living local composer, set up the equipment—and urged Johannes Brahms to play something on the piano. Brahms is often depicted as a reticent and reactionary figure. But he was fascinated with new technology (including another Edison invention, the light bulb) and sat down enthusiastically for just over a minute to perform part of his Hungarian Dance No. 1 in G Minor.

The wax cylinder preserving this moment was damaged at some point in the early twentieth century, but recent techniques of digital restoration and "denoising" allow us an extraordinary glimpse of Brahms playing his own music. His performance of the Hungarian Dance is not only full of passion and energy, but is highly nuanced in tempo, rhythm, dynamics, and touch. Brahms often plays the left hand slightly before the right, a kind of rubato that was characteristic of many pianists of the period, but is rarely encountered today. Brahms captures the Gypsy style of the dance more vividly than many modern pianists, who stick closer to the notated score. In the passage shown in Example 13.1, Brahms thumps the bass strongly and exaggerates the syncopations. He increases the tempo at the sixteenth-note runs, then tosses off the cadence with a still more rapid flourish.

Example 13.1: *Brahms, Hungarian Dance No. 1 in G Minor, mm. 1–5*

Brahms was giving an impromptu demonstration, not a formal concert. But we can learn much from this bit of recorded sound, most importantly, perhaps, how little the printed page—what Brahms and other composers actually wrote down—communicates about the aural experience of music and about historical styles of performance. Brahms's rendition of the Hungarian Dance is literally "authentic," coming from the author or composer, but it also deviates considerably from the notated score. Should pianists of today striving for a historically accurate performance re-create Brahms's own effects, or should they stay closer to the printed notes? Such questions raise fundamental issues about our understanding of nineteenth-century music.

Music is above all sound, sound that has a direct impact on our senses. Music displays more than any other art form what has been called "presence," a quality of immediacy that can bypass conscious or intellectual processes. Because sounds are ephemeral, decaying in time, musical presence is by its very nature impossible to capture. It has often been ignored or downplayed in writings about music (including textbooks), which tend to focus on more permanent and readily analyzable phenomena like the score, or historical and biographical facts. Yet presence, and the performer or performance that generates it, are as much a part of music's context as any of these, and thus merit consideration in the present volume.

The opera houses, symphony halls, and piano salons of the nineteenth century that we have discussed in this book are silent to us now, as are the singers and instrumentalists who filled them with sound. And yet we have ways of glimpsing the presence of nineteenth-century music. For the past few decades, much discussion and activity has focused on the area of historical performance practice. Nineteenth-century instruments are often very different from their modern counterparts. Playing on these instruments, if they have been well preserved or intelligently restored or replicated, can offer a good idea of the music's original sound world. Also relevant are issues of interpretation like tuning, tempo, phrasing, balance, articulation, bowing, pedaling, and breathing. Here, treatises, commentaries, letters, memoirs, or other written documents from the nineteenth century can be of much help. No less valuable are recordings. The cylinder of Brahms at the piano is exceptional for its early date, but there are many recordings made nearer the end of the nineteenth century, or in the first decades of the twentieth, by composers or artists who worked closely with them. Although primitive by modern digital standards, such recordings, like older instruments and written evidence about interpretation, reveal musical values and styles quite unlike those we experience today.

PIANOS

Let us look first at the technology—the instruments—that artists in the nineteenth century used to produce sounds and to bring scores to life. The piano is arguably the premier instrument of the era, in both the private and public spheres. Every middle-class parlor had a piano, and on concert stages across the world piano recitals became increasingly common. Some of the most vivid musical images of the nineteenth century are of piano virtuosos like Franz Liszt executing pyrotechnics at the keyboard (see Fig. 13.1). The piano underwent a dramatic evolution over this period. In the way that technology often works, these developments were in part spurred by composers' demands for a keyboard with greater range and power. Then, in turn, the enhanced instrument stimulated composers to write for it in new ways.

When Beethoven began giving recitals in Vienna in the 1790s, he was playing the locally built instruments of the day, whose light action favored the speed and clarity characteristic of much late-eighteenth-century music. The range of these Viennese pianos was typically five octaves, their frame was wooden, and the hammers were covered with a thin layer of leather. Such instruments could barely hold up to the unusual force with which Beethoven played. He became famous for

Figure 13.1: *Franz Liszt at piano, Berlin, 1842. After silhouette by Varnhagen von Ense*

popping strings and splitting hammers. Beethoven's friend and pupil Ferdinand Ries later recalled that "the pianofortes of the period (until 1810), still extremely weak and imperfect, could not endure his gigantic style of performance." One contemporary reported that Beethoven's "playing tore along like a wildly foaming cataract, and the conjurer constrained his instrument to an utterance so forceful that the stoutest structure was scarcely able to withstand it."

While Viennese pianos remained similar in style well into the nineteenth century, their counterparts in England and France developed into robust instruments. In 1817, the English firm Broadwood sent Beethoven just such a piano, free of charge, with the composer's name inlaid in ebony above the keys. Beethoven was thrilled and wrote to Thomas Broadwood: "I have never felt a greater pleasure than your announcement of the arrival of this piano, with which you are honoring me as a present. I shall look upon it as an altar upon which I shall place the most beautiful offerings of my spirit to the divine Apollo." Beethoven kept this instrument for the rest of his life, and it survives today (Fig. 13.2). Later in the century it belonged to Liszt, and upon his death it was given to the Hungarian National Museum.

Figure 13.2: *Broadwood piano owned by Beethoven from 1817 until his death in 1827*

Beethoven's Broadwood has a span of six octaves, and its frame is supported by four metal bars, allowing for triple stringing (three strings per note) and thicker, heavier hammers covered in cloth. It also has a true *una corda* (or soft) pedal, which shifts the hammers to allow them to strike only one string. Beethoven's piano was restored in the early 1990s, and recordings made on it reveal a big, thick tone, and the possibility of a wide dynamic range that Beethoven would have wanted for his music—though by the time he got the piano he was almost certainly too deaf to appreciate it fully. It is a mistake to think Beethoven wanted only power and volume. He continued to admire Viennese instruments. In 1825 he received a specially made Graf piano, which spanned six and a half octaves and was also with him until his death.

The Romantic piano repertory of the next few generations—music composed by Schubert, Mendelssohn, Schumann, Chopin, Liszt, and Brahms—was inspired by further developments in the piano. Especially important was the arrival of an iron frame, which could support heavier strings wound at greater tension, and thicker hammers covered in felt. In the 1820s the French maker Erard pioneered many of these innovations, including metal studs to anchor the strings and, more important, double escapement, a system of levers between the key and the hammer that allowed for a very quick response time. A player could now repeat a single note rapidly without waiting for the key to rebound fully, so that only his technique limited the rate of repetition. Such improvements were richly exploited by the virtuoso pianist-composers working in Paris, including Chopin and Liszt, as can be seen in Liszt's étude after Paganini from 1851, *La campanella* (The Bell), with the quick repeated notes in the right hand for which Liszt himself wrote in the fingering (Ex. 13.2).

Example 13.2: *Liszt*, Grandes études de Paganini, *No. 3,* La campanella, *mm. 61–63*

By the 1860s, with the pianos manufactured by the firm of Steinway & Sons in the United States, the modern piano had pretty much arrived. Steinway pianos featured a frame cast as a single piece of iron, three pedals, and a span of seven octaves and a third. They also used cross-stringing, in which the base strings placed above the others and on the diagonal. This allowed for longer strings in a shorter space, which in turn created a richer array of overtones. Steinway had created an instrument that was consistent and could be manufactured on a large scale. By the end of the nineteenth century more than 3,500 Steinways were being produced every year. Other makers adopted most of the Steinway innovations, including cross-stringing. Today, Steinways dominate the worldwide

piano scene. It has been estimated that 98 percent of professional classical performers use Steinway pianos. Pianists like knowing that wherever they perform
around the world, they can rely on a Steinway. But this reliability comes with a
cost. Steinways sound similar to each other, and not that different from other
pianos that have adopted Steinway technology. In the 1830s, composers, players, and audiences could choose from an Erard, a Graf, a Broadwood, and other
pianos with distinct personalities. In a more homogeneous (and homogenized)
world, we have lost that variety of sonority—and presence.

CHOPIN AT THE KEYBOARD

The relationships between technology, technique, and musical style are nowhere better exemplified than in the case of one of the nineteenth century's great
pianist-composers, Frédéric Chopin, whose music we discussed in Chapter 6.
Chopin, who mostly avoided the concert career of his virtuoso contemporaries,
was a much sought-after teacher in Paris. His pupils, and others who heard him,
left compelling accounts of his teaching and playing, often quoting directly
comments that he made. When reading these descriptions, we have a strong
sense of presence and sometimes feel we are at the keyboard with Chopin.

Many of Chopin's pianistic innovations were stimulated by the instruments
of the early Romantic period. According to Liszt, Chopin "particularly cher-
ished" Pleyel pianos "for their silvery and slightly veiled sonority and their
lightness of touch." Chopin himself called Pleyel "the last word in perfection."
(One of Chopin's own Pleyel instruments resurfaced in 2007 in a country manor
in England. He had brought it with him for a tour in 1848.) Accounts of Chopin's
playing are consistent in emphasizing the light, elegant style enabled by the
Pleyel. But he was also capable of getting a rich and deep sound, with plenty
of power. A description of Chopin's playing by Ferdinand Hiller, a renowned
German musician, is especially evocative:

> Nobody before had stirred the keys of a grand piano like that, nor known
> how to release such countless sonorities from it. Rhythmic firmness was
> combined with freedom in the declamation of his melodies, so that they
> would seem to have occurred to him at that very moment. What in the
> hands of others was elegant embellishment, in his hands became a co-
> lourful wreath of flowers; what in others was technical dexterity seemed
> in his playing like the flight of a swallow. All thought of isolating any one
> quality—novelty, grace, perfection, soul—fell away; it was simply Chopin.

Chopin's ideal for piano sound, especially for melodies, came not from the
world of instruments, but (as discussed in Chapter 6) from the great Italian bel

canto tradition of the 1830s, especially the operas of Bellini. "You must sing if you wish to play," he told students, and he urged them to imitate singers like Giuditta Pasta (Chapter 4).

The first half of the nineteenth century saw the emergence of several styles or "schools" of piano technique, each promoted by leading artists working in major cities. In London there were Muzio Clementi and John Field, in Paris Friedrich Kalkbrenner and Johann Pixis. Many published instruction "methods" and exercises. (What budding pianist has not spent many hours struggling through the studies in Clementi's *Gradus ad Parnassum*? Debussy even parodies it in *Doctor Gradus ad Parnassum* from the *Children's Corner Suite* of 1908.) Chopin distanced himself from this trend, feeling that adherence to any one approach and to hours of repetitive, mechanical exercises was meaningless. In his teaching Chopin concentrated on touch and fingering. "Everything is a matter of knowing good fingering," he wrote in a draft of a piano manual never completed. For him, this involved finding the most practical and comfortable succession of fingers for a given passage. In doing so, as evidenced by what his pupils report and by the fingerings he put into some of his own pieces, Chopin revolutionized piano technique.

For example, Chopin liberated the thumb to play on the black keys and participate actively in melodies. Or the third, fourth, and fifth fingers of the right hand would cross over one another without the help of the thumb, as in the Étude, Op. 10, No. 2 (Ex. 13.3, with Chopin's fingering). One pupil reports that, going against tradition, Chopin "often used the same finger to play two adjoining notes consecutively (and this not only when sliding from a black key to a white key), without the slightest noticeable break in the continuity of the line." For Chopin, such fingerings offered an infinite variety of possible legato touches. "Caress the key, never bash it!" he told his pupils. "You should, so to speak, mould the keyboard with a velvet hand and feel the key rather than striking it!" Unlike other teachers and virtuosos of the day, Chopin urged students to concentrate on the fingers, and not play from the arms or elbows.

Example 13.3: *Chopin, Etude in A Minor, Op. 10, No. 2, mm. 1–2*

THE ROMANTIC TENOR

The sound is unmistakable even after only a few notes, and unforgettable: the throbbing, passionate tenor voice of Luciano Pavarotti (1935–2007). Pavarotti was the most famous opera singer of the later twentieth century. Earlier in the century that status belonged to another tenor, Enrico Caruso (1873–1921). Both men sang with an intensity and urgency that created immediate presence; their sound went straight to the heart and soul. Caruso and Pavarotti were best known for singing roles in the Italian operas of Donizetti, Verdi, and Puccini. Their characters—ardent lovers, bold rebels, brave soldiers—all embody the romantic tenor. Rarely are tenors in nineteenth-century opera cast as villains; that function is usually reserved for basses and baritones.

Today we take for granted these associations between voice type and character, but the romantic tenor was developed only in the nineteenth century. In eighteenth-century *opera buffa*, male lovers were often cast as tenors, but these were mainly lighter voices in secondary roles, like Don Ottavio in Mozart's *Don Giovanni* (1787) or Ferrando in the same composer's *Così fan tutte* (1790). Up until the last few decades of the eighteenth century, the male romantic lead in *opera seria* was most often sung by a castrato, whose genitals had been surgically altered before puberty to keep his voice in the high range of a soprano or mezzo-soprano (see Chapter 4). After this barbaric practice was discontinued, composers of serious opera—who still needed to write music for warriors, lovers, and heroes—relied on the so-called *contralto en travesti*, a woman singing in a lower range and dressed up as a man. So-called trouser roles also existed in comic opera, such as the page Cherubino in Mozart's *Marriage of Figaro* (1786). But here too there is a difference from serious opera: Cherubino and similar characters are young boys, not mature lovers.

Composers continued to search for ways to reinvent the male romantic lead. Here Gioachino Rossini was a pioneer (as discussed in Chapter 4). From about 1815 to 1830 he experimented with different male voice types, both low and high. When Rossini came to Paris in 1823, a type of male tenor had been in place for many years, a specifically French one called the *haute-contre*. But this high, light tenor was not suited for full-blooded romantic leads. Rossini thus worked to create tenor parts with more thrust and force. His successors in French and Italian opera, Meyerbeer, Donizetti, Bellini, and Verdi, expanded the scope of the Romantic tenor. Gilbert Duprez (1806–1896), who created the role of Edgardo in Donizetti's *Lucia di Lammermoor* (1835), was the prototype of what became known as the *tenore di forza* (tenor of force, or sometimes *tenore robusto*). Duprez famously introduced the use of a high C sung from the chest rather than the head.

Near the end of his career, in 1887, Verdi created his last great role in this style for Otello in the opera of that name based on the Shakespeare play (see Chapter 12). At once a lover, a warrior, and a tragic figure caught up in jealous fury, the character of Otello calls for a particularly powerful *tenore di forza*. Verdi wrote the role for Francesco Tamagno (1850–1905), one of the leading Italian tenors of his day. Toward the end of his life, in 1903–5, Tamagno recorded a few excerpts from *Otello*. Although he was obviously not in his vocal prime, Tamagno sings with ringing clarity and force. His diction is crisp, and his rhythm is firm. We get a good sense of what a powerful Otello he must have been when creating the role, and also of how a Romantic tenor was supposed to sound at the end of the nineteenth century.

Although Caruso did not originate the most famous Italian romantic tenor roles of the nineteenth century, he sang them throughout his career. That career coincided with the rise of recordings, and Caruso made many between 1902 and his death in 1921 (these are now available complete in a set of twelve CDs). It has been suggested that his recordings helped gain acceptance of the medium as appropriate for opera. At the same time, they made Caruso the most famous opera singer in the world. In the best of his recordings, we can hear superb breath control, ringing high notes, and solid intonation. Caruso moves comfortably between sensuous lyricism and fiery declamation. Above all there is passion and presence. In Caruso's recordings we can hear the direct inheritance of the nineteenth-century Italian operatic style.

Each national tradition of opera developed its special type of romantic tenor in the nineteenth century. In France, whether in grand opera, opéra comique, or operetta, tenor voices remained lighter than in Italy. Even the roles of Faust or Roméo in Gounod's famous operas (*Faust* and *Roméo et Juliette*, 1859 and 1867, respectively), or that of Don José in Bizet's *Carmen* (1875), call for a more purely lyric tenor who will use a head voice more frequently than in the Italian style.

In Germany, Richard Wagner was responsible for the development of a tenor voice that extended the capabilities of the *tenore di forza* into what became known as a *Heldentenor* or heroic tenor. The roles of Tristan in *Tristan und Isolde* (1859) and Siegfried in the last two *Ring* operas, *Siegfried* and *Götterdämmerung* (1856–74), demanded enormous power and stamina. Each opera is five hours long. Tenors who had sung the bigger roles in Meyerbeer, Weber, or Verdi were the best suited to undertake these Wagner parts, and the composer worked closely with them to develop both vocal and dramatic skills. Wagner's ideal heroic tenor was Ludwig Schnorr von Carolsfeld (1836–1865), who created the role of Tristan in June 1865 and whom Wagner also heard in *Tannhäuser* and *Lohengrin*. As can be seen from contemporary photographs, Schnorr was a hefty man, but he was also apparently a compelling singer-actor (Fig. 13.3).

Only weeks after premiering Tristan, Schnorr von Carolsfeld developed a serious fever, and he died at the age of 29. Wagner was devastated by this loss. In a memoir about the singer, he described the qualities of his voice and put it in historical context—one framed by Wagner's own prejudices. For Wagner, the Italian model of male singing, embodied by the castrato and enduring well into the nineteenth century, was based merely on "sensuous pleasure, without a spark of nobler passion." He explained that "any male-singing organ merely trained for physical force will succumb at once . . . when attempting to fulfill the tasks of newer German music, such as are offered in my own dramatic works, if

Figure 13.3: *The tenor Ludwig Schnorr von Carolsfeld as Tristan in Wagner's* Tristan und Isolde, *Munich, 1865*

the singer be not thoroughly alive to their *spiritual* significance." By spiritual, Wagner meant primarily the expressive and emotional dimensions of the roles. For him, Schnorr von Carolsfeld had stood alone among heroic tenors, "tireless in the service of spiritual understanding."

ORCHESTRAS IN THE NINETEENTH CENTURY

Although its size varied widely according to function and locale, over time the nineteenth-century orchestra experienced a great increase in numbers and in richness of color and sonority. In the early 1800s most orchestras retained modest proportions typical of the eighteenth century, even for works like Beethoven's mature symphonies. We are used to hearing the Third (*Eroica*) and Fifth Symphonies in robust performances from modern orchestras of over 100 players, with blazing brass, lush strings, and thundering percussion. While the number of winds and brass is fixed in these scores (usually two of each) and has not usually changed in performances over time, the string forces—and thus the proportion of winds and brass to strings—have varied widely. In 1811 Beethoven called for an orchestra that numbered in the low thirties; it had only 16 strings (including violins, violas, cellos, and double basses), where a modern orchestra might have 70. The instrumentation of Beethoven's *Eroica* is not fundamentally different from that of Haydn's later symphonies, with the exception of a third horn. What makes the *Eroica* so revolutionary is Beethoven's expansion of the form, his rhythmic and harmonic language, and his highly contrapuntal way of writing for the orchestra.

Orchestral expansionism—especially affecting the string sections—was already in the air in the first decade of the nineteenth century. In 1810 the composer-conductor Louis Spohr led a performance of Haydn's *Creation* in Germany with an orchestra of 106 players. Beethoven himself caught the bug, and at an 1814 concert in Vienna, his Seventh and Eighth Symphonies were played by an orchestra of over 80. One proponent of bigger numbers was also one of the greatest composers for orchestra of the nineteenth century, Hector Berlioz. For his colossal Requiem (1837), intended to be performed in a large church, Berlioz called for 4 flutes, 2 oboes, 2 English horns, 4 clarinets, 8 bassoons, 12 horns, 4 cornets, 4 tubas, 16 timpani (10 players), 2 bass drums, 10 pairs of cymbals, 4 tam-tams, 25 first violins, 25 second violins, 20 violas, 20 cellos, and 18 contrabasses. To these forces are added four satellite orchestras (to be placed north, south, east, and west) that include another 12 trumpets, 4 cornets, 16 trombones, 2 tubas, and 4 ophicleides. This makes for a grand total of 212 players. Then there is the chorus of 40 sopranos, 40 altos, 60 tenors, and 70 basses. Berlioz's Requiem was clearly intended to make an earth-shattering sound, and indeed it still does so in performances on the grand scale envisioned by the composer.

By the end of the nineteenth century, most professional orchestras in Europe and the United States numbered in the 80–100 range, a size that allowed them to play the standard repertory. In Figure 13.4 we see a photograph taken in 1890 of the American conductor Theodore Thomas (discussed in Chapter 11) and an orchestra of about 100 players. But bigger was not always better. In Germany some smaller municipalities or private courts had small orchestras that attracted great composers and great music. Two of Brahms's symphonies were first played by orchestras of no more than 50 players. The First was premiered at Karlsruhe in southwestern Germany in 1876, the Fourth in Meiningen in central Germany in 1885. The Meiningen orchestra was under the command of Hans von Bülow, one of the greatest pianists and conductors of his age, who made it into one of the finest ensembles in Europe before going on to lead the much larger Berlin Philharmonic.

It is revealing to hear Brahms's Fourth played by an orchestra of the dimensions of Meiningen (as will be discussed below), but we should never insist that such a performance is the most "authentic." Like many composers of the nineteenth century, Brahms made do with what was available, especially if it was an ensemble as good as Meiningen. But he was also eager to have his orchestral music played by larger forces. Brahms's Second and Third

Figure 13.4: *Theodore Thomas and his Orchestra of about a hundred players at Steinway Hall in New York City, 1890*

Symphonies were premiered by the 100-strong Vienna Philharmonic under the distinguished conductor Hans Richter. And during the months after their premieres with the smaller orchestras, the First and Fourth Symphonies were both played by a range of orchestras of different sizes in Germany and Austria, including the Vienna Philharmonic.

INSTRUMENTAL COLOR: THE CASE OF THE BRASS

In much music of the nineteenth century, as we have seen in this book, color and sonority are as important as structure, harmony, and melody. Like the piano, orchestral instruments underwent considerable change in the course of the century. The shapes and materials of woodwind instruments changed, keys were added, and ranges increased. The English horn and piccolo became regular colors in the orchestra. Adolphe Sax (1814–1894) improved or invented woodwind instruments, most famously the saxophone (actually made of brass), which bears his name and was patented in 1846. String instruments changed less dramatically, but still significantly. Chin rests were added for violins and violas. Some older instruments were retrofitted with longer necks and fingerboards and higher and rounder bridges, all improvements made (as with pianos) with the goal of increasing power and projection. In the later nineteenth century gut strings began to be replaced by steel ones.

Perhaps nowhere was change more visible and audible than in the brass family, where the most important development was the introduction of valve systems. Prior to the 1820s, most brass instruments were tuned by means of "crooks," curved pieces of tubing that permitted playing in different (but not all) keys. Individual pitches were sounded by changing lip tension and, in the case of the horn, by changing the position of the hand in the bell. Valves allowed a player to press down a lever or button that would in effect change the length of the column of air and thus allow a fuller range of chromatic notes.

Valved horns and trumpets opened up a whole new range of possibilities for composers. But the natural horn continued to coexist alongside the newer one until near the very end of the century. Berlioz, himself very much a fan of the valve horn, reported in the 1840s that some composers objected to it because they found its timbre inferior to that of the natural horn. Brahms certainly felt this way. He wrote for natural horn to the end of his career (most evocatively in the Horn Trio, Op. 40), even though he accepted the fact that most orchestras would play his symphonic works with valve horns.

In some cases, composers had to experiment with brass instruments to get the effects they desired, especially to obtain the very lowest pitches. The bass trombone often filled that purpose, but players were rarely up to the challenge of more difficult parts. For his Requiem in Berlin, Berlioz found German trombonists inadequate: "Impossible! Quite impossible! We have to give up the attempt. Can you imagine it? It's enough to make one batter one's head against the wall." In France and England, some composers turned to the serpent, which was indeed shaped like a snake: an old and imposing wooden instrument with a brass-type mouthpiece, originally from the sixteenth century. In the early nineteenth century, serpents, fitted with chromatic keys, were used mainly in military bands and in the church. An English critic recalled playing violin in a church next to a serpent, which "emitted the most appalling sounds that ever pretended to be music." For Berlioz the serpent had "a truly barbaric tone . . . better suited for the bloody cult of the Druids than for that of the Catholic Church."

With the serpent considered too crude for orchestral or concert music, Berlioz and others sometimes turned for those lowest brass notes to the more reliable ophicleide. This instrument appeared in Paris in 1817 and was patented in 1821 (Fig. 13.5). The name of the ophicleide in fact comes from the Greek word for serpent, *ophis*, but the ophicleide differed significantly from the serpent. The eleven keys on most ophicleides allowed for a full chromatic range across three octaves. Berlioz and Mendelssohn wrote parts for the ophicleide—Berlioz in the *Symphonie fantastique* and Requiem, and Mendelssohn in his oratorio *Elijah* and the Overture to *A Midsummer Night's Dream*. In the 1840s in London the ophicleide part of *Elijah* was played by the virtuoso Jean Prospère Guivier on a giant, specially made instrument that appears to have been about nine feet tall. A critic reported on the final chorus of Part 1 of the oratorio:

Figure 13.5: *An ophecleide being played, from an illustration of 1837*

One felt as if the Divine Presence had been evoked, so impressive, so awe-inspiring was its effect upon the listeners. The marvellous effect of the rain and rushing of waters given by the violins, and the stupendous bass F fortissimo, was beyond human conception. I think Prospère with his monstrous ophicleide added materially to this splendid tone effect.

In the finale of the original version of the *Symphonie fantastique*, Berlioz calls for *both* the serpent and ophicleide to join the bassoons in playing the *Dies irae* chant amid the infernal Witches' Sabbath. Here the purpose is the inverse of Mendelssohn's: mockery of the sacred and solemn.

In the second half of the nineteenth century, the valve tuba rapidly displaced the serpent and ophicleide to become the instrument of choice for the lowest brass parts. Berlioz found the tone of the tuba "full and vibrant and well matched with the timbre of trombones and trumpets, to which it serves as a true bass, blending perfectly with them." Thus the search for the most reliable low brass instrument effectively came to an end. The valve tuba remains standard in orchestras to this day. The story involving bass trombone, serpent, ophicleide, and tuba is a vivid example of the complex relationship between music and technology. Instruments develop or change in response to composers' demands and at the same time can stimulate composers to explore new sonorities and colors.

THREE WORKS, THREE RECORDINGS

Descriptions like those cited above can make us want to go back in time and hear spectacular and colorful works like Berlioz's Requiem or Mendelssohn's *Elijah* in their original contexts. Some modern performances and recordings have attempted to re-create nineteenth-century works in that spirit. To conclude this chapter we will consider important recordings of works by Berlioz, Wagner, and Brahms.

Two of the conductors, Roger Norrington (b. 1934) and John Eliot Gardiner (b. 1943), have made recordings with orchestras they hand-picked and trained. Both began their careers as conductors of Baroque music, carefully researching historical instruments, tuning, articulation, tempo, seating arrangement, and the like. By the mid-1980s, Norrington and Gardiner had expanded their projects into the nineteenth-century repertory. In treating Schubert, Berlioz, Mendelssohn, Schumann, Wagner, and Brahms as "early" music, worthy of the same careful study as Monteverdi or Bach, they brought fresh perspectives to works that make up the bulk of the modern symphonic repertory.

In 1991, Gardiner recorded Berlioz's *Symphonie fantastique* with his group Orchestre Révolutionnaire et Romantique (Philips 434 402-2). "Fundamental to the performance," Gardiner wrote in his liner note, "is our intention to recapture as precisely as possible the sound of the instruments in Berlioz's orchestra, for which he wrote with such specific instructions to create aural pictures of unique immediacy and clarity." Gardiner made his recording in the very room at the Paris Conservatoire where the premiere had taken place in 1830. In the *Symphonie fantastique* he sought to highlight, in a way that modern orchestras cannot, Berlioz's juxtaposition of old-fashioned and contemporary sounds, which he compares to manipulating the manuals of an organ. Thus in the finale the serpent plays alongside the modern ophicleide and bassoon. And in the fourth movement, the *March to the Scaffold*, Gardiner uses the *cornet à pistons*, a version of the valve trumpet introduced in Paris in 1827–28, only two years before the *Symphonie fantastique*. The sonic results of Gardiner's efforts are breathtaking, especially in the last two movements. It is as if coats of varnish or grime have been taken off an old painting to reveal original colors. The even balance between the different sections (strings, winds, brass) of the orchestra allows us to hear inner parts more clearly.

In 1995 Roger Norrington and his London Classical Players tackled a different nineteenth-century warhorse, the Prelude and Transfiguration (still today, and on this recording, mistakenly called the Love Death) from Wagner's *Tristan und Isolde* (EMI 5-55479-2). In his liner note, Norrington discusses four areas on which he focused in creating a historically accurate performance: instruments, orchestral size, playing style, and tempo and interpretation. "In this recording . . . we aim for the sounds, the gestures, the speeds which Wagner may have intended for his music," Norrington explains. "At the same time, of course, we try not to sacrifice the mystery and dreamlike beauty which are so important a part of his personality." The strings play with almost no vibrato—the throbbing sound we tend to associate with passionate expression—and Norrington's tempos are much faster than any modern listener is accustomed to. Most recordings of Wagner's Prelude last between ten and eleven minutes; Norrington's clocks in at 6:59.

Some might feel that Norrington's approach actually wipes away the "mystery and dreamlike beauty" of Wagner that he seeks to retain. But he argues that because the Tristan Prelude is in a $\frac{6}{8}$ meter, it should retain a feeling of two beats in a measure, which cannot be sustained at a very slow tempo (see Ex. 1.1 in Chapter 1). Moreover, Norrington suggests, the Prelude "fits into a long tradition of love scenes in slow waltz time." The critic Richard Taruskin has called Norrington's ideas about Wagner performance "ludicrous" and has written that the conductor, while claiming to be true to Wagner's intentions, is in reality imposing on the music an entirely Modernist aesthetic of anti-sentimentalism. While many will be put off by Norrington's performance of Wagner, we should appreciate that, as with Gardiner's Berlioz, he is inviting us to hear Wagner's Prelude with fresh ears.

The third recording is of the four Brahms symphonies made in 1997 by Charles Mackerras and the Scottish Chamber Orchestra (Telarc 80450). Unlike Gardiner and Norrington, Mackerras (1925–2010) was known neither as an "early music" conductor nor as one who aimed to give historically informed performances. With this recording Mackerras had three main goals: to give some sense of the instrumental color, especially of winds and brass, characteristic of Austro-German orchestras from Brahms's day to our own; to re-create the proportions and balance of the Meiningen Orchestra, which premiered the Fourth Symphony in 1885; and to shape the music according to interpretive guidelines passed down from the composer's era through the early twentieth century.

Mackerras employed so-called Vienna horns, rotary-valve trumpets, and narrow-bore trombones. The horns, still in use in Viennese orchestras today, produce a liquid legato; they have valves like modern horns but are closer in design to the older natural instrument, with a narrow internal diameter, removable crooks, and a natural horn mouthpiece. The trumpets have a more tapered attack and decay, and a warmer, less brilliant and incisive tone, than the instruments with piston valves common in the United States. These instruments give Mackerras's recordings a special sheen.

The Scottish Chamber Orchestra uses 54 players, just slightly above the 49 reported as being at Meiningen in the 1880s. The string complement is 34, and first and second violins are divided on either side of the podium, as was customary in the nineteenth century. Because the strings and other instruments are more evenly matched than in modern orchestras, we hear a balanced sonority very different from most recordings. Instrumental colors are less blended and less homogenized than we are accustomed to hearing. As with Gardiner's

Berlioz and (more controversially) Norrington's Wagner, it is as though a painting by an old master has been cleaned and its vibrant original colors restored. Mackerras's Brahms reveals the rich inner voices and the contrapuntal fabric so characteristic of the composer's orchestral music.

Perhaps the most striking aspect of the Mackerras recordings is the great flexibility of tempo, which was also, we recall, a distinctive feature of Brahms's performance of his Hungarian Dance. Fluctuation and the avoidance of metronomic regularity were performance values that Brahms shared with Wagner. Brahms greatly admired the conductor Fritz Steinbach (1855–1916), who succeeded Hans von Bülow as director of the Meiningen Orchestra. Steinbach's conducting scores of Brahms contained detailed indications about how he performed the symphonies. These markings confirm that Steinbach conducted Brahms with nuance and plasticity; as one critic said, "through every performance there surged the pulse of a terse, fundamentally musical rhythm, which is the unmistakable sign of a true and complete master." Without ever simply playing by the book, Mackerras re-creates many of the subtle tempo shifts recommended by Steinbach. He brings us closer than any other modern conductor to the flow of musical time imagined by Brahms.

The same basic impulse—the desire to capture and preserve a significant musical performance—enabled Brahms's playing to be captured on cylinder in the 1880s and Mackerras to re-create something of Brahms's symphonic world on CD just over a hundred years later. Both documents suggest the enormous impact recording technology has had during the past 150 years. Recordings give us the ability to experience a wide range of music across historical time and geographical space. As such, they enhance both the diachronic and synchronic dimensions of music history that we identified in Chapter 1. In his volume in this series, Joseph Auner explores in more detail the role played by technologies of sound in the twentieth and twenty-first centuries, with the advent of noise-generating machines, radio, tape recorders, synthesizers, and, more recently, computers and digital media.

But we can linger briefly in the nineteenth century. Much of the music that we have examined in this book, from Beethoven to Debussy, still forms the core of the concert, opera, and classical recorded repertory. Sound and visual media can help enhance our historical appreciation of this music, as this chapter has suggested. But so can words on the page, in empathetic writing that shows how music of the nineteenth century was an integral part of its various cultures. We have tried to do this by exploring the scores, composers, promoters, institutions, critics, performers, and consumers of that era—from Metternich's Vienna, to Risorgimento Italy, to the United States in the Gilded Age, to France in the Third Republic. In this endeavor we do not try to turn back the clock or re-create the past. Rather, we reinforce the conviction held and practiced today across the world in every culture: that whatever music people love and listen to, it really "matters," always has, and always will.

FOR FURTHER READING

Brown, Clive, *Classical and Romantic Performing Practice, 1750–1900* (Oxford and New York: Oxford University Press, 1999)

Eigeldinger, Jean-Jacques, *Chopin, Pianist and Teacher: As Seen by His Pupils,* trans. Krysia Osostowicz and Naomi Shohet, ed. Roy Howat (Cambridge and New York: Cambridge University Press, 1986)

Good, Edwin M., *Giraffes, Black Dragons, and Other Pianos: A Technological History from Cristofori to the Modern Concert Grand,* second ed. (Stanford: Stanford University Press, 2001)

Koury, Daniel J., Orchestral *Performance Practices in the Nineteenth Century: Size, Proportions, and Seating* (Ann Arbor: UMI Research Press, 1986)

Performing Brahms: Early Evidence of Performance Style, ed. Michael Musgrave and Bernard Sherman (Cambridge and New York: Cambridge University Press, 2003)

Piano Roles: 300 Years of Life with the Piano, ed. James Parakilas (New Haven: Yale University Press, 1999)

Potter, John, *Tenor: History of a Voice* (New Haven: Yale University Press, 2009)

Taruskin, Richard, *Text and Act: Essays on Music and Performance* (Oxford and New York: Oxford University Press, 1995)

Ⓢ Additional resources available at wwnorton.com/studyspace

absolute music Music, usually instrumental, that is independent of words, drama, visual images, or anything representational. It expresses ideas that are only musical in nature.

accidental Sign that calls for altering the pitch of a note: a ♯ raises the pitch a half step, a ♭ lowers it a half step, and a ♮ cancels a previous accidental.

acoustics Branch of physics concerned with the properties, production, transmission, and aural reception of sound.

anti-Romanticism A viewpoint characteristic of the middle of the nineteenth century that believed Romanticism was limited, self-involved, and not enough concerned with the real world.

appoggiatura Dissonant (literally, "leaning") note usually occupying a strong beat and lying above or below a chord note, to which it resolves by step.

aria Lyrical number for solo voice in an opera or oratorio.

aria di baule (Italian, "suitcase aria") Aria that a principal singer might substitute for another in Italian opera to display the special qualities of her voice.

arpeggio Chord in which the individual pitches are sounded one after another instead of simultaneously.

art-religion (German: *Kunstreligion*) Nineteenth-century concept treating the contemplation of art as a substitute for religious worship.

augmentation Statement of a theme in longer note values, often twice as slow as the original.

ballade Type of longer character piece for piano associated with Chopin, in several continuous sections that resemble the narrative form of the poetic ballad.

barcarolle Song associated with Venetian gondoliers, in $\frac{6}{8}$ or $\frac{12}{8}$ meter with a rocking accompaniment, adapted by nineteenth- and twentieth-century composers.

barline Vertical line used in a musical score to indicate a division between measures.

baton Thin stick used by conductors to direct musicians.

beat Unit of regular pulsation in musical time.

bel canto (Italian, "beautiful singing") Vocal style characterized by florid and smoothly lyrical melodic lines, associated with early-nineteenth-century Italian opera.

binary form Musical form comprising two complementary sections, each of which is repeated. The first section usually ends on the dominant or the relative major key; the second section returns to the tonic.

brass instrument   Wind instrument with a cup-shaped mouthpiece, a tube that flares into a bell, and slides or valves to vary the pitch.

cabaletta   In the scene structure developed in early-nineteenth-century Italian opera, the fast final section, featuring brilliant vocal writing.

cadence   Melodic or harmonic succession that closes a musical phrase, section, or composition.

cantabile   (Italian, "songful") In the scene structure developed in early-nineteenth-century Italian opera, the slow, lyrical section.

cantata   Multimovement work for solo singers, chorus, and instrumentalists, based on a lyric or dramatic poetic narrative.

castrato   (plural, *castrati*) Male singer castrated before puberty to preserve his high vocal range, featured prominently in eighteenth-century opera.

chaconne   Form originating in the Baroque period, in which variations unfold over a repeated bass line.

chamber music   Music for a group of up to about ten players, with one person to a part.

character piece   Short piece, usually for piano and often in ternary form, that projects a single principal mood or spirit, often conveyed by its title.

chorale   Strophic hymn in the Lutheran tradition, intended to be sung by the congregation.

chord   Combination of three or more pitches, heard simultaneously.

chromatic scale   Scale built of all twelve pitches in the octave.

chromaticism   Musical vocabulary employing all or most of the chromatic pitches, originally as an expansion of a major or minor key.

coda   Final part of an instrumental movement, usually coming after the standard parts of the form are completed.

comprimario   (plural, *comprimari;* Italian, literally "with the principal[s]") Singer of a secondary role in Italian opera.

concert aria   Aria for voice and orchestra written for performance as an independent composition.

concerto   Instrumental work in several movements for solo instrument (or instrumental group) and orchestra.

conductor   Person who, by means of gestures, leads performances of musical ensembles.

consonance   Combination of pitches that provides a sense of stability in music.

contralto en travesti   (Italian, "contralto cross-dressed") In opera, a woman singing in a lower range and dressed up as a man.

counterpoint   The art of combining in a single texture two or more melodic lines.

crook   An exchangeable segment of tubing in a brass instrument, used to change the length of fixed tube, altering the key in which it plays.

cross-stringing   Method of positioning strings inside a piano in a vertically overlapping slanted arrangement.

cyclic form   Musical structure in which thematic material from one movement recurs in a later movement, often at the end of the work.

cylinder   (recording) Cylinder-shaped object upon whose outside surface (made of tin or wax) an audio recording is engraved, developed by Thomas Edison in the late nineteenth century.

decadence   In the late nineteenth century, originally a pejorative label for an artistic style characterized by a perceived decline of moral and ethical standards; the name was then adopted by many artists and writers.

Deutsche   (German, "German") A term indicating a variety of triple-meter dance types popular around 1800 in German-speaking realms.

development   In a sonata form, the second section, in which the thematic material is fragmented and undergoes modulation through a range of keys.

diatonic   Built from the seven pitches of a major or minor scale.

diminished seventh chord   Chord built of a diminished triad and a diminished seventh, occurring naturally on the raised seventh step of a minor scale.

dissonance   Combination of pitches that sounds unstable, in need of resolution.

diva   Leading female opera singer.

dominant In tonal music, the pitch a perfect fifth above the tonic, or the chord based on that note.

dominant seventh chord The chord form that occurs naturally on the dominant of a major key, consisting of a major triad and a minor seventh.

double escapement Type of piano action, invented by Sébastien Érard in 1821, incorporating a lever that permits a note to be repeated rapidly without lifting the key completely.

double fugue Fugue in which two different themes or "subjects" are developed simultaneously.

double stop The playing of two pitches simultaneously on a bowed string instrument.

dumka (plural, *dumky*) Slavic name for a vocal or instrumental folk piece that is ruminative or melancholic in character and proceeds in alternating sections of slow and fast tempos.

dynamics Element of musical expression relating to the degree of loudness or softness, or volume, of a sound.

écossaise (French, "Scottish") A dance in duple meter popular around 1800 and used by some classical composers.

English horn Double-reed woodwind instrument, larger and lower in range than the oboe.

ensemble In opera, an extended number with multiple singers.

exoticism In music, a style in which the rhythms, melodies, or instrumentation are designed to evoke the atmosphere of foreign countries or cultures.

exposition Opening section of a sonata form, in which the principal thematic material is set out: the first theme group is in the tonic key, and the second is generally in the dominant or the relative major.

falsetto Vocal technique whereby a man can sing above his normal range, producing a lighter sound.

fermata Symbol placed over a note, chord, or rest indicating it is to be sustained longer than the indicated time value, at the performer's discretion.

feuilleton (French, "little leaf") In the nineteenth century, a portion of a French newspaper devoted to commentary on politics, culture, and the arts.

finale Last movement of an instrumental work, or the last, extended section of an act in an opera.

folk music Music of unknown authorship from a particular region or people, passed down through oral tradition.

form Structure and design in music, based on repetition, contrast, and variation.

four-hand piano music Music written or arranged for two performers playing at one piano.

fugue Polyphonic form in which one or more themes or "subjects" are treated in imitative counterpoint.

Gesamtkunstwerk (German, "total artwork") Term coined by Richard Wagner for an opera in which poetry, scenic design, staging, action, and music all work together toward one artistic expression.

glee Type of unaccompanied part-song, typically for male voices, that flourished in England from about 1750 until World War I.

grand opera Type of opera developed in nineteenth-century Paris with emphasis on spectacle, and featuring historical plots, crowd scenes, and ornate costumes.

habanera Moderate duple meter dance of Cuban origin, based on a characteristic rhythmic figure, and popular in the nineteenth century.

half step Distance between two adjacent pitches on a piano.

half-diminished seventh chord Chord constructed of a diminished triad and a minor seventh; most commonly encountered in the minor mode as a ii^7 harmony that leads to the dominant (V).

harmonic progression Series of chords that are directed toward a harmonic goal, usually a stable, consonant sonority.

harmonic sequence A melodic-harmonic pattern that is restated successively at different pitch levels.

harmony Aspect of music that pertains to simultaneous combinations of notes, the intervals and chords that result, the succession of chords, and the underlying principles.

harpsichord　Keyboard instrument, in use between the fifteenth and eighteenth centuries, in which the strings are plucked by quills instead of being struck with hammers like the piano.

haute-contre　(French, "high counter [tenor]") High tenor voice in French opera of the eighteenth and nineteenth century.

Heldentenor　(German, "heroic tenor") Rich, powerful tenor voice especially suited for performance of Richard Wagner's operatic roles.

historicism　Intellectual or philosophical position, especially important in the nineteenth century, including among composers and critics, that the study of the past is necessary for an understanding of, and artistic creation within, the present.

hornpipe　Lively dance from the British Isles, said to have begun on ships in imitation of bodily movements familiar to sailors.

hymn　Song in praise of God, often involving congregational participation.

idealism　Philosophy of the late eighteenth and early nineteenth centuries that maintains that reality is in the mind, of which the external world is a projection.

idée fixe　(French, "fixed idea" or "obsession") Term applied by Hector Berlioz to the melody, representing the beloved, that is transformed throughout his *Symphonie fantastique*.

impresario　Businessman who manages an opera house and oversees the production of operas.

Impressionism　Term originally applied to the movement in French painting that sought to capture the changing qualities of color and light; also used for the contemporaneous musical style that evokes moods and visual imagery through colorful harmony and instrumental timbre.

impromptu　Musical composition, usually for piano or other solo instrument, intended to suggest the character of an improvisation, as if prompted by the spirit of the moment.

interval　Relationship or distance between two pitches.

inversion　(1) Reversal of the upward or downward direction of each interval of a theme. (2) In a musical texture, reversal of the relative position of two melodies, so that the one that had been lower is now above the other.

irony　Rhetorical device of saying the opposite of what one means, adapted by Romantics as a literary and musical strategy.

Kapellmeister　German term for the director or conductor of an orchestra.

key　In tonal music, the organization of pitches and chords around a central pitch, the tonic.

key signature　Sharps or flats placed at the beginning of a piece to show the key or tonal center of a work.

ländler　Austro-German folk dance in triple meter, adapted by eighteenth- and nineteenth-century composers.

leitmotif　(German, "leading motive") In Wagner's operas, a short theme associated with a character, idea, object, or place, which returns continually in different transformations.

libretto　(Italian, "little book") Text of an opera or oratorio.

lied　(German, "song"; plural, *lieder*) A setting of a poem for solo singer or several singers, with the accompaniment of a piano, sometimes supplemented by other instruments.

liturgy　The body of texts to be spoken or sung, and ritual actions to be performed, in a religious service.

major scale　Scale consisting of seven different pitches in a specific pattern of whole and half steps. It differs from a minor scale primarily in that its third degree is raised half a step.

mass　Musical setting of the texts from the most important service of the Catholic Church; usually in five movements, consisting of the Kyrie, Gloria, Credo, Sanctus, and Agnus Dei.

materialism　A view that holds that we can only assume to exist that which we can observe or experience directly through the senses.

mazurka Polish folk dance in triple meter, characterized by accents on the second or third beat and often by dotted figures on the first beat.

measure Recurring temporal unit that contains a fixed number of beats, indicated on the musical staff by barlines.

melody Succession of pitches, usually in several phrases that are perceived as a coherent, self-contained structure.

meter Recurring patterns of strong and weak beats, dividing musical time into units of equal duration.

metronome Mechanical or electrical device used to indicate tempo by sounding regular beats at adjustable speeds.

Mighty Handful Group of five Russian composers in the later nineteenth century, including Mily Balakirev, Aleksandr Borodin, César Cui, Modest Musorgsky, and Nikolay Rimsky-Korsakov, who fostered a distinctly Russian art music.

mimetic effect Musical sound that is intended to imitate a sound of the natural or human world, such as a bird call or clock chimes.

minor scale Scale consisting of seven different pitches in a specific pattern of whole and half steps. It differs from the major scale primarily in that its third degree is lowered.

minstrelsy Popular form of musical theater in the United States during the mid-nineteenth century, in which white performers blackened their faces and impersonated African Americans.

Modernism Movement in the arts that began in the last decades of the nineteenth century and continued into the twentieth; in music it stressed innovation in harmony, rhythm, and formal design.

motive Short melodic or rhythmic idea; the smallest fragment of a theme that forms a recognizable unit.

movement Complete, self-contained segment of a larger musical work.

Musikdrama (German, "music drama") Term often applied to Wagner's mature operas, suggesting a carefully planned coordination of music, words, and scenic presentation.

nationalism Attitude or outlook that posits an identity for a group of people through characteristics such as common language, shared culture, historical tradition and institutions, and musical elements derived from folk or indigenous styles.

natural horn Ancestor of the modern French horn, characterized by lack of valves.

nocturne (French, "night piece") Type of character piece, with slow tempo, flowing accompaniment, and broad lyrical melodies, associated especially with the solo piano music of John Field and Frédéric Chopin.

octatonic scale Scale composed of alternating half and whole steps, favored by some late-nineteenth- and early-twentieth-century Russian composers.

octave Interval between two pitches seven diatonic pitches apart; the lower note vibrates half as fast as the upper.

opera Musical stage work that is generally sung throughout, combining the resources of vocal and instrumental music with poetry and drama, acting and pantomime, scenery and costumes.

opéra bouffe Genre of nineteenth-century French comic opera, associated with Offenbach, with witty spoken dialogue and sparkling, light music.

opera buffa Italian comic opera, sung throughout, with recitatives, arias, and ensembles.

opéra comique Term for a French stage work, whether serious or humorous, with vocal and instrumental music and spoken dialogue; distinguished from grand opera.

opera house Theater or hall where opera is regularly performed, usually designed to accommodate an orchestra, sets, and other stage equipment.

opera seria Italian serious opera, on a serious subject but normally with a happy ending, and without comic characters and scenes.

operetta Broad term for light opera in which musical numbers are interspersed with spoken dialogue.

ophicleide Nineteenth-century instrument with finger holes and a brass mouthpiece, used by Berlioz among others; the parts are generally played today on tuba.

opus number (abbrev. *op.*; plural, *opera* [*opp.*]) Number designating a work in chronological relationship to other works by the same composer.

oratorio Large-scale genre originating in the Baroque, with a libretto of religious or serious character; similar to opera but unstaged, performed by solo voices, chorus, and orchestra.

orchestra Performing group generally consisting of groups or "sections" of string instruments, with single, paired, or multiple woodwind, brass, and percussion instruments.

orchestra society Organization or institution that presents orchestral concerts on a regular basis, often by subscription.

orchestration The study or practice of writing music for instruments, or adapting for orchestra music composed for another medium.

Orientalism Term describing a Western view of a non-Western or non-European culture from a position of superiority and prejudice; in Western music, the use of non-Western or exotic elements, sometimes implying their lesser status.

overtone Constituent higher pitch that is part of a sounding tone: any instrumental or vocal pitch produces a characteristic set of overtones that help create the tone color or timbre.

parola scenica (Italian, "stage word") Giuseppe Verdi's term for short phrases in an opera libretto, set to music in a memorable way that captures or focuses a dramatic situation.

part-song Secular vocal composition, unaccompanied, in three or more parts.

patronage Sponsorship of an artist or a musician, undertaken in the nineteenth century primarily by a member of the aristocracy or middle class.

pentatonic scale Five-note pattern (usually scale degrees 1–2–3–5–6) used in some non-Western musics and adopted by Western composers in the nineteenth and twentieth centuries.

perfect cadence Cadence that moves from a dominant to a tonic harmony, with chords in root position.

phrase Unit of a melody or of a succession of notes that has a distinct beginning and ending and is followed by a pause or other articulation.

piano cycle Series of short piano pieces intended to be played together, often with recurring musical material.

piano quartet Chamber ensemble of piano, violin, viola, and cello, or a composition written for that ensemble.

piano trio Chamber ensemble of piano, violin, and cello, or a composition written for that ensemble.

pianoforte (Italian, "soft-loud") Early name for the piano, so called because of its ability to produce gradations of dynamics.

pizzicato Performance direction to pluck a string of a bowed instrument with the finger.

plainchant Monophonic, unmeasured vocal melody, usually part of the liturgy of the early Roman Catholic Church.

poetic-musical period Wagner's term for the structural unit that replaced traditional numbers in his operas.

polonaise Stately Polish processional dance in triple meter.

polyphony Musical texture featuring two or more lines or voices.

popular music Type of music that aims for broad appeal, often avoids complexity, and is usually sold in printed or recorded form.

prelude (1) Name sometimes used for an instrumental movement preceding an opera or other large-scale vocal work. (2) Type of independent short piece for piano or other solo instrument.

prima donna (Italian, "first lady") Leading female singer in Italian opera.

primo (plural, *primi*) Singer of a principal role in Italian opera.

print culture Set of cultural values and practices, especially prominent up through the eighteenth and early nineteenth centuries, that emphasizes printed forms of communication.

program music Instrumental music that is based on a narrative or a poetic idea, which is often explained in an accompanying text or program that is meant to be read by the listener before or during the performance.

range Distance between the lowest and highest pitches of a melody, an instrument, or a voice.

realism Mid-nineteenth-century movement in the arts that stressed naturalistic depiction of people, situations, and objects; in music, often an emphasis on naturalistic opera plots or declamation of a sung text.

recapitulation In a sonata form, the third section, where material from the exposition is restated, now in the tonic key.

recital Concert given by one or two performers.

recitative Speech-like type of singing, with minimal accompaniment, that follows the natural rhythms of the text; used in opera and oratorio.

relative major Scale or key whose initial note lies a minor third above the tonic of a minor scale, with which it shares all pitches.

relative minor Scale or key whose initial note lies a minor third below the tonic of a major scale, with which it shares all pitches.

rhythm The particular pattern of short and long durations.

ricochet In string playing, a technique in which the bow is bounced upon the string to produce a series of rapid notes.

Romanticism A nineteenth-century reaction against Enlightenment values of rationality and universality, celebrating subjectivity, spontaneity, and the power of emotions; in music, associated with a turn to smaller and more flexible forms, as well as increased chromaticism and melodic expressivity.

rondo Musical form in which the first section recurs, usually in the tonic, between subsidiary sections.

rubato (from Italian *tempo rubato*, "stolen time") Technique common in nineteenth-century music in which the performer holds back or accelerates the written note values.

sacred music Religious or spiritual music, for church or devotional use.

salon Gathering in a private home for a semipublic musical or literary event, attended by both aristocracy and the bourgeoisie.

saxophone Single-reed woodwind instrument made of brass, invented by Adolphe Sax in 1846.

scale Series of pitches arranged in ascending or descending order according to a specific pattern of intervals.

scherzo (Italian, "joke") Composition in ternary (ABA) form, usually in triple meter; often a part of a multimovement chamber or orchestral work.

Schubertiad Informal gathering of Franz Schubert and his friends at which the composer's music was performed.

score The written form of a musical composition, containing musical notation as well as verbal and graphic indications for performance.

secondary dominant Dominant chord that resolves to or is directed toward a harmony that is not the tonic.

sequence Restatement of a musical idea or motive at a different pitch level.

serenade Multimovement work for large instrumental ensemble, usually lighter in mood than a symphony.

serpent A bass wind instrument and ancestor of the tuba, with a long wooden cone bent into a snakelike shape, and finger holes; in the nineteenth century, used in military bands and church music.

seventh chord Four-note combination consisting of a triad with another third added on top, spanning a seventh between its lowest and highest pitches.

Singspiel (German, "singing play") Genre of opera in Austria and Germany, featuring spoken dialogue interspersed with arias, ensembles, and choruses.

sonata Work for solo instrument or ensemble; especially, multimovement work for piano or for other solo instrument with piano.

sonata form The design of the opening movement of most multimovement instrumental works from the later eighteenth through the nineteenth centuries, consisting of themes that are stated in the first section (exposition), developed in the second section (development), and restated and transformed in the third section (recapitulation).

song cycle   Group of art songs or lieder, meant to be performed in succession, usually tracing a story or narrative.

spiritual   Type of religious song that originated among slaves of the American South and was passed down through oral tradition.

Stabreim   (German, "root rhyme") Wagner's term for the alliteration or repetition of similar vowel sounds used in his librettos.

stretta   Section at the end of an Italian operatic ensemble where tempo is increased.

string quartet   Chamber music ensemble consisting of two violins, viola, and cello; or a multimovement composition for this ensemble.

strophic   Song or aria structure in which the same music is repeated for every stanza (strophe) of the poem.

subdominant   In tonal music, the pitch a perfect fourth above the tonic, or the chord based on that pitch.

suite   Multimovement work made up of a series of contrasting movements, usually dance-inspired and all in the same key.

Symbolism   Movement originating in French literature in the late nineteenth century in which events, feelings, or objects are presented by suggestion and allusion; in music, associated with composers' blurring of harmonic, melodic, and formal structures.

symphonic poem   Term coined by Franz Liszt for a one-movement work for orchestra that conveys a poetic idea, story, scene, or succession of moods.

symphony   Large work for orchestra, usually in four movements.

syncopation   Temporary shifting of the accent to a weak beat or a weak part of a beat.

tempo   (Italian, "time" or "movement") Speed of a musical composition, or the designation of such in a musical score.

tempo d'attacco   (Italian, "opening movement") First section of the scene structure developed in early-nineteenth-century Italian opera, usually using recitative.

tempo di mezzo   (Italian, "middle movement") Middle section of the scene structure developed in early-nineteenth-century Italian opera, usually using recitative.

tenore di forza   (Italian, "tenor of force") Ringing, powerful tenor voice in nineteenth-century Italian opera.

ternary form   Musical form comprising three sections, with the outer sections being essentially the same, contrasting with a middle section: ABA.

texture   The interweaving of melodic and harmonic elements in a musical work.

thematic transformation   Presentation of a recurring motif, such as an *idée fixe*, that keeps its basic shape and contour but returns in varied mood, instrumentation, meter, or tempo.

theme   Melody or other well-defined musical element used as basis for a composition or movement; in a fugue, the theme is often called a subject.

theme and variations   See **variation form**.

through-composed   Descriptive term for songs that are composed from beginning to end, without repetitions of large sections.

timbre   The sound quality or character that distinguishes one voice or instrument from another.

tinta   (Italian, "tint") Giuseppe Verdi's term for an opera's special coloration, imparted by the orchestration and certain kinds of melodic and harmonic gestures.

tonality   The system by which a piece of music is organized around a central note, chord, and key (the tonic), to which all the other notes and keys in the piece are subordinate.

tone poem   Term coined by Richard Strauss to describe his one-movement orchestral works in the tradition of the symphonic poem.

tonic   (1) The first and central pitch of a scale. (2) The main key area in which a piece or movement begins and ends and to which all other keys are subordinate.

tremolo   Rapid repetition of a tone or alternation between two pitches.

triad   Common chord type, consisting of three pitches, normally a third and a fifth apart. The common forms are major, minor, diminished, and augmented.

trio (1) Piece for three players or singers. (2) The second of two alternating sections in a minuet or scherzo movement.

triple stop Three notes played simultaneously on a violin or other bowed string instrument.

triplet Group of three equal-valued notes played in the time of two.

"Tristan" chord The first chord heard in the Prelude to Wagner's *Tristan und Isolde,* a dissonant chord that recurs throughout the opera and also became widely known and quoted by other composers.

tritone Interval spanning three whole steps or six half steps, such as F to B, and a component of the diminished seventh chord.

trouser role Operatic role in which a woman plays a male character and appears in the clothing of a man.

una corda (Italian, "one string") The soft pedal on a piano, which on modern grand pianos shifts the action to the right, so that hammers strike only two of the three strings.

valve instruments Brass instruments in which valves are pressed to change the length of tubing, allowing the player to reach the notes of various harmonic series.

variation form, variations Musical form that presents a series of transformations of a theme, usually preserving the length and phrasing, but altering melody or harmony. Also referred to as *theme and variations*.

verismo (Italian, "realism") Late-nineteenth-century operatic movement in Italy that presents everyday people in familiar situations, often depicting sordid or brutal events.

vernacular The everyday language spoken by the people, as distinguished from the language of literature or religious liturgy; in music, the term is used to distinguish folk music, popular music, jazz, and other music not considered "classical."

vibrato Small, rapid fluctuation of pitch used as an expressive device to intensify a sound.

virtuoso Performer of extraordinary technical ability.

visual culture A set of values and practices, especially characteristic of the nineteenth and twentieth centuries, that emphasize visual forms of communication, including opera, photography, and film.

Wagner tuba Brass instrument developed by Richard Wagner for his Ring cycle, combining elements of French horn and tuba.

Wagnerism A trend in the arts in the later nineteenth century influenced by the music and writings of Richard Wagner.

waltz Ballroom dance type in triple meter; in the nineteenth century, often a character piece for piano.

waltz operetta Operetta whose numbers consist largely of waltzes that are danced or sung.

whole step Musical interval equal to two half steps.

woodwind Musical instrument that produces sound when the player blows air through a mouthpiece that has a sharp edge or a reed, causing the air to vibrate in a resonating column.

CHAPTER 1

5. "one of the most charming and honorable accomplishments for young ladies": Ruth Solie, *Music in Other Words: Victorian Conversations* (Berkeley and Los Angeles, University of California Press, 2004), p. 89.

7. "*La bohème*, just as it left no impression on the minds of its listeners": Julian Budden, *Puccini: His Life and Works* (Oxford and New York: Oxford University Press, 2002), p. 155.

CHAPTER 2

13. "Do you know it? Do I?": Peter le Huray and James Day, *Music and Aesthetics in the Eighteenth and Early-Nineteenth Centuries* (Cambridge and New York: Cambridge University Press, 1981), p. 409.

13. "The word 'romantic' has come to mean so many things": *English Romantic Poets: Modern Essays in Criticism,* ed. M. H. Abrams (Oxford and New York: Oxford University Press, 1975), p. 6.

14. "Myself alone": Jean-Jacques Rousseau, *Confessions,* trans. Angela Scholar (Oxford and New York: Oxford University Press, 2000), p. 5.

14. "Poetry is the spontaneous overflow of powerful feelings": William Wordsworth and Samuel Taylor Coleridge, *Lyrical Ballads and Other Poems,* ed. Martin Scofield (Ware: Wordsworth Editions Ltd., 2003), p. 21.

15. Winckelmann (1717–1768) extolled Greek art for its "noble simplicity": *German Aesthetic and Literary Criticism: Winckelmann, Lessing, Hamann, Herder, Schiller, and Goethe,* ed. H. B. Nisbet (Cambridge and New York: Cambridge University Press, 1985), p. 42.

17. "Other kinds of poetry are complete": Le Huray and Day, *Music and Aesthetics*, p. 246.

17. the term derived from "romance": Le Huray and Day, *Music and Aesthetics*, p. 195.

17. "The poetry of the ancients": Le Huray and Day, *Music and Aesthetics*, pp. 269–70.

18. "Christianity leads poetry to the truth": *Prefaces and Prologues to Famous Books* (New York: Collier & Son, 1910), pp. 345–46.

22. SR 160:1193; 6/13:151: Throughout the text, these citations refer to *Strunk's Source Readings in Music History*, Leo Treitler, general editor (New York: W. W. Norton, 1998). The first reference is to selection and page number in the one-volume edition. The second is to the volume in the seven-volume set, with selection and page number: in this case, volume 6 (*The Nineteenth Century,* ed. Ruth A. Solie), selection 13, page 151.

19. "the passage from this state of melancholy reverie": Hector Berlioz, *Fantastic Symphony,* ed. Edward T. Cone (New York: W. W. Norton & Company, 1971), p. 23.

22. But music, "since it passes over the Ideas": Arthur Schopenhauer, *The World as Will and*

Representation, trans. E.F.J. Payne (New York: Dover, 1969), vol. 1, p. 257.

26. which he dubbed "trifling with everything": Georg Wilhelm Friedrich Hegel, *Lectures on the History of Philosophy*, trans. E. S. Haldane (Lincoln: University of Nebraska Press, 1995), vol. 1, p. 401.

29. "ruthless, undismayed": *The Complete Poetical Works of William Wordsworth*, ed. Henry Reed (Philadelphia: Hayes & Zell, 1854), pp. 534, 531, 261.

CHAPTER 3

34. "Today's youth cannot imagine": Leon Botstein, "Realism Transformed: Schubert and Vienna," in *The Cambridge Companion to Schubert*, ed. Christopher Gibbs (Cambridge and New York: Cambridge University Press, 1997), p. 22.

34. Schubert had "chimed in against the authorized official": Cited in Christopher H. Gibbs, *The Life of Schubert* (Cambridge and New York: Cambridge University Press, 2000), p. 67.

34. "What charm there is in the intimate sociability": Ruth Solie, *Music in Other Words: Victorian Conversations* (Berkeley and Los Angeles: University of California Press, 2004), p. 128.

36. "We must consider the public": Friedrich Rochlitz, "On the Occasion of," *Allgemeine musikalische Zeitung* 30 (23 and 30 July 1828), cols. 485–95 and 501–9; translation courtesy of Robin Wallace.

39. the genuine artist "sees unfortunately that art has no limits": Maynard Solomon, *Late Beethoven: Music, Thought, Imagination* (Berkeley and Los Angeles: University of California Press, 2003), p. 95.

40. "It was his [Beethoven's] will": Ignaz Xaver Seyfried, "Review," *Caecilia* 9 (August 1828), pp. 217–43; translation courtesy of Robin Wallace.

47. "Wölffl, on the contrary": *Thayer's Life of Beethoven*, revised and edited by Elliot Forbes (Princeton: Princeton University Press, 1970), pp. 206–7.

49. "Herr P. is without a doubt": Paul Metzner, *Crescendo of the Virtuoso: Spectacle,*

Skill, and Self-Promotion in Paris during the Age of Revolution (Berkeley and Los Angeles: University of California Press, 1998), p. 124.

49. Paganini once "stood up suddenly": Metzner, *Crescendo of the Virtuoso*, p. 126.

CHAPTER 4

52. "complicated machine": Hervé Lacombe, "The 'Machine' and the State," in *The Cambridge Companion to Grand Opera*, ed. David Charlton (Cambridge and New York: Cambridge University Press, 2003), p. 21.

52. "a great industry": Roger Parker, "The Opera Industry," in *The Cambridge History of Nineteenth-Century Music*, ed. Jim Samson (Cambridge: Cambridge University Press, 1991), p. 87.

55. "Madame Pasta's incredible mastery": Stendhal, *Life of Rossini*, translated and annotated by Richard N. Coe (Seattle: University of Washington Press, 1972), pp. 371–72, 376.

56. "I own all my original manuscripts": Philip Gossett, *Divas and Scholars: Performing Italian Opera* (Chicago and London: University of Chicago Press, 2006), p. 75.

56. "The revolution inaugurated by Rossini": Stendhal, *Life of Rossini*, p. 353.

56. "It is prohibited": Hilary Poriss, *Changing the Score: Arias, Prima Donnas, and the Authority of Performance* (Oxford and New York: Oxford University Press, 2009), p. 23.

57. "The most striking quality in Rossini's music": Stendhal, *Life of Rossini*, p. 404.

57. "Rossinian scores": Stendhal, *Life of Rossini*, p. 405.

58. "Music is a sublime art": Rodolfo Celletti, *A History of Bel Canto*, trans. Frederick Fuller (Oxford and New York: Oxford University Press, 1991), p. 136.

63. "a subject with variety and offering opportunities": Herbert Schneider, "Scribe and Auber: Constructing Grand Opera," in *Cambridge Companion to Grand Opera*, p. 168.

63. "An opera in five acts can come to life": Schneider, "Scribe and Auber," p. 170.

64. "the libretto is not necessary": Anselm Gerhard, *The Urbanization of Opera: Music Theater in Paris in the Nineteenth Century,*

trans. Mary Whittall (Chicago and London: University of Chicago Press, 1998), p. 148.

65. "Oh for a newly created German opera!": John Warrack, *German Opera: From the Beginnings to Wagner* (Cambridge and New York: Cambridge University Press), p. 85.

70. "She was a pale woman": Henry Chorley, *Thirty Years' Musical Recollections* (London: Hurst and Blackett, 1862), vol. 1, p. 55.

70. "She cared not whether she broke the flow": Henry Chorley, *Modern German Music: Recollections and Criticisms* (London: Smith, Elder, 1854), vol. 1, p. 343.

CHAPTER 5

73. "generation of the 1830s": Charles Rosen, *The Romantic Generation* (Cambridge, MA: Harvard University Press, 1995).

74. "Become a doctor!": *The Memoirs of Hector Berlioz*, trans. and ed. David Cairns (New York: Knopf, 2002), p. 18.

75. "a set of copper wires connecting a battery": Hugh Macdonald, *Berlioz's Orchestration Treatise: A Translation and Commentary* (Cambridge: Cambridge University Press, 2002), p. 353.

76. "Ten years on the stage": Hector Berlioz, *Evenings with the Orchestra*, trans. Jacques Barzun (Chicago and London: University of Chicago Press, 1973), pp. 68–69.

76. "Motionless, with downcast eyes": Berlioz, *Evenings with the Orchestra*, pp. 239–40.

77. "Our fundamental attitude . . . is simple": John Daverio, *Robert Schumann: Herald of a "New Poetic Age"* (Oxford and New York: Oxford University Press, 1997), p. 119.

79. "Eusebius came in quietly": Robert Schumann, *On Music and Musicians*, ed. Konrad Wolff, trans. Paul Rosenfeld (New York: W. W. Norton & Company, 1969), pp. 126–28.

79. "Don Juan, Zerlina, Leporello, and Masetto": Schumann, *On Music and Musicians*, p. 128.

80. "There inevitably must appear a musician": Schumann, *On Music and Musicians*, p. 253.

81. "nothing but a rather pleasant 'means of amusement'": "Liszt on the Artist in Society,"

trans. Ralphe Locke, in *Franz Liszt and His World*, ed. Christopher Gibbs and Dana Gooley (Princeton: Princeton University Press, 2006), p. 291.

81. "Isn't he always a stranger among men?": Franz Liszt, *An Artist's Journey: Lettres d'un bachelier ès musique, 1835–1841*, trans. Charles Suttoni (Chicago and London: University of Chicago Press, 1989), pp. 28–29.

81. "The happy times have passed": Liszt, *An Artist's Journey*, pp. 29–30.

81. "the forceful, austere art of the Middle Ages": Liszt, *An Artist's Journey*, p. 30.

84. "not only the sacred work of our time": R. Larry Todd, Foreword to Mendelssohn, *Elias* (Stuttgart: Carus, 1995), p. vii.

86. "She seized upon the spirit of the composition": R. Larry Todd, *Fanny Hensel: The Other Mendelssohn* (Oxford and New York: Oxford University Press, 2010), p. 219.

87. "But *persuade* her to publish something I cannot": Marian Wilson Kimber, "The 'Suppression' of Fanny Mendelssohn: Rethinking Feminist Biography," *19th-Century Music* 26 (2002): 129.

90. "She taught us to play with truth": Adelina de Lara, "Clara Schumann's Teaching," *Music & Letters* 26 (1945): 145.

90. "We think we are correct in saying that no pianist": Nancy B. Reich, "Schumann, Clara," *Grove Music Online/Oxford Music Online*, http://www.oxfordmusiconline.com/subscriber/article/grove/music/25152 (accessed May 27, 2010).

CHAPTER 6

93. The term *absolute music* was coined by Richard Wagner: Carl Dahlhaus, *The Idea of Absolute Music*, trans. Roger Lustig (Chicago and London: University of Chicago Press, 1989), pp. 18–21.

94. "The composer's intention has been to develop": Hector Berlioz, *Fantastic Symphony*, ed. Edward T. Cone (New York: W. W. Norton & Company, 1971), p. 21.

95. "*Part Five: Dream of a Witches' Sabbath*. He sees himself": Berlioz, *Fantastic Symphony*, pp. 22–25.

97. "The aim of the program": Berlioz, *Fantastic Symphony*, p. 28.

97. "since the composer of this symphony is convinced": Berlioz, *Fantastic Symphony*, p. 29.

99. "The composer of instrumental music never thinks": Eduard Hanslick, *The Beautiful in Music*, trans. Gustav Cohen (New York: Liberal Arts Press, 1957), p. 57.

100. "No instrumental composition can describe": Hanslick, *The Beautiful in Music*, pp. 24–25.

100. "The essence of music is *sound and motion*": Hanslick, *The Beautiful in Music*, p. 48.

101. he "imagined shepherds who live a simple life": Adapted from Kenneth DeLong and Adrienne Simpson, "Tomášek, Václav Jan Křtitel," *Grove Music Online/Oxford Music Online*, http://www.oxfordmusiconline.com/subscriber/article/grove/music/28077 (accessed May 31, 2010).

102. the "form of their representation": Cited in Charles Rosen, *The Romantic Generation* (Cambridge, MA: Harvard University Press, 1995), p. 130.

106. "I admit that I do not understand": Frédéric Chopin, *Preludes, Opus 28*, ed. Thomas Higgins (New York: W. W. Norton & Company, 1973), p. 96.

CHAPTER 7

114. "We have been beaten and humiliated": *The Revolutions in Europe, 1848–1849: From Reform to Reaction*, ed. R.J.W. Evans and Hartmut Pogge von Strandmann (Oxford and New York: Oxford University Press, 2000), pp. 45–46.

114. "The political gravity of the present situation": *Music and Aesthetics in the Eighteenth and Early-Nineteenth Centuries*, ed. Peter le Huray and James Day (Cambridge and New York: Cambridge University Press, 1981), p. 565.

114. "Is there such a thing as a republican or monarchical harmony": *Music and Aesthetics in the Eighteenth and Early-Nineteenth Centuries*, p. 566.

115. "We are and remain, whatever names we have": Norbert Meurs, *Neue Bahnen? Aspekte*

der Brahms-Reception 1853–1868 (Cologne: Studio Verlag, 1996), p. 92 (translation mine).

116. "life no longer dwells in the whole": Friedrich Nietzsche, *The Birth of Tragedy and the Case of Wagner*, trans. Walter Kaufmann (New York: Vintage, 1967), p. 170.

116. "We are justified in maintaining that only what is in ourselves": Immanuel Kant, *Critique of Pure Reason*, trans. Norman Kemp Smith (New York: St. Martin's Press, 1965), pp. 344–45.

117. "The crude material which the composer has to fashion": Eduard Hanslick, *The Beautiful in Music*, trans. Gustav Cohen (New York: Liberal Arts Press, 1957), p. 47.

118. Up to now music had "withdrawn itself from treatment": Hermann von Helmholtz, *Science and Culture: Popular and Philosophical Essays*, ed. David Cahan (Chicago and London: University of Chicago Press, 1995), p. 46.

118. "in a musical work of art the movement follows the outflow": Helmholtz, *Science and Culture*, p. 75.

120. Zola claimed his goal as "first and foremost a scientific one": Gerald Needham, "Naturalism," in *Grove Art Online/Oxford Art Online*, http://www.oxfordartonline.com/subscriber/article/grove/art/T061451 (accessed Feb. 17, 2011).

120. "She was fruit of the charnel house": Emile Zola, *Nana* (New York: Grosset & Dunlap, 1931), p. 521.

122. "My music must be an artistic reproduction of human speech": *The Musorgsky Reader: A Life of Modeste Petrovich Musorgsky in Letters and Documents*, ed. and trans. Jay Leyda and Sergei Bertensson (New York: W. W. Norton & Company, 1947), p. 113.

123. photography created "spatial continuum" of objects and images: *The Nineteenth-Century Visual Culture Reader*, ed. Vanessa R. Schwartz and Jeannene M. Przyblyski (New York: Routledge, 2004), p. 60.

129. "On the way home, Smetana turned his moist eyes": *Music in the Western World: A History in Documents*, ed. Piero Weiss and Richard Taruskin, second ed. (Belmont CA: Thomson Schirmer, 2008), p. 333.

129. "The work tells of *the flow of the Moldau*": Adapted from A. Peter Brown, *The Symphonic*

Repertoire, vol. 4: *The Second Golden Age of the Viennese Symphony: Brahms, Bruckner, Dvořák, Mahler, and Selected Contemporaries* (Bloomington and Indianapolis: Indiana University Press, 2003), p. 447.

151. "The essential trait of Symbolist art": *Kingdom of the Soul: Symbolist Art in Germany 1870–1920*, ed. Ingrid Ehrhardt and Simon Reynolds (Munich, London, and New York: Prestel, 2000), p. 9.

CHAPTER 8

134. "In my ninth year I went to the Dresden Kreuzschule": *Wagner on Music and Drama*, trans. William Ashton Ellis, ed. Albert Goldman and Evert Sprinchorn (New York: Da Capo Press, 1988), p. 239.

136. a myth is timeless and universal; it "is true for all time": *Wagner on Music and Drama*, p. 90.

137. the end of "the real *life history of opera*": *Wagner on Music and Drama*, p. 106.

137. "The last symphony of Beethoven is the redemption of Music": *Wagner on Music and Drama*, p. 160.

138. "the great, the speaking plainness": Richard Wagner, "On Franz Liszt's Symphonic Poems," in *Judaism in Music and Other Essays*, trans. William Ashton Ellis (Lincoln and London: University of Nebraska Press, 1995), p. 251.

140. "The new form of dramatic music will have the unity": *Wagner on Music and Drama*, pp. 229–30.

142. "We called this the 'mystic chasm'": Geoffrey Skelton, "Bayreuth," in *Grove Music Online/ Oxford Music Online*, http://www.oxfordmusiconline.com/subscriber/article/grove/music/40950 (accessed Feb. 21, 2011).

143. "It is republican to begin with": *Bayreuth: The Early Years*, ed. Robert Hartford (Cambridge and New York: Cambridge University Press, 1980), pp. 141–42.

146. "genuine ardent longing for death": *Wagner on Music and Drama*, p. 271.

147. "creaking, squeaking, buzzing snuffle": Richard Wagner, "Judaism in Music," in *Judaism in Music and Other Essays*, p. 85.

147. "the Jew musician hurls together the diverse forms": Wagner, "Judaism in Music," p. 92.

149. "a genius such as appears on earth once every thousand years": *Wagnerism in European Culture and Politics*, ed. David C. Large and William Weber (Ithaca and London: Cornell University Press, 1984), p. 152.

CHAPTER 9

157. the *parola scenica* "sculpts and makes the situation precise and evident": *A Verdi Companion*, ed. William Weaver and Martin Chusid (New York: W. W. Norton & Company, 1979), p. 132.

168. "The spectators leaning on the balconies garnish the walls": Rebecca Harris-Warrick et al., "Paris," in *The New Grove Dictionary of Opera*, ed. Stanley Sadie. *Grove Music Online/ Oxford Music Online*, http://www.oxfordmusiconline.com/subscriber/article/grove/music/O005519 (accessed June 16, 2010).

170. "I persisted, explaining that ours would be a softer, tamer Carmen": Susan McClary, *Georges Bizet: Carmen* (Cambridge and New York: Cambridge University Press, 1992), pp. 19–20.

171. "a savage; a half Gypsy, half Andalusian": McClary, *Georges Bizet: Carmen*, p. 112.

CHAPTER 10

177. "most of our orchestras believe they have discharged their obligations": Walter Frisch, *Brahms: The Four Symphonies* (New Haven and London: Yale University Press, 2003), p. 20.

177. "everything must be cast more grandly": Frisch, *Brahms: The Four Symphonies*, p. 3.

178. "we find many too close imitations [of Beethoven]": Robert Schuman, *On Music and Musicians*, ed. Konrad Wolff, trans. Paul Rosenfeld (New York: W. W. Norton & Company, 1969), p. 62.

178. "I will never compose a symphony!": David Brodbeck, *Brahms: Symphony No. 1* (Cambridge: Cambridge University Press, 1997), p. 15.

180. "Brahms's symphonies do not inspire and delight": Margaret Notley, *Lateness and Brahms: Music and Culture in the Twilight of Viennese Liberalism* (Oxford and New York: Oxford University Press, 2007), p. 32.

180. found Bruckner's symphonic work "strange": Eduard Hanslick, *Hanslick's Music Criticisms*, trans. and ed. Henry Pleasants (New York: Dover, 1988), p. 288.

180. "Brahms is unique in his resources": Eduard Hanslick, *Hanslick's Music Criticisms*, p. 243.

181. "Brahms seems to favour too one-sidedly": Hanslick, *Hanslick's Music Criticisms*, p. 127.

182. "What would you think about a symphony written on this theme": Frisch, *Brahms: The Four Symphonies*, p. 131.

183. "even before Herr Bruckner raised the baton": Andrea Harrandt, "Bruckner in Vienna," in *The Cambridge Companion to Bruckner*, ed. John Williamson (Cambridge and New York: Cambridge University Press, 2004), p. 31.

186. "It is permissible to say that on that date": James Harding, *Saint-Saëns and His Circle* (London: Chapman and Hall, 1965), p. 120.

187. "form a complete summary of the history of music": Gordon A. Anderson et al., "Paris," in *Grove Music Online/Oxford Music Online*, http://www.oxfordmusiconline.com/subscriber/article/grove/music/40089pg7 (accessed June 22, 2010).

192. Tchaikovsky was reported as being "utterly happy and content": Alexander Poznansky, *Tchaikovsky's Last Days* (Oxford and New York: Oxford University Press, 1996), p. 55.

CHAPTER 11

196. "While in our country almost every institution": Charles Hamm, *Music in the New World* (New York: W. W. Norton & Company, 1983), p. 100.

197. the performance's "superiority to any ever before given": Richard Crawford, *America's Musical Life* (New York: W. W. Norton & Company, 2001), p. 293.

199. Their performance "had neither feet nor head": Owen da Silva, *Mission Music of California* (New York: Da Capo, 1978), pp. 30–31.

199. "In saecula saeculo-ho-horum": Da Silva, *Mission Music of California*, p. 12.

201. "I have just finished . . . my last tour of concerts": Louis Moreau Gottschalk, *Notes of a Pianist*, ed. Jeanne Behrend (Princeton: Princeton University Press, 2006), p. 174.

201. music "is one of the most powerful means of ameliorating and ennobling": Gottschalk, *Notes of a Pianist*, p. 111.

201. "In fact, you are better, your heart is in some way purified": Gottschalk, *Notes of a Pianist*, p. 112.

202. "Pianos and guitars groan with it": Hamm, *Music in the New World*, p. 230.

204. "I find that by my efforts I have done a great deal": Hamm, *Music in the New World*, p. 240.

206. "a strange medley of manners and deportment": John Dizikes, *Opera in America: A Cultural History* (New Haven and London: Yale University Press, 1993), p. 52.

207. "The opera—the ballet—the acted drama": Dizikes, *Opera in America*, p. 161.

208. "Across the stage with pallor on her face": Walt Whitman, "Proud Music of the Storm," in *Leaves of Grass* (Boston: Small, Maynard: 1904), p. 312.

209. "the music of the high hour of Human Brotherhood": Ora Frishberg Saloman, *Beethoven's Symphonies and J. S. Dwight: The Birth of American Music Criticism* (Boston: Northeastern University Press, 1995), p. 170.

209. "In Germany, songs grow": Dizikes, *Opera in America*, p. 153.

209. "the advancement of instrumental music": Howard Shanet, *Philharmonic: A History of New York's Orchestra* (Garden City, NY: Doubleday, 1975), p. 84.

209. "We must undoubtedly reckon Wednesday evening last": Hamm, *Music in the New World*, p. 208.

209. "life was never the same afterward": Crawford, *America's Musical Life*, p. 310.

210. "The Musical Director is to determine the character": Crawford, *America's Musical Life*, pp. 311–12.

211. "There is nothing in the whole range of composition": *Dvořák in America, 1892–1895*, ed. John C. Tibbetts (Portland, OR: Amadeus Press, 1993), pp. 355–56.

211. "How then can folk songs attributed to the negro or Indians be distinctively, peculiarly American?": Adrienne Fried Block, "Amy Beach's Music on Native American Themes," *American Music* 8 (1990): 145.

211. "their laments . . . their romance": Adrienne Fried Block, *Amy Beach, Passionate*

Victorian: The Life and Work of an American Composer, 1867–1944 (Oxford and New York: Oxford University Press, 1998), pp. 87, 91.

213. "I do not believe in 'lifting' a Navajo theme": Kara Anne Gardner, "Edward MacDowell, Antimodernism, and 'Playing Indian' in the *Indian Suite*," *Musical Quarterly* 87 (2004): 370.

213. "The promise of our national musical art": Hamm, *Music in the New World*, p. 417.

tav *Mahlers Sinfonien* (Berlin: Schuster & Loeffler, 1921; rpt. Tutzing: Hans Schneider, 1969), p. 62.

233. "There is no theory": *Music in the Western World: A History in Documents*, ed. Piero Weiss and Richard Taruskin, second ed. (Belmont, CA: Thomson Schirmer, 2008), pp. 355–56.

234. "*taches sonores*": Edward Lockspeiser, *Debussy: His Life and Mind* (Cambridge and New York: Cambridge University Press, 1978), vol. 2, pp. 16, 18.

CHAPTER 12

215. "the transient, the fleeting, the contingent": *Modernism: An Anthology of Sources and Documents*, ed. Vassiliki Kolocotroni, Jane Goldman, and Olga Taxidou (Chicago and London: University of Chicago Press, 1998), p. 107.

218. "Five worm-eaten steps lead up": Walter Frisch, *German Modernism: Music and the Arts* (Berkeley and Los Angeles: University of California Press, 1995), pp. 39–40.

220. "Richard Strauss, the productive artist": *Gustav Mahler–Richard Strauss: Correspondence, 1888–1911*, ed. Herta Blaukopf, trans. Edmund Jephcott (Chicago and London: University of Chicago Press, 1996), p. 105.

220. "beyond all question a gigantic work": Willi Schuh, *Richard Strauss: A Chronicle of the Early Years*, trans. Mary Whittall (Cambridge and New York: Cambridge University Press, 1982), p. 98.

221. "I have found myself in a gradually ever-increasing contradiction": Bryan Gilliam, *The Life of Richard Strauss* (Cambridge and New York: Cambridge University Press, 1999), pp. 42–43.

224. "the sudden outburst . . . of despair": Constantin Floros, *Gustav Mahler: The Symphonies*, trans. Vernon Wicker (Portland, OR: Amadeus Press, 1993), pp. 39–40.

224. "I have experienced the way the audiences have been set on the wrong track by them": Gustav Mahler, *Selected Letters*, ed. Knud Martner, trans. Eithne Wilkins, Ernst Kaiser, and Bill Hopkins (New York: Farrar, Straus and Giroux, 1979), p. 177.

225. it seems to arrive from some place outside the symphony: Paul Bekker, *Gus-*

CHAPTER 13

239. Beethoven's "playing tore along like a wildly foaming cataract": *Thayer's Life of Beethoven*, rev. and ed. Elliot Forbes (Princeton: Princeton University Press, 1967), pp. 369, 206.

239. "I have never felt a greater pleasure": Cited in the original French in *Thayer's Life of Beethoven*, p. 694.

241. Chopin himself called Pleyel "the last word in perfection": Jean-Jacques Eigeldinger, *Chopin, Pianist and Teacher: As Seen by His Pupils*, trans. Krysia Osostowicz and Naomi Shohet, ed. Roy Howat (Cambridge and New York: Cambridge University Press, 1986), p. 25.

241. "Nobody before had stirred the keys": Eigeldinger, *Chopin, Pianist and Teacher*, p. 270.

242. "You must sing if you wish to play": Eigeldinger, *Chopin, Pianist and Teacher*, p. 14.

242. "Everything is a matter of knowing good fingering": Eigeldinger, *Chopin, Pianist and Teacher*, p. 19.

242. "You should, so to speak, mould the keyboard": Eigeldinger, *Chopin, Pianist and Teacher*, pp. 40, 31.

244. "sensuous pleasure, without a spark of nobler passion": Richard Wagner, "My Recollections of Ludwig Schnorr von Carolsfeld," in Wagner, *Art and Politics*, trans. William Ashton Ellis (Lincoln and London: University of Nebraska Press, 1995), pp. 238–39.

248. "Impossible! Quite impossible!": *The Memoirs of Hector Berlioz*, trans. and ed. David Cairns (New York and Toronto: Knopf, 2002), p. 352.

248. "emitted the most appalling sounds": Daniel J. Koury, *Orchestral Performance Practices in the Nineteenth Century: Size,*

Proportions, and Seating (Ann Arbor: UMI Research Press, 1986), pp. 98–99.

249. "One felt as if the Divine Presence had been evoked": Koury, *Orchestral Performance Practices*, p. 100.

249. "full and vibrant and well matched": Koury, *Orchestral Performance Practices*, p. 100.

251. Norrington's ideas about Wagner performance "ludicrous": Richard Taruskin, *The Danger of Music and Other Anti-Utopian Essays* (Berkeley and Los Angeles: University of California Press, 2009), p. 83.

252. "through every performance there surged the pulse": Alexander Berrsche, cited in Walter Frisch, "In Search of Brahms's First Symphony," in *Performing Brahms: Early Evidence of Performance Style*, ed. Michael Musgrave and Bernard Sherman (Cambridge and New York: Cambridge University Press, 2003), p. 283.

CREDITS

INDEX

Note: Page numbers in *italics* indicate illustrations or musical examples.